Entrepreneurship

IN THEORY
AND PRACTICE

Paradoxes in Play

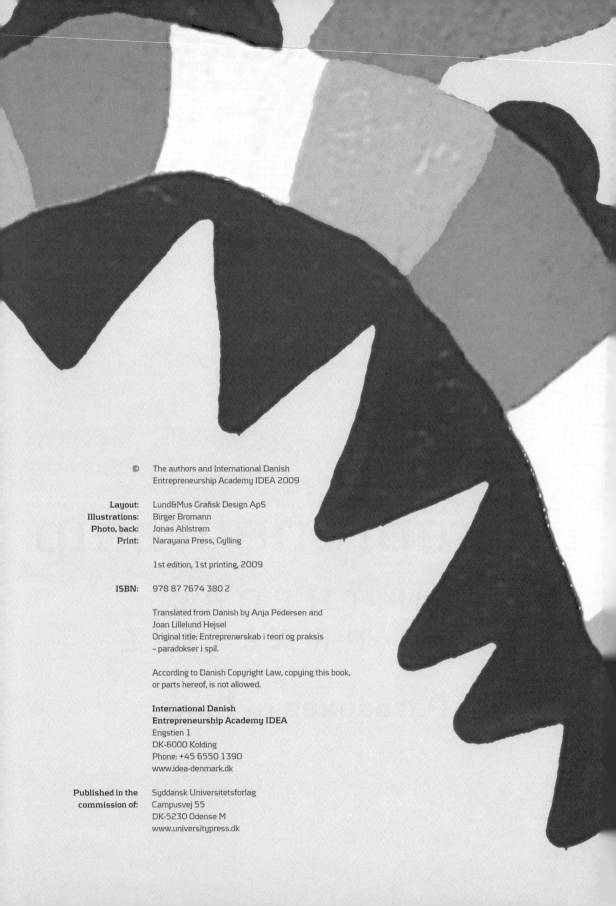

©   The authors and International Danish
Entrepreneurship Academy IDEA 2009

Layout: Lund&Mus Grafisk Design ApS
Illustrations: Birger Bromann
Photo, back: Jonas Ahlstrøm
Print: Narayana Press, Gylling

1st edition, 1st printing, 2009

ISBN: 978 87 7674 380 2

Translated from Danish by Anja Pedersen and
Joan Lillelund Hejsel
Original title: Entreprenørskab i teori og praksis
– paradokser i spil.

**International Danish
Entrepreneurship Academy IDEA**
Engstien 1
DK-6000 Kolding
Phone: +45 6550 1390
www.idea-denmark.dk

**Published in the
commission of:**   Syddansk Universitetsforlag
Campusvej 55
DK-5230 Odense M
www.universitypress.dk

Table of contents

Figures and tables

Entrepreneurship in theory and practice

11

12

Preface

These days the global market of textbooks is swarming with books dealing with entrepreneurship, company establishment and business development.

In many ways, this book differs from the traditional textbooks about entrepreneurship.

Firstly, it is not a "cookery book" supplying cocksure recipes for how to become a successful entrepreneur. That is why this textbook is so inspiring. It is an introduction to a world of paradoxes. It incites to dialogues and discussions, and it guides the readers to develop their own unique understanding of what entrepreneurship means to them and inspires them to find their own recipe for how to create a company, project or initiative of their own.

Secondly, this textbook offers a number of big and small examples of entrepreneurship, picked from Denmark. These examples are used for pedagogical ends. Consequently, the practical entrepreneurship examples influence the entire textbook and the practice employed throughout the various chapters.

Thirdly, this book breaks with the traditional and dominating approach to the understanding of entrepreneurial behaviour and actions as filtered through the perspective of traditional management theories. In this book, the core theoretical approaches to the entrepreneurship field are emphasised.

Therefore, the book offers a varied insight into the many different conceptions which influence the understanding of the drivers behind entrepreneurial behaviour and practice.

The eleven chapters of the book are organised around three crucial issues: interpretations of the nature of entrepreneurship, understandings of the entrepreneurial process and explanations of the role of the entrepreneurial context. Thus, the reader is guided through the practical core of entrepreneurship and paradoxes from discovery or creation through evaluation to organising of new opportunities.

Throughout the book, the reader is kept in a learning circle which moves from practical examples through the immediate interpretation of the examples to the possible theoretical interpretations and finally towards experimental exercises on the basis of what has been learned.

In the final chapter of the book, chapter 11, which is a scoop in terms of learning and theory, the many paradoxes of the chapters are summed up, and a suggestion for a synthesis is given. In this synthesis, two completely different approaches to the understanding of entrepreneurship are enumerated: the objectified and the subjectified interpretation. The synthesis is simple: Do not consider the two different approaches as "either or" but as "both and". In other words, it is about finding your balance in a world of practical as well as theoretical paradoxes. When the balance is obtained, you will be strengthened as an enterprising human being.

The book is relevant to students in many different study fields at universities and institutions of higher education because the core issue of the book is that such students and graduates will need more than their disciplinary knowledge in order to get on in tomorrow's society. No doubt, whether they choose a career as entrepreneurs or wage earners, they will all end up working in interdisciplinary connections and with new projects and ideas. Their challenge can be businesslike but it can also be professional, cultural or social. This is where entrepreneurship is able to offer the students something extra, not only an extra course but also an entrepreneurial approach to their own discipline and to the creation of their own career. Their career is not just waiting out there. They have to create it themselves.

It is fantastic to read a book that in a plain language is able to represent the theories of entrepreneurship and entrepreneurial behaviour in a manner well aligned to the theoretical field itself.

Poul Rind Christensen
Professor and Managing Director of IMEET,
International Master in Entrepreneurship Education & Training
Aarhus School of Business, Aarhus University

16

Introduction
– the idea of the textbook

It is a pleasure for us to present one of the first Danish textbooks dealing with entrepreneurship. Entrepreneurship is important and eventful. The creation of new organisations and innovation in already existing organisations is the key to the creation of new jobs and growth in our modern society. Furthermore, it is exciting that the subject is about creating something new. Entrepreneurs are exciting people who make a difference.

The present book differs in many ways from the typical textbook about entrepreneurship. First of all we define entrepreneurship as a broad phenomenon. The field of entrepreneurship is basically about the creation of new opportunities and the evaluation and organising of those. Such behaviour can lead to the creation of a new and independent organisation. But entrepreneurship can also take place within many other organisational contexts (labour unions, public institutions, existing companies etc.). We demonstrate how entrepreneurship has many different appearances in different contexts. Typical textbooks tend to have a delimited understanding of entrepreneurship as the creation of new organisations.

Moreover, we emphasise the theory and knowledge that is prevalent to entrepreneurship. Most other textbooks focus on "How to" develop and run new and small businesses by referring to theory already well-known from the management literature.

Last but not least, we offer an exciting but alternative pedagogical approach to entrepreneurship education. The approach is important since it takes its starting point in concrete entrepreneurial narratives. You will meet "real life entrepreneurs" and you will be challenged to make decisions on behalf of them which basically implies that you will have to put yourself in their place. Not until this point, will theories and concepts attributed to entrepreneurship be presented. The approach also includes your presentation of your own attempts of testing the generated theory and knowledge in new entrepreneurial situations. The pedagogy that is characteristic of other textbooks is typically more traditional and focuses primarily on presenting theory in addition to empirical examples. Our pedagogical approach is solely an offer. However, if you wish, the textbook can easily be used as a traditional textbook. We have also connected the book to IDEA-Textbook which is a website that gives you access to video cases, papers, exercises and articles which back up the book. This aspect will be clarified further on.

Below, you will find a presentation of the target audience of the book, the principal ideas, the contents, the structure and the pedagogical approach. When we employ the concept entrepreneurship we refer to a broad concept that encapsulates the overall subject field of the book. In the introductory part, entrepreneurship is defined as discovery or creation of new opportunities that are being evaluated and exploited through a process of organising. Closely related to the concept entrepreneurship is the concept the entrepreneurial process. We define the process as the movement from discovering or creating an opportunity, evaluating this opportunity to finally exploiting it through organising. The process of organising can lead to a new organisation. It can either be an independent organisation or a new organisation within the framework of an existing society, public institution or company. A third and widely used concept is entrepreneur. The concept refers to the individual who initiates, strives for and creates entrepreneurship. Many other concepts will continuously be introduced in the book.

■ **Target audience**
Who is the target audience of the book? Due to the fact that the book has an introductory purpose, its target audiences are all of you students who have not already been taught entrepreneurship. It is a book that addresses all those who want to become entrepreneurs and everybody else. It is possible to talk about a specific target group consisting of people who want to start (their own) business and a broader target group counting people who wish to develop their entrepreneurial way of thinking. If you belong to the first group, the book will supply you with a useful insight in how entrepreneurs behave and benefit economically from their behaviour. Your understanding of start-up processes will increase and you will probably be looking for instrumental and very concrete competences. If you, on the contrary, belong to the last mentioned broad target group, you will most likely find the value of the book in its introduction to a lot of principles that can be employed in all situations that deal with aspects of creating something new. It does not matter if the situation is related to design, humanistic studies, politics or another field of subject. Hopefully, you will develop your way of thinking towards becoming more entrepreneurial and as far as your learning process is concerned you will probably seek to understand how you discover, evaluate and organise opportunities. The table below shows some basic differences between the two target groups.

Table I: Differences between target groups

	Specific target group	Broad target group
Career ambitions	People with concrete ambitions about starting their own business	People with ambitions of dealing with entrepreneurial issues
Overall purposes	To understand start-up-processes	To develop an entrepreneurial way of thinking
Learning needs	Seek concrete and instrumental competences	Seek an ability to discover, evaluate and organise opportunities

No matter what kind of target group you belong to, studying entrepreneurship is important to you. Students who have received this type of teaching distinguish themselves from their fellow students. It turns out that those students are more likely to start up new organisations in comparison to students in general. In addition, they are, in comparison with other students, more effective in terms of accumulating financial assets, they receive a higher salary and furthermore, to a considerable extent, they participate in the process of developing products and other research and development activities (Autio 2007).

■ **The idea of the book: theory and practice in play**

A lot seems to suggest that teaching in entrepreneurship should be different from your usual teaching. The reason is that entrepreneurship is about teaching you to create something that does not already exist. Traditional teaching typically concentrates on how to behave in the context of something that is already created. An example could be how to behave within an already existing organisation or on a well-known market. In teaching entrepreneurship there should be room for stimulating entrepreneurial imagination, willingness to take risks, orientation towards action and independence to take a stand. That is why it is not sufficient that you acquire academic skills and proficiencies. You must also be able to employ knowledge and put it into perspective to your own situation, activities, experiences and creativity. The book will help you to capture the complex, creative and creating nature of entrepreneurship.

The idea of the book is inspired by Kolb's (1984) learning circle – a circle that pushes you into the entrepreneurial practice. You will not only be reading about it. The circle also means that you will be presented with entrepreneurship from a thorough and theoretical perspective. Practice as well as theory, experimental learning and reflexion are in play. Enjoy!

Kolb's learning circle consists of four activities. 1) The learning circle takes its starting point in narratives closely connected to entrepreneurship in practice which in the book takes the form of text cases of which some are complemented by a video case. By this, your learning process is activated. 2) Then focus is put on your immediate reflexion and interpretation of what is happening in the narrative and why. 3) Not until this point will we introduce relevant theory and provide you with an example of how the narratives can be interpreted in the light of the theory. 4) In the light of these three learning activities, you are finally ready to experiment with the knowledge you have acquired by reading the chapter. We offer some exercises that you can go through in order to test your new knowledge. The learning circle, which is illustrated in figure I, can then start again.

Figure I: The use of the learning circle in the book

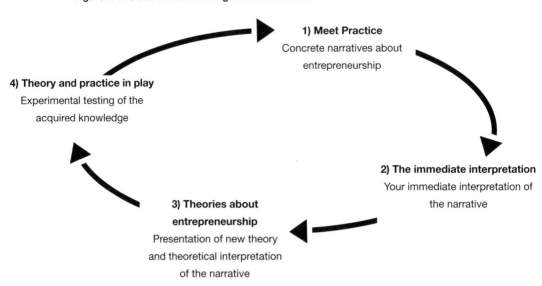

1) **Meet Practice**
Concrete narratives about
entrepreneurship

4) **Theory and practice in play**
Experimental testing of the
acquired knowledge

2) **The immediate interpretation**
Your immediate interpretation of
the narrative

3) **Theories about
entrepreneurship**
Presentation of new theory
and theoretical interpretation
of the narrative

Source: Inspired by Kolb (1984).

■ The structuring of the chapters into four parts

The chapters in the book are structured in agreement with the logic of the learning circle. In effect that means that various types of language are employed – you will find theoretical language as well as you will find everyday language. In addition, every chapter in the book is divided into four parts, which are in accordance with the dimensions of the learning circle. The four parts are:

Meet practice

The chapters begin with concrete narratives about entrepreneurship in text format. Videos are often available via www.idea-textbook.dk which also contains interviews with the entrepreneurs in addition to the text.

The immediate interpretation

Subsequently, exercises follow which guide you to reflect about and create your immediate interpretation of the entrepreneurs' narratives. What happens in the narratives and why?

Theories of entrepreneurship

Then relevant theories of entrepreneurship are introduced for the purpose of interpreting the narratives further and to supply them with theoretical perspectives. This part focuses on presenting theory in a sophisticated way. For that reason, the presentation of theory is composed in accordance with a paradox. The paradox supplies you with all-round and exciting theoretical tools for interpreting the entrepreneurial narratives.

Practical tests of the theory

The last part of the chapter comes up with proposals for how the knowledge and theory that so far have been discussed in the chapter can be tested in another entrepreneurial context. How can we understand the acquired knowledge and theory in the light of other situations than exactly those that are accentuated in the narratives which are initially presented in each chapter?

■ Entrepreneurship: a world of paradoxes

Theories of entrepreneurship are characterised by tensions and dilemmas which at first sight can seem conflicting. For instance, many theories present the entrepreneurial process as a purposeful action which is possible for the entrepreneur to plan in advance. That is to say that the entrepreneur is capable of predicting the process and in effect what has to be done in order to reach the goal. Think of a puzzle. These theories assume that from the beginning, a picture of the puzzle, which shall be put together, exists. The entrepreneurial process is about making the right plans and making the optimal decisions so that the puzzle can be completed.

Other theories emphasise that the entrepreneur is not capable of predicting in advance what goal to achieve and how he or she can achieve it. The picture of what the entrepreneur will create does not already exist. Entrepreneurship is simply too unpredictable which in effect means that it is not possible to plan everything in advance – it is about creating a future in terms of a product, market or something similar which we do not already know. Instead, the entrepreneur must improvise and feel his way step by step. Think of a patchwork. Such a patchwork is created gradually by collecting a lot of new and old materials (fabrics, silk ribbons, embroidery, buttons etc. which are to be found in a wealth of colours and qualities) and making it into a meaningful pattern. From this starting point, many different, beau-

tiful and not so beautiful patchwork creations can be created. From this perspective, the entrepreneurial process is about how the entrepreneur through small steps
and by improvising creates an entrepreneurial process with the materials that are
available to him or her. The results of the process can be many different organisations, products or markets.

In this way, the book presents theories of entrepreneurship as a collection of
paradoxes. Generally, a paradox is a conflicting statement which in the book will
be presented as two conflicting theoretical perspectives. Thus, the perspectives
can be perceived as contrasts to each other. In that way, we wish to emphasise
the contradictory nature of the theories which furthermore reflects the dilemmas
that the entrepreneur meets in his daily life. As an entrepreneur, you will often find
yourself in an ambiguous situation that requires you to make up your mind about
which of the perspectives applying to the paradox that is useful for the purpose of

understanding entrepreneurship. You must be critical and capable of making up your own mind.

However, the paradoxes in the book are not only "either or"-paradoxes in spite of the fact that they are often presented in relatively extreme versions. The purpose is to distinguish the perspectives of the paradox from each other. Basically, they can be characterised as stylised interpretations. But in practice you will often find that a combination of both perspectives that apply to the paradox are useful in terms of understanding what is happening in the entrepreneurial process.

■ **The structure of the book**

You can choose to read the book as a unified whole. However, its structure also makes it possible for you to choose the parts of the book you find most relevant in the light of your professionalism, your interests etc. Therefore, the book is structured around four main sections which can each be employed independently. The sections are:

Section 1: **Welcome to entrepreneurship**
Section 2: **The entrepreneurial process**
Section 3: **The entrepreneurial content**
Section 4: **The entrepreneurial context**

Each section is composed of a minor group of chapters. These chapters deal with a core subject area in the context of entrepreneurship. As you can see from table II, we have chosen crucial theoretical paradoxes related to each subject area.

Table II: The structure of the book, sections and chapters

Sections	Chapters	Paradoxes
Welcome to entrepreneurship	1 What is entrepreneurship? 2 Who is the entrepreneur?	Introduction – no paradox Born or Made?
The entrepreneurial process	3 Creation of opportunities 4 Evaluation of opportunities 5 Organising of opportunities	Discovered or created? Instrumental or legitimate? Planning or improvising?
The entrepreneurial content	6 Resources 7 Network 8 The business plan	Exploit or explore? Rational or embedded? A management tool or a creativity curb?
The entrepreneurial context	9 Intrapreneurship 10 Social entrepreneurship	Top-down or bottom-up? Business or a better world?

Section 1: Welcome to entrepreneurship

In the first section of the book, you will be confronted with two chapters. Chapter 1 introduces the entrepreneurial phenomenon. Why is this phenomenon important from an individual, organisational and social point of view? Last but not least, you will gain an insight into crucial concepts that underpin the book.

In chapter 2, emphasis is on the decision about making an entrepreneurial career. Why do some people and not others decide to become entrepreneurs? Who is the entrepreneur? Is it possible to point him or her out in the crowd? Are you born to become an entrepreneur or is it something that all of us have a potential to become? Especially the paradox "Born or Made?" will be discussed.

Section 2: The entrepreneurial process

Emergence, evaluation and organising of new opportunities are three key activities which are related to the creation and realisation of the entrepreneurial process. In the second section of the book, you will meet three chapters. The first (chapter 3) discusses the conditions that lead to the emergence of a new opportunity. In particular, it will be discussed whether opportunities are always around us, just waiting to be discovered. Or are opportunities created by the individual? Thus, the paradox is whether opportunities are discovered or created.

The second chapter of the section (chapter 4) provides you with an insight in how the entrepreneur can evaluate his or her opportunities. Evaluation is about relating an opportunity to the market: how it makes sense in the context of the market or what needs to be done in order to add sense to it. It is discussed whether evaluation of opportunities is a systematic and analytic process, or to what extent evaluation can be perceived as a justification process in which the entrepreneur via interaction with the market attempts to gain legitimacy for his or her activities. Thus, the chapter presents evaluation of opportunities in the light of the paradox: instrumental or legitimate?

The last chapter of the section (chapter 5) emphasises how opportunities can be organised. Opportunities do not become visible to the investors, customers and others until they are organised. Thus, every entrepreneurial process involves the development of structures and routines which can back up the organising that can lead to an independent organisation or a new unit within an already existing organisation. Is it possible to plan and predict this organisational effort or is the process characterised by being improvising in character? This is a question that will be dealt with in chapter 5 in the discussion about: planning or improvising?

Section 3: The entrepreneurial content

The third section of the book focuses on topics which account for core issues in the entrepreneurial process where opportunities are created, evaluated and organised. In the first chapter of the section (chapter 6), you will be confronted with the issue of resources. What are resources? In the chapter, resources are divided into three types: financial, human and social. It is discussed how the value of a resource can be estimated. It is also discussed whether the entrepreneur should exploit the resources which he or she at some point controls for the purpose of exploiting an opportunity or whether the entrepreneur should employ these resources for the purpose of exploring new and more opportunities. In that way, the following paradox will be discussed: to exploit or explore?

The following chapter of the section (chapter 7) deals with network and the concept of networking. The entrepreneur's social and business networks are important. The chapter goes through different types of networks, which the entrepreneur makes use of, and investigates how different challenges that attribute to the entrepreneurial process create a need for different types of networks. Are we supposed to perceive network as a rational tool which is available to the entrepreneur or should we perceive networks as a condition that surrounds the entrepreneur and is hard to control? Thus, the paradox that will be discussed is: rational or embedded?

Chapter 8 provides you with an insight into the business plan which is a core topic in entrepreneurship. The role of the business plan in the entrepreneurial process and its significance will be discussed. Is the business plan an effective management tool in the often chaotic entrepreneurial process, a tool that supports the entrepreneur and promotes a structured and holistic understanding of the idea and its potential? Or is the business plan more an impediment for the maturing of the idea and for the consideration of new opportunities in the process? Put differently, the paradox is whether the business plan is a management tool or a curb of creativity.

Section 4: The entrepreneurial context

The last section in the book pinpoints that the entrepreneurial process does not take place in a vacuum. Different contexts contribute to shape the process. The chapters in the section go through two interesting contexts for entrepreneurship. The first chapter (chapter 9) presents entrepreneurship within the context of an already existing organisation. This phenomenon is often called intrapreneurship. New ideas, which are to be discovered or created, evaluated and organised, emerge not only in the creation of new independent organisations but also in the context of already existing organisations. But the question is, does this happen by virtue of processes that are initiated and supported by the management or is it rather the employees' initiative and engagement that create intrapreneurship? Therefore, crucial to this chapter is the discussion of the paradox: "top-down" or "bottom-up"?

Chapter 10 provides you with an understanding of the social entrepreneur who forms or creates a new organisation for the purpose of achieving social goals or contributing to social activities so that better conditions for people at the local or global level can be created. The chapter deals with the issue of social entrepreneurship. But how is social entrepreneurship created? Is social entrepreneurship driven by the creation of a better world where social ends are the only ends an entrepreneur has in view? And does this involve that profit and commercial exchange are completely out of place? Or does the creation of a better world mean that an economically sustainable business has to get going in order to let the social entrepreneur contribute to social activities? This means that the social ends no longer are the primary but only secondary ends because priority is given to profit and commercial exchange. Thus, the paradox in the chapter is: business or a better world?

In addition to these ten chapters, the book contains a summing up chapter (chapter 11). The chapter sums up the discussions in the book. Emphasis is put on the paradoxes which have been treated in the book. The chapter discusses whether there exists a deeper connection between the presented paradoxes which can enhance our understanding of entrepreneurship.

■ Additional material

Exercises in the book refer teachers and students to online materials that can be found on this web page: www.idea-textbook.dk. Here you have the possibility to download video segments that back up your learning process and make the teaching situation and your learning process more lively and exciting. You can also find relevant literature, exercises and information about the evaluation tool IDEA VIQ™. Apart from evaluating opportunities, you can also use the tool to write a business plan. We have provided the book with a minidisc containing the IDEA VIQ™ tool.

■ Feedback

We will appreciate very much to receive your feedback if you have some comments on the structure of the book, its tone, content or scope of application. Your feedback can help us improve the book. Please send your reactions via www.idea-textbook.dk.

Introduction - the idea of the textbook

Literature

Autio, E. (2007). Entrepreneurship Teaching in Öresund and Copenhagen Regions. Copenhagen: Danmarks Tekniske Universitet.

Kolb, D. A. (1984). Experimental Learning: Experience as the Source of Learning and Development. Englewood Cliffs: Prentice-Hall.

30

Chapter 1

What is entrepreneurship?

Entrepreneurship is around us all the time and we often talk about it. But what is it actually? How would you define entrepreneurship? On the face of it, it might seem an easy task but it definitely is not. By reading newspapers or watching television, you easily get the impression that entrepreneurs are the heroes in our time. You are confronted with stories about the inventive hero who starts his own organisation and as a result of this becomes rich and famous. Just think of Lars Larsen – the story of a young and energetic man from a rural area in Northern Denmark who for small money starts his own chain of bedlinen outlets. However, the message of this book is that entrepreneurship is much more than starting an independent organisation. Entrepreneurship is a complex phenomenon that takes place in many different contexts and the extent as well as the process and output differ.

The purpose of this chapter is first of all to define: What is entrepreneurship? There is not a single answer to that question. The entrepreneurial phenomenon is wide and has many faces; *"... there are many entrepreneurships in terms of focus, definitions, scope and paradigms"* (Steyaert & Hjorth 2003: 5). A reason for the many different "entrepreneurships" is the fact that entrepreneurship is studied in many different disciplines (economics, psychology, sociology, management etc.). In fact, every author seems to have his own definition of entrepreneurship. By reference to Saxes' (1916-1987) story of the blind men who touch an elephant in different places (trunk, tail etc.) and as a result of this end up telling completely different stories about the elephant, Gartner (2002) asks, *"Is there an Elephant in Entrepreneurship?"*

Is there an elephant in entrepreneurship?

■ An elevator-pitch for entrepreneurship

However, before we begin to define entrepreneurship, we will supply you with a short "Elevator-Pitch". This concept is often used in the context of entrepreneurship. Conventionally the concept applies to a little sales speech or an oral monologue from one person to two or more persons where a given topic is introduced in the time it takes taking an elevator. The concept is American and is often used in connection with networking in the context of business arrangements. On such occasions, you only have a few seconds to sell your idea, product or something similar effectively and quickly.

In the following, we will raise your interest for the idea of studying entrepreneurship. However, we will not expose you to an "Elevator-Pitch" in the formal sense but it is still a relatively short sales speech for entrepreneurship. Entrepreneurship has great value to individuals as well as to already existing organisations and to society. Thus, entrepreneurship is of great value to you as an individual, for the organisations that you are perhaps going to create or work for and for the people who are all around you.

Elevator-Pitch for you

Entrepreneurship is of different value to different people. What would the value be for you to become an entrepreneur? That question was posed in 2006 to 1,747 students at Aalborg University and other institutions of higher education in the north of Jutland. The most common answers were, *"I will be able to control my own life, make my own decisions"*; *"I have a desire to create"* and *"I want personal development and learning."* To a minor extent, the students were motivated by the prospect of earning a lot of money (Sørensen et al. 2006). Despite the fact that you often notice that entrepreneurs are primarily motivated by other things than money, it is important to keep in mind that entrepreneurs, in order to carry out their entrepreneurial processes, need to establish an organisation which is economically sustainable. This means that earning money is always important for successful entrepreneurship.

You might think that entrepreneurship has no specific value for you. But think of the changes on the labour market. The development moves towards more free agents, frequent job switching, a faster technological development, more options and more unclear job structures. Effectively this means that every one of us, to a greater extent than earlier, must act like entrepreneurs in educational and career connections: We must to a higher degree create a career instead of just having a career. Normally, we can choose between many educational offers and there are often more career tracks to follow after having finished a study, for instance the choice between different wage earner existences and a career as an entrepreneur. Earlier, it was more frequent that children picked the same career as their parents, which meant that you were almost born to a certain career. Despite of the fact that it is still possible to find such a career model today, the young generations are nowadays more challenged to create their own future. As Down says, *"We are entrepreneurs of the self"* (Down 2006: 5). Therefore, it is important to young people in general to know what entrepreneurship involves and be trained in it.

Last but not least, entrepreneurship is exciting. As an entrepreneur you participate in creating something new, typically in association with others who find it challenging and instructive working in the pioneer phase where new things come into existence.

Elevator-Pitch for existing organisations

Entrepreneurship is also of great value for existing organisations. The thing is that organisations can have difficulties surviving if they are not able to differentiate and renew themselves, which is essential in a globalised world. In the context of our globalised world, it is about competition in everything and from everywhere. It is also a world that has no speed limits (Nordström 2000). One of the consequences of the technological development is that the products and services offered by the organisations constantly become obsolete. Therefore, organisations constantly have to renew themselves (new products, materials, markets, technologies, processes etc.).

Differentiation and renewal require organisations to be capable of creating or discovering new opportunities and go for them which is exactly the heart of entrepreneurship. That is why organisations often seek employees who have something more to offer than the traditional management competencies which focus on the ability to plan, organise and coordinate. What the organisations want are employees who are entrepreneurial, innovative, adaptable and creative. Thus, entrepreneurship is also of value to you who are going to become an employee in an already existing organisation.

Elevator-Pitch for society

The value of entrepreneurship to society as a whole is also worth considering. Especially since the 1970s, entrepreneurship has been perceived as a tool that can be used to generate jobs, economic growth and wealth in society. In the seventies, especially Bolton (1971) and Birch (1979) proposed the revolutionary thought that small companies are more important to the economy than the big ones are. They are to a higher extent taking part in creating economic growth. The thought still lives and the importance of entrepreneurship in a socio-economic perspective is often highlighted. In Entrepreneur Index 2007 it says for instance: *"Annually, about 20 percent of all new jobs in Denmark are created in new companies. Especially the growth-oriented entrepreneurs contribute to the creation of new jobs. The growth-oriented entrepreneurs only represent about 5 percent of the surviving companies but they create almost half of the jobs of a year's cohort of entrepreneurs"* (Erhvervs- og Byggestyrelsen 2007: 7).

From this perspective, it is not surprising that it is a political objective to increase the numbers of entrepreneurs in Denmark, especially the numbers of entrepreneurs who focus on growth. And there is certainly room for improvement. With respect to the percentage of the population who starts new organisations and the percentage of entrepreneurs who create growth, Denmark is lagging behind the best countries (Schøtt 2007).

In addition, entrepreneurship is famous for taking part in developing a healthy competition in the economy because of the fact that the entrepreneur constantly pushes new ideas, products, services and processes into the market. Indeed, new areas of business and markets emerge as a result of the entrepreneurial behaviour. Alternative energy via wind turbines can be mentioned as an example of a Danish entrepreneurial fairytale that has created a new area of business of great importance to our ability to solve environmental and climate problems now and in the future.

Therefore, through entrepreneurship education, you come to understand a phenomenon that is exciting and important to you, existing organisations and society. Do we need to say more? Entrepreneurship is worth studying.

■ A historical flashback

Nothing comes to this world from nothing. All phenomena are part of a longer historical process of learning. This feature also applies to entrepreneurship. Entrepreneurship also has a history. Let us go on a journey back in time in order to delve into this history. You will gain a better understanding of what entrepreneurship is and how the phenomenon can be defined. We have divided the field into four traditions: 1) the economic tradition; 2) the social-psychological tradition; 3) the emergence tradition; and 4) the opportunity tradition.

The economic tradition

Entrepreneurship is an old phenomenon. Thus it has developed differently in different societies. When we look back in time – back to ancient Rome – personal wealth was highly respected if it was not created directly from participation in commercial activities. These activities were reserved for previous slaves and other emancipated men. Wealth and prestige could go hand in hand only if the wealth was created through private property, yields from loans and investments or political benefits. Obviously, it influenced the development of entrepreneurship in ancient Rome. Later on, warfare and conquering of land were considered kinds of entrepreneurship. Thus, conquering and taking over resources were considered as natural parts of the endeavours to discover and exploit new opportunities (Baumol 1990).

Not until around 1755, does the entrepreneurial phenomenon get formally introduced in the literature of trade, economy and business development. Cantillon (1680-1734) is often emphasised as an important pioneer within the entrepreneurial context (Landström 1999). To him, the function of entrepreneurship was to equalise discrepancies between supply and demand by buying something cheap for the purpose of selling it again at a price that as far as possible was higher. Therefore, the entrepreneur is a person who is getting hold of and allocates resources by running a risk and consequently balances the economy (Murphy et al. 2006). In the late 18th century, the concept of entrepreneurship is extended to include a perception of the entrepreneur as a person who plans, supervises, organises or even owns production factors. This perception is a contrast to how the 19th century distinguishes between those who provide means and those who create profit (Coulter 2003).

An important person of the 20th century is Knight. He pinpoints that the entrepreneur should be able to cope with certain aspects of uncertainty (Sarasvathy et al. 2005).

■ The first type of uncertainty appears when different outcomes in the future both exist and are known. In such case, it is required of the entrepreneur to calculate the possibilities and make decisions on the basis of those. It might be compared with the way in which meteorologists determine when the sun rises and sets.

■ The other type of uncertainty appears in cases when the outcomes of the future exist but are unknown in advance. An example could be your own dying day. You know that you shall die but when it will be is unknown. In these situations, the entrepreneur will have to estimate the outcome of the future in the light of experiments that have been repeated over and over again and finally make decisions in the light of those.

■ The last type of uncertainty, which Knight refers to as the true uncertainty, appears when the outcomes of the future are not existing which means that it is not possible to know anything about them. The entrepreneur receives profit as compensation for coping with the true uncertainty.

So the entrepreneur is willing to spend time, capital and risking his career by dealing with uncertain projects. He or she is the investor, the owner of the economic resources. Uncertainty is present in each economy because decisions about input must be made immediately in order to create output in the future where the demand is an unknown factor. The consumer is not willing to commit himself or herself to an uncertain demand in the future which leaves the investor in a risky position (Casson 1982).

Anyway, it is the function which Schumpeter (1934) attributes to the entrepreneur that really has given rise to today's understanding of entrepreneurship. According to Schumpeter, the economic uncertainty does not attribute to the entrepreneur as a capitalist who allocates means to the entrepreneur. Instead, the entrepreneur is an innovator who by combining something existing creates new opportunities and organisations in the economy – he or she is the main source leading to the development of the economy. Schumpeter presupposes that the starting point is a balanced economy until an entrepreneur by combining something existing creates new opportunities and thereby creates an imbalance in the market. But at the same time the imbalance contributes to the development of the economy. The new opportunity can be:

■ Introduction of new products or the quality subscribed to these
■ Introduction of new methods of production
■ Opening of new markets
■ Exploitation of new contractor relationships
■ Reorganising of a business

Schumpeter assumes that the new factors will oust existing organisations and create waves of change in the economy. He talks about this process in terms of creative destruction. All the time, new projects and organisations are created while others close down. If an entrepreneur is successful, imitators will imitate the entrepreneur and enter the market. In line with the fact that the market becomes satisfied, a new equilibrium will emerge in the economy. Of course, critique can be raised against Schumpeterian theory. One possible objection could be: Are the new things always better than the old ones? Why is uncertainty not attached to the entrepreneur's actions? However, there is no doubt that Schumpeter made a crucial point about the link between entrepreneurship, innovation and economic growth.

The social-psychological tradition

In the years between 1960 and the 1980s, entrepreneurship is often defined from a psychological perspective. Especially, McClelland's (1961) work: "The Achieving Society" gives rise to these thoughts. This work presents the story about why some people concentrate on financial affairs and as a result of that are rich while others are not. In addition to this, it is a story about why some societies manage better financially than other societies, in spite of the fact that they have similar starting points. The need to achieve among the players in a given society is pinpointed as the key to the mystery. This need is linked to the entrepreneurial personality which effectively means that psychological explanations gain ground in the entrepreneurial research field. Especially psychological differences between entrepreneurs and non-entrepreneurs are of scientific interest (Carland 1984). One of the first investigations of the personal characteristics of successful entrepreneurial individuals is made by Hornaday and Bunker (1970). They emphasise many different entrepreneurial qualities, for instance "energetic participation in endeavour", "confidence", "desire for being your own boss" and "need to achieve".

But from the mid-80s this literature fades away. Especially three aspects of criticism emerge:

- By studying individual qualities, such as the need to achieve, one seems to ignore the influence that personal qualities have on each other and how environmental factors tend to shape the entrepreneurial behaviour.

- In addition, the psychological perspective has given rise to so many personal characteristics and factors that the entrepreneur has been characterised as an "everyman".

■ Finally, the studies have not empirically made it possible to point out the entrepreneurial personality in the crowd. Especially the article: "Who is the Entrepreneur? Is the Wrong Question" (Gartner 1988), has contributed to the criticism of the psychological approach.

Over the years the psychological research tradition has been supplemented with a sociological tradition. The sociological tradition focuses on interpersonal relations more than on the individual. Therefore, it is possible to talk about a social-psychological tradition which is interested in man as an individual and social entrepreneurial actor (Aldrich 1999). The social-psychological tradition will be further discussed in chapter 2.

The emergence tradition
Recent theory has put emphasis on understanding entrepreneurship as an organising process that leads to a certain output, namely the creation of a new organisation. The facts that tend to distinguish entrepreneurs from non-entrepreneurs are not personal qualities but the fact that entrepreneurs create new organisations. This consideration was introduced in the theoretical field in the 1980s. Thus, entrepreneurship is considered as an organisational phenomenon; entrepreneurship is *"... synonymous with the behavioural act of new venture creation"* (Pittaway 2003: 22).

By defining entrepreneurship as an organisational emergence process, entrepreneurship is synonymous with the shaping of new structures because the organisations are characterised by a certain extent of formal structure, administrative procedures and objectives (Bakka & Fiveldal 2004). However, an important boundary exists as conventional organising theory *"... begins at the place where the emerging organization ends"* (Kats & Gartner 1988: 429). This means that the entrepreneurship research field primarily concentrates on the process that leads to the creation of a new organisation while organising theory primarily focuses on what happens when the organisation has been created and is further developed.

From the very beginning, this literature has by nature, to a great extent, been behaviour-oriented. This means that it has focused on what activities the entrepreneur is dealing with in the process of creating a new organisation. Carter et al. (1996) analyse for instance what kind of activities 71 entrepreneurs are preoccupied with in the start-up process.

The opportunity tradition

However, the emergence tradition has a competitor. We call the competitor the opportunity tradition. Instead of defining entrepreneurship as a field dealing with organisation creation, the opportunity tradition defines entrepreneurship as: *"… discovery, evaluation and exploitation of opportunities to introduce new goods and services, ways of organizing, markets, processes and raw materials"* (Shane 2003: 4). From that perspective, opportunity or opportunity emergence is likely to be seen as the heart of the entrepreneurial process. In addition, it makes it possible for entrepreneurial activities to end in different outputs, as for instance an independent organisation. Another possible output one could think of is entrepreneurship in the context of already existing organisations, voluntary organisations and public institutions.

The opportunity tradition sees innovation as crucial in order to talk about entrepreneurship. Entrepreneurial actions involve creativity and have the potential for changing the already existing economic market conditions. According to Eckhardt and Shane (2003), entrepreneurship involves the creation of new opportunities, objectives, means or means-ends chains.

It is not enough to optimise existing objectives, means or means-ends chains. Entrepreneurship is characterised by the creation or identification of new objectives, means or means-ends chains, implying that emphasis is on the minority of organisations, either new or existing, which give rise to new products, production methods, markets and reorganisations. This is based on opportunities that contribute something new to the world that we already know. Thus, the concept of opportunity is a very crucial concept to the opportunity tradition. Eckhardt and Shane define opportunity: *"… as situations in which new goods, services, raw materials, markets and organizing methods can be introduced through the formation of new means, ends, or means-ends relationships"* (Eckhardt & Shane 2003: 336).

■ The starting point of the book

From a historical perspective, a wide range of understandings of what entrepreneurship is has existed. Many of these understandings live side by side today and they are still developing. Effectively, this pinpoints how important it is that you position yourself within the range of understandings when you write a project or express something about entrepreneurship. In the following section, the understanding which we align with in this book will be outlined and positioned.

A complementary approach

The literature on entrepreneurship supplies us with many different suggestions for the way in which the entrepreneurial process is likely to be perceived. Some think that this process can be illustrated as a phase or life cycle sequence. From this point of view, all entrepreneurial processes develop through the same phases which it is possible to point out in advance. Some examples of these phases are: 1) initiation, 2) development, 3) growth 4) maturity and 5) decline (Kroeger 1974). Reynolds (1997) suggests the following phases: 1) conception, 2) gestation, 3) infancy 4) adolescence. In spite of the fact that it is assumed that the phases attributing to these models are universal, the phases vary in number and content across the different models.

Today, the emergence and opportunity traditions represent two dominating perspectives in the entrepreneurial research, aiming to improve our understanding of the entrepreneurial process. They are often presented as competing perspectives. However, the starting point of the book is that the two traditions can be encountered as complementary. The argument is that the entrepreneurial process in practice involves emergence (discovery or creation) of opportunities, evaluation of opportunities as well as organisation of opportunities. Opportunity emergence means that the entrepreneur discovers or creates a business opportunity, for instance by combining something already existing into a completely new or improved product. On the other hand, opportunity evaluation focuses on the evaluation of the opportunity in relation to whether it is attractive or not to the market. Opportunity organising appears when the entrepreneur attempts to make use of the opportunity by implementing it so the market actors can be aware of it, understand it and act in accordance with it.

The fact that the emergence and opportunity tradition can be encountered as complementary approaches is also pinpointed by Bygrave and Hofer's definition of the entrepreneur: He or she is a person *"… who perceives an opportunity and creates an organization to pursue it"* (Bygrave & Hofer 1991: 14). Or Shane's (2003) perception of the essence of entrepreneurship: *"Entrepreneurship is an activity that involves the discovery, evaluation and exploitation of opportunities to introduce new goods and services, ways of organizing markets, processes and raw materials through organizing efforts that previously had not existed"* (Shane 2003: 4).

The complementary nature that characterises the two traditions can be illustrated by the establishment of a new association. Associations often reflect a political interest among a group, as for instance students who are interested in environmentalism or the relation between industrialised and developing countries. A group of politically engaged students might for instance consider how to optimise their opportunities for influencing top decision-makers through establishment of a new association. What might be important here is to consider whether there is "room" left for one more student association traditionally established, or if there is an opportunity for an alternative way of organising through for example a virtual network. From the perspective of the emergence tradition, it is possible to understand this case as a traditional collective organising process while from the perspective of the opportunity tradition it could be perceived as a different and new way of organising an association. Both traditions hence contribute to the understanding of a specific case.

Figure 1.1 illustrates the perception of entrepreneurship applied in this book as a three-part process that involves emergence, evaluation and organising of opportunities. Thus, both the emergence and opportunity traditions are in play. The figure is designed as a spiral to underpin that the book dissociates itself from the idea that the process is linear. The process is not made up of clear and definable phases that naturally build on each other. Instead, it is often iterative, parallel and overlapping.

Figure 1.1: How entrepreneurship is construed in the context of this book

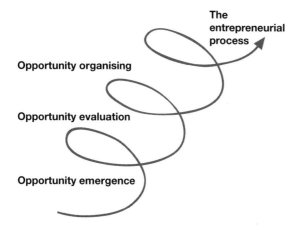

The entrepreneurial process

Opportunity organising

Opportunity evaluation

Opportunity emergence

Chapters 3, 4 and 5 will go into details about this figure. Chapter 3 focuses on opportunity emergence and the perspectives of discovery or creation. Chapter 4 deals with opportunity evaluation and chapter 5 focuses on opportunity exploitation through organising.

Core topics

The processes linked to emergence, evaluation and organising of new opportunities are extremely complex. Different factors play a part, such as environments, demography, the entrepreneur's previous experiences, career, personality, self-perception, strategic decisions etc. Particularly, the book wants to emphasise four topics that influence the process. The topics are: 1) the individual, 2) resources, 3) networks and 4) the business plan. The topics are illustrated in figure 1.2.

Figure 1.2: Core topics for entrepreneurship

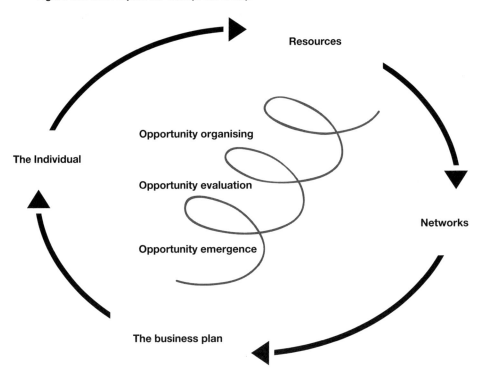

Why are these topics important? The entrepreneurial individual is of great importance for the development of entrepreneurship. After all, it is the individual or a
smaller group of individuals who take the initiative and carry through the process.
And imaginative and creative processes take place in the minds of individuals.
Resources are important inputs in the attempt towards discovering or creating a
new opportunity and organising it. They are the material that is the starting point
for entrepreneurship. Resources are likely to be encountered broadly as human,
social and financial resources.

Social relationships – networks – are of great importance. In spite of the fact that
entrepreneurship in many ways is a lonely journey, it is emphasised over and over
again that this process to a higher extent is a network journey. The entrepreneur
constantly interacts with others (bank employees, potential customers, advisers
and other entrepreneurs etc.) and creates networks. These networks are absolutely
crucial in the sense that they give him or her access to knowledge, resources etc.
which are essential to the development of entrepreneurship.

The business plan perceived as a written document is not necessarily a part of all
entrepreneurial processes but a certain degree of planning is present in all of these
processes. The business plan is also likely to have different meanings. At times, its
meaning is to create a foundation for the acquiring of resources or for the evaluation of the entrepreneurial process. At other times, the purpose of the business
plan is to support the entrepreneur in the planning process.

As it appears from the table of contents, chapters 2, 6, 7 and 8 of the book will
treat each of the four topics in more detail which explains why they are only
superficially touched upon here. Thus in the process of reading the book, you will
not only gain a greater insight into crucial activities in the entrepreneurial process,
namely the emergence, evaluation and organising of opportunities, you will also
come to understand the important topics which influence these activities.

The importance of the context
So far, we have dealt with entrepreneurship as a phenomenon that takes place in a
vacuum. We have not touched upon the way in which the entrepreneurial process
is influenced by the unique context that surrounds it. A tendency to ignore the context is also prevalent to entrepreneurship research. Emphasis is on the flower (the
new organisation) and the gardener (the entrepreneur) while the garden itself (the
context) and its influence remain a mystery. That is an important shortcoming.

It makes a difference what kind of context entrepreneurship takes place within, especially because the context influences what networks and resources the entrepreneur has access to in his opportunity emergence, evaluation and organising process. Additionally, different contexts will have an affect on the entrepreneur's opportunity to act. For example, contexts with entrepreneurship furthering norms and values give rise to a higher level of entrepreneurial activity among its members (Gnyawali & Fogel 1994). Finally, heterogeneous contexts will confront the entrepreneur with different barriers and opportunities.

An entrepreneur within the university context can feel inhibited by the academic norms and their emphasis on details and generation of knowledge in preference to action and commercialisation. This can cause tensions in the entrepreneurial process. But the university context also provides the entrepreneur with a lot of opportunities, for instance in terms of unique knowledge which he or she can use for the purpose of developing his or her opportunity. Last but not least, when breaking with their familiar contexts, entrepreneurs can experience a feeling of loneliness if the context does not legitimise their entrepreneurial actions. A professor from the University of Aalborg who has started his own organisation says: *"I compare entrepreneurship with going to war. When you go to war, you are either a loser or a winner… that is very obvious because of the fact that you are at war. To be an innovator is like this. It feels very dangerous because you might go to war against the old-fashioned research culture or you might join the battle in order to win a market. If you are able to create a success then you have won. But your little company can also go under and then you lose. Experiencing such a thing will inevitably make you feel lonely."*

The importance of the context has made us work out two significant chapters in this book – chapters which are not often included in textbooks about entrepreneurship, namely a chapter about intrapreneurship (chapter 9) and a chapter about social entrepreneurship (chapter 10).

■ Ready for departure

We hope that at this point you have a better understanding of how valuable it is to study entrepreneurship, what entrepreneurship is and how the book comprehends the phenomenon. In any case, it was the aim of the introductory chapter. Now you are going on an exciting journey where you will have the opportunity of scrutinising crucial topics for entrepreneurship from a practical as well as a theoretical point of view. You know the itinerary. However, before the final departure we will make sure that you have packed your suitcase with the right concepts. Therefore, we supply you with an overview of crucial concepts which are essential for your understanding of the book.

- *Entrepreneurship* = Broad concept that generally speaking can be defined as: discovery or creation of new opportunities which are evaluated and exploited through organising
- *The emergence tradition* = A tradition within the context of entrepreneurship that emphasises: the creation of new organisational structures which function as a frame for an opportunity related to a specific market demand.
- *The opportunity tradition* = Another tradition within the context of entrepreneurship that focuses on: the break with existing structures via identification and creation of new opportunities
- *The entrepreneurial process* = The movement from discovering or creating an opportunity to evaluation of the opportunity to finally exploiting it through organising
- *Entrepreneur/intrapreneur* = The individual who initiates, strives for and organisess entrepreneurship
- *Paradox* = A conflicting statement which will be introduced in the book as two conflicting theoretical perspectives
- *Perspective* = A theoretical approach which represents one of the two statements that pertain to the paradox
- *Opportunity* = An idea which is evaluated as capable of creating value for others
- *Opportunity emergence* = The process in which the opportunity emerges led by individuals who discover or create the opportunity
- *Opportunity evaluation* = The process in which the entrepreneur evaluates to what extent the idea represents an attractive opportunity
- *Opportunity organising* = Creation of some meaningful structures that support the realisation of the opportunity, for instance to collect resources, to coordinate activities and to involve others so that the wanted output can be obtained

Literature

Aldrich, H. E. (1999). Organizations Evolving. London: Saga.

Bakka, J. F. & Fivelsdal, E. (2004). Organisationsteori: Struktur, kultur og processer. Copenhagen: Handels-højskolens Forlag.

Baumol, W. J. (1990). Entrepreneurship: Productive, Unproductive and Destructive, Journal of Political Economy, 98(5), 893-921.

Birch, D. L. (1979). The Job Generation Process. Cambridge: MIT Program on Neighbourhood and Regional Change.

Bolton, J. E. (1971). Small firms: Report of the Committee of Inquiry on Small Firms. London: Her Majesty's Stationery Office.

Erhvervs- & Byggestyrelsen (2007). Iværksætterindeks 2007 – Vilkår for iværksættere i Danmark. Copenhagen: Erhvervs- og Byggestyrelsen.

Bygrave, W. D. & Hofer, C. W. (1991). Theorizing About Entrepreneurship, Entrepreneurship Theory & Practice, 16(2), 13-22.

Carland, J. W. (1984). Differentiating Entrepreneurs from Small Business Owners: A Conceptualization, Academy of Management Review, 9(2), 354-359.

Carter, N. M., Gartner, W. B. & Reynolds, P. D. (1996). Exploring Start-up Event Sequences, Journal of Business Venturing, 11, 151-166.

Casson, M. (1982). The Entrepreneur. Totowa, NJ: Barnes and Noble Books.

Coulter, M. (2003). Entrepreneurship in Action. Upper Saddle River, NJ: Prentice Hall.

Down, S. (2006). Narratives of Enterprise: Crafting Entrepreneurial Self-identity in a Small Firm. Cheltenham: Edward Elgar.

Eckhardt, J. T. & Shane, S. (2003). Opportunities and Entrepreneurship, Journal of Management, 29(3), 333-349.

Gartner, W. B. (1988). Who is the Entrepreneur? Is the wrong Question, American Journal of Small Business, 12(4), 11-32.

Gartner, W. B. (2001). Is There an Elephant in Entrepreneurship? Blind Assumptions in Theory Development, Entrepreneurship Theory & Practice, 25, 27-39.

Gnyawali, D. R. & Fogel, D. S. (1994). Environments for Entrepreneurship Development: Key Dimensions and Research Implications, Entrepreneurship: Theory and Practice, 18, 43-62.

Hornaday, J. A. & Bunker, C. S. (1970). The nature of the entrepreneur, Personnel Psychology, 23(1), 47-54.

Kats, J. & Gartner, W. B. (1988). Properties of Emerging Organizations, Academy of Management Journal, 13(3), 429-441.

Kroeger, C. V. (1974). Managerial Development in Small Firm, California Management Review, 17(1), 41-47.

Landström, H. (1999). The Roots of Entrepreneurship Research, New England Journal of Entrepreneurship, 2, 9-20.

McClelland, D. C. (1961). The Achieving Society. Canada: D. Van Nostrand Company Ltd.

Murphy, R. J., Liao, J. & Welsch, H. P. (2006). A Conceptual History of Entrepreneurship Thought, Journal of Management History, 12(1), 12-35.

Nordström, K. (2000). Funky Business: Talent Makes Capital Dance. London: BookHouse.

Pittaway, L. (2003). Paradigms as Heuristics: A Review of the Philosophies Underpinning Economic Studies in Entrepreneurship, Lancaster University Management Scholl, 1-30.

Reynolds, P. D. (1997). Who Starts New Firms? Preliminary Explorations of Firms-in-gestation, Small Business Economics, 9, 449-462.

Sarasvathy, S., Dew, N., Velamuri, S. R. & Venkataraman, S. (2005). Three views of entrepreneurial opportunities. In Acs, Z. J. & Audretsch, D. B. (Ed.), Handbook of Entrepreneurship Research (pp. 141-160). Springer.

Schumpeter, J. A. (1934). The Theory of Economic Development. Cambride: Harvard University Press.

Shane, S. (2003). A General Theory of Entrepreneurship: The Individual-opportunity Nexus. Cheltenham: Edward Elgar.

Steyaert, C. & Hjorth, D. (2003). New Movements in Entrepreneurship. Cheltenham: Edward Elgar.

Sørensen, S., Sørensen, O. J. & Pedersen, L. M. (2006). Iværksætterpulsen 2006: Har alle nordjyske studerende entreprenant vokseværk, eller gør uddannelsesmæssig tilknytning en forskel? Institut for Erhvervsstudier: Aalborg Universitet.

What is entrepreneurship?

48

Chapter 2

Who is the entrepreneur?

Without a person who initiates and shapes the entrepreneurial process the entre-preneurial process does not exist. If new opportunities are to be created whether it is new opportunities that will lead to a new organisation or a radically different way of handling things within the context of an existing organisation, it must be initiated and maintained by individuals or groups of individuals. Especially in the start-up phase where the new opportunity must stand its test, the individual plays an important part. At this point, the new opportunity depends on the individual because no processes or activities function automatically yet. Not until the later phases of the lifecycle of an opportunity – the phases where the opportunity has been organised, generally known and accepted, does the individual begin to play a less important part.

In other words, individuals or groups of individuals leave their clear marks on the way in which new opportunities emerge, are evaluated and organised. In entrepre-neurship, a lot depends on the entrepreneur and it becomes very crucial to exa-mine what kind of qualities the entrepreneur has. Who is the individual that creates entrepreneurship? Kilby writes in a famous article: The entrepreneur is *"... a rather large and important animal. He has been hunted by many individuals using various trapping devices, but no one has so far succeeded in capturing him. All who claim to have caught a sight of him report he is enormous, but disagree on his particu-lars"* (Kilby 1971: 1). Apparently, it remains a mystery who the entrepreneur is. But let us see if we shall manage to find an answer to the above mentioned question.

■ Meet entrepreneurship in practice

Below, you will be introduced to two entrepreneurs. In many ways, their situation probably reminds you of your own situation. The two entrepreneurs involved are Thomas and Mette who develop their opportunities, evaluate and organise them while they are still students.

To have a dream

"I actually think that it is something that you get aware of early in life (...). You seek for something that is unique for your person." That is how Thomas, a 24-year-old man, substantiates why he at one time became an entrepreneur. He is now the owner of a successful company in Aalborg (a town in the Northern part of Den-mark). The company, Bodyman.dk sells vitamin supplements to food, street- and fitness wear and more through two sales channels: the internet and a big physical store in Aalborg city. He headhunted his employees where he studied. Thomas's partner, Kåre, is a fellow student to Thomas. They met at their first semester at the

university. When we meet Thomas, he studies a masters degree in business economics, specialising in financial management and informatics at his 7th semester.

Early in life, it comes to you
Thomas has been aware of the entrepreneurial career since he was a child. *"I think
my father has always had a dream of becoming an entrepreneur. But he never
dared to take the plunge. Therefore, at home we always talked about how fantastic
it was that some people did dare to run the risk. Thus, it was something that we
admired and if I should make my father happy, then I should do it (…). I do not think
that you are born to do things but you are influenced by something or someone
and I was just influenced by the point of view that people who are entrepreneurs
are admirable."* Obviously, early in life, Thomas had a good mind to become an
entrepreneur.

Becoming an entrepreneur is apparently also something that is linked to Thomas's
personality. He feels best when he is charged with the task of motivating people
and making them follow his advice. As chairman of the pupils' council at upper
secondary school, he initiates the collection of money for the purpose of having
Kashmir (a music band) to play in connection with one of the parties taking place
at the school. But he is definitely not a control-freak. In groups, he appears as the
creative person who brings many ideas. Furthermore, Thomas reacts negatively
towards authorities. Once in connection with an exam, he was picked out to hand-
write a document instead of using one of the computers at the school. He refused
to participate. It made no difference that the head master met him with serious
threats.

What is a dream without an opportunity?
Before becoming entrepreneurs, when Thomas and Kåre attended lectures, they
discussed possible ideas. In the course of time, many ideas have appeared, such
as a housing site on the internet, sale of second-hand study books over the internet etc. However, none of the ideas represents real opportunities. But then something happens: *"Kåre never has money. So one day he came to me saying, 'If you
buy for 1,000 kroner of vitamin supplements to food on your visa card in Germany,
then I promise that during the next three days I will sell all of it and then you get
1,500 kroner back.'"* Three days later, Thomas receives 1,500 Danish kroner. They
continue the game. They deposit the profit in a bank account. When the account
has been filled with a sufficient amount of money, the two students buy a bigger
amount of food supplements and a home page. The sale is growing. Soon they
invest money in a small shop and stock facilities.

However, other entrepreneurs soon imitate their success. The reaction of the two students is an extension of the assortment. Now they also sell fitness clothing. The interesting thing is that the two students apparently never would have started their organisation if Kåre had not borrowed money from Thomas. *"We had a lot of ideas of what we could possibly do. But I do not think that we had ever started if it was not for that event. It was not planned that it should happen. But then we had that chance and then it happened."*

Because of the fact that the start-up process is quite short and unpredictable, the market analysis is not a part of the process: *"We jumped into it."* Not until now when they look back, can they begin to express what the idea, mission and business concept of their organisation is.

A part of the past
In spite of the fact that Thomas has now started his own company, he is constantly aware of new opportunities. This means that during the last year he has been involved in one more entrepreneurial adventure. This adventure gets started by Thomas and three other young and successful entrepreneurs from Aalborg. The organisation is called Concept Investors A/S which is a common platform for development and commercialising of the four entrepreneurs' future business concepts. Especially the concept "Meet Your Messenger" is important. This is a virtual overview which all messenger users of the world can register for in order to secure existing networks and create new networks. However, Thomas has resigned from the project in spite of the fact that it is an enormous commercial success. Now he is back full time in Bodyman.dk. He does no longer see himself as an entrepreneur because he works at improving Bodyman.dk within the frames of an existing strategy. To him, an entrepreneur is a person who starts new things. *"I no longer see myself as an entrepreneur because these days I only run the company. The new things we do are all within an already defined strategy."*

Engineer in a foreign territory
Here is Mette's story. A group of engineering students who are soon about to finish their masters degree are joined around a project topic that their instructor has formulated. Everything is as usual. What they are dealing with is only one of many project exercises which the students have to write in order to pass their exam. The project topic is clear. The purpose is to measure acceleration on offshore constructions. Wind and waves make these constructions move. The consequences can be very expensive cracks in the construction. Therefore, it is an important but also a burdening task to inspect these constructions. The group is to develop a measu-

ring method that can reduce the uncertainty and the costs associated with these inspections.

Pushed into entrepreneurship
"It was actually our instructor who himself had a company that started pushing us. He said, 'I hope you are aware of the fact that you have invented something here. What about starting a company?'" The students begin to play with the thought in spite of the fact that Mette is sure that, *"... it would be easy to find someone who is more truly an entrepreneur than I am."* She and other group member have never before considered becoming entrepreneurs.

When the students graduate, they have not seriously got into the process of starting the organisation. They have primarily focused on developing the idea, trying to figure out to what extent the idea may result in savings in comparison with traditional offshore measuring equipment. The instructor recommends the students to apply for a wage-earner job. He will work on commercialising their opportunity. He will call them soon.

Other parties get interested
The instructor has found a group of Business Angels who would like to hear more about the students' idea. Business Angels are private individuals who invest their own means in new ventures in which they also function as active sparring partners. The group of Business Angels are interested. But they also have a question: What kinds of activities are carried out in connection with the inspections of off-shore constructions and does the students' idea make commercial sense in this light? The students choose to send scientific articles out to key players in the business in order to get some statements that testify the existence of a foundation for their idea – the idea is a potential opportunity.

Now, the students also begin to look for knowledge about how to start their own organisation. They start at an entrepreneur course, they write a business plan and they get attached to a hardened businessman who functions as their mentor. But unfortunately, in spite of the fact that the articles in general cause positive feedback, the related business sector doubts that the idea may result in a business. It simply does not reduce the costs associated with the inspection of off-shore constructions. However, the students go far in their efforts towards uncovering the business potential – Norwegian Hydro, Maersk etc. They also win the business plan competition arranged by Venture Cup in the central and northern part of Jutland. But at last, they conclude that it is not possible to carry out the idea.

Now they are wage earners ·

The students return to jobs as wage earners. But even today, Mette often thinks of the idea and its potential. These days, she works for a consultative engineering company. When Mette looks back, she believes that it is possible that others would have been able to start a company on the basis of the idea. The students did not have the required entrepreneurial enthusiasm as they did not really dream of becoming entrepreneurs. *"If Casper and I had been more true entrepreneurs of the heart, it is possible that we had managed to start our own company. In the middle of the process, too little emphasis was on the aspect of actually getting something started. It might have been different if it originally had turned us on."* However, the experience has influenced Mette in the way that she more than ever feels like starting her own company.

■ Your immediate interpretation

What do the stories tell you about the entrepreneurial individual? How will you understand it at first sight? The exercises listed below will support you in creating your own interpretation of the two stories.

- ■ Make a list and discuss the character features which find expression in the two stories. Who are the two entrepreneurs?
- ■ Imagine that the two entrepreneurs present their stories to you and your fellow students. Your teacher asks you to give a short account of how far both entrepreneurs can actually be defined as entrepreneurs. What seems to confirm that it is the case? What seems to speak against it? How would you define an entrepreneur?
- ■ One of your fellow students pinpoints that the two entrepreneurs do not start up alone but together with others. Does it tell you something about the entrepreneurial individual? Why do you think that entrepreneurs often start up in teams instead of starting alone?
- ■ You have decided to start your own organisation but you prefer starting it with others. As regards your efforts to make up the perfect start-up team, what will you take into account? What character features, competencies, networks etc. should be attached to the other members of your start-up team?
- ■ You meet one of your friends. She has already started two organisations. You discuss what it takes to create an entrepreneurial person. She claims that she was born to be an entrepreneur. What do you think of this argument?

■ Theories of entrepreneurship

In 2007, 5.4 percent of the Danish population were active entrepreneurs in the sense that they were starting or had just started their own independent organisations (Schøtt 2007). But what characterises these entrepreneurial individuals? The theory can give us some answers. But it points in different directions. Some theories claim that the entrepreneur possesses a particular personality – a personality that she or he is more or less born with. The logic is that the personality which individuals are equipped with from birth makes them act in a certain way. Other theories emphasise that the entrepreneurial individual is created through different types of dynamics – some related to the individual and others to the environment. This also means that individuals are not necessarily born to be entrepreneurs. Over time they can become entrepreneurs. Depending on what kind of situations and experiences the individual is exposed to through his or her life, these will shape the starting point for whether the individual will be motivated to measure his or her strengths towards an entrepreneurial career or not. In short, through this chapter you will be introduced to the paradox to what extent entrepreneurs are:

Born or Made?

When you read the chapter you must remember that the entrepreneur is not only an entrepreneur. It is possible to talk about different types of entrepreneurs. Entrepreneurs are often divided into six different groups:

- ■ "Novice" entrepreneur (a person without entrepreneurial experience)
- ■ "Habitual" entrepreneur (a person with previous entrepreneurial experience)
- ■ "Nascent" entrepreneur (a person who is in the process of creating a new organisation – he or she can both be "novice" and "habitual")
- ■ "Serial" entrepreneur (a person who constantly establishes and sells organisations)
- ■ "Portfolio" entrepreneur (a person who owns several organisations at the same time)
- ■ Intrapreneur (a person who acts entrepreneurially in the context of an existing organisation). This type of entrepreneur will be discussed thoroughly in chapter 9.

The entrepreneur is a character in disguise

Who is the individual that creates entrepreneurship? This is, as already mentioned, a crucial question in this chapter. In the economic tradition which was introduced in chapter 1, we discussed the entrepreneurial function attached to the entrepreneur. However, the economic tradition has primarily focused on the entrepreneur's function in the economy. It has not emphasised who the entrepreneur is. As Hérbert and Link write in the light of an analysis of economic theory: *"… referred to often but rarely ever studied or even carefully defined, the entrepreneur winds his way through economic history, producing results often attributed to faceless institutions or impersonal market structures"* (Hérbert & Link 1988: 11). Especially one economist, Schumpeter (1934) goes into details as regards the function which the entrepreneur has for the economy. He explains how the entrepreneur is an innovator who by means of creative destruction creates new waves of economic growth. But according to Schumpeter, not everybody has the ability to carry out creative destruction. Schumpeter pinpoints that entrepreneurs are individuals who have:

- A wish to establish a private kingdom: *"First of all, there is the dream and the will to found a private kingdom, usually, though not necessarily, also a dynasty."*

- A will to conquer: *"Then there is the will to conquer: The impulse to fight, to prove oneself superior to others, to succeed for the sake, not of the fruits of success, but of success itself. From this aspect, economic action becomes akin to sport – there are financial races, or rather boxing-matches."*

- A delight in creating: *"Finally, there is the joy of creating, of getting things done, or simply of exercising one's energy and ingenuity"* (Schumpeter 1934: 93-94).

According to Schumpeter, the described entrepreneur is different from the ordinary person. The ordinary person acts on the basis of routine. It reflects how the economists divide people into two groups: *"… those who lead and those who follow"* (Hérbert & Link 1988: 12). The entrepreneur is a member of the first group. The idea of the entrepreneur as a special person has given rise to a lot of discussions. But is it really true that it is required of you to be a special person in order to be an entrepreneur?

Entrepreneurs are Born

To discover or create opportunities, evaluate and pursue them through organising involves a certain extent of willingness to run risks, an ability to find creative solutions, a need of achieving, personal ambitions and much more. They all sound like character features attached to the personality. The question is whether some people are more inclined to have these character features or not? And are there others who prefer a more secure and conformist career model?

As mentioned in chapter 1, the entrepreneurship research field has been inspired by psychology from around 1960 until the 1980s. The main emphasis has namely been to describe the entrepreneurial person as a set of qualities or character features that attribute to the personality. Hence the psychological tradition has looked for fixed features pertaining to the entrepreneurial person and it has differentiated the population of entrepreneurs from other groups in society (Begley & Boyd 1987). To consider personality as the crucial factor that makes us act in a certain way is a way of thinking that applies to the psychological tradition. Thus, some people have some features that tend to optimise the probability that they will discover or create an opportunity and go for it through the process of organising. Personality features are: *"... constructs to explain regularities in people's behavior, and help to explain why different people react differently to the same situation"* (Llewellyn & Wilson 2003: 342).

The line of personality features that in the course of time have been identified as pertaining to the entrepreneurial person is long: inclined to run a risk, a need to achieve, independent, aggressive, leader, a belief in his/her own abilities, oriented towards actions and results, innovative, intelligent, creative, tolerant towards uncertainty and with a wish to earn money (Gartner 1988). Thus, the tradition has ended up presenting the entrepreneur as an extraordinary super-human being – a hero or a heroine.

The tradition assumes that the personality features concerned are stable over time and that the entrepreneur has acquired these more or less from birth. Just like in H.C. Andersen's fairytale of the Ugly Duckling, it is origin and not growing up that decides who you are and what you become. *"Being born in a duck yard does not matter, if only you are hatched from a swan's egg."* The consequence is *"... once an entrepreneur, always an entrepreneur, since an entrepreneur is a personality type, a state of being that doesn't go away"* (Gartner 1988: 12). As a follow-up on this, the entrepreneurial gene is wanted these years (Nicolaou et al. 2005). However, such a gene has not yet been identified.

If we take it to its logical conclusion, the result of the personality oriented thinking is that only a limited number of entrepreneurs exist in a given society because only some people are born with the appropriate character features. Furthermore, as a logical consequence, entrepreneurship education makes less sense because entrepreneur is something that you are. It is not something you can learn or develop into.

Growing up and demography in focus
Other researchers take another approach to the entrepreneurial personality. They do not think that the entrepreneurial personality is formed only by descent, they also ascribe meaning to the first years of growing up and to demographic factors. The sociological tradition represents this way of thinking. Again emphasis is on finding regularities in order to be capable of pointing out the entrepreneur in the crowd. It is presumed that factors such as birth order, independent parents, encouraging parents, working experience, education, gender, age etc. influence whether you become an entrepreneur or not (Hisrish & Peters 2001). In the search for fixed features that are exceptional to the entrepreneur's life situation, it is concluded that entrepreneurs are typically *"… first-born children, generally male, college-graduated, in their thirties at the time of their first significant venture"* (Hérbert & Link 1988: 2-3). Thus, what is of interest is not only who the entrepreneur is from the perspective of personality; also his or her social and demographic background is of interest.

The characterisation of the typical entrepreneur is in agreement with empirical research results from Denmark. They also show that the typical entrepreneur is a man, middle-aged, well educated and with self-employed parents (Schøtt 2006). Moreover, the Danish results show that a typical Danish entrepreneur, in comparison with others, is more than willing to run a risk because he or she considers opportunities as more attractive than others do and because he or she possesses more competences and knowledge about how to start a new organisation than others.

But the psychological as well as the sociological tradition have received much criticism. As a result of this, and as mentioned in chapter 1, since the 1980s, attempts have emerged towards toning down the idea of behaviour as something that is only determined by personality, upbringing or demography.

Entrepreneurs are Made
As a reaction to the outlined criticism, research of the entrepreneurial person in a wider context is initiated. Now, a number of factors with which the entrepreneur interacts in order to discover, create, evaluate and organise opportunities, become matters of great importance. Thus, the entrepreneur is perceived as formed in interaction with other individuals and other factors. In the interaction, the entrepre-

neur's market situation and life situation, networks, character features, type of organisation, experience, demography etc. play a role in determining who becomes
an entrepreneur and who does not. The theoretical approaches are extended in
order to pin down the essence of what creates an entrepreneur.

For the purpose, contingency theories rendered as systems that consist of different components in interaction, are employed. That the theory is contingent means
that something is "determined by the situation". Whether an individual becomes
an entrepreneur or not therefore depends on the situations and experiences that
he or she is exposed to. In addition, the interaction between the components of
the theories makes it possible for completely different entrepreneurial processes
and entrepreneurs to be created. The consequence is: *"The process of starting a
business is not a single well-worn route marched along again and again by identical entrepreneurs. New venture creation is a complex phenomenon: Entrepreneurs
and their firms vary widely"* (Gartner 1985: 697).

One of the well-known contingency theories in the field of entrepreneurship is
Gartner's (1985) model, illustrated in figure 2.1. The model shows that the entrepreneurial process must be regarded as a result of an interaction between four
components (the individual, the organisation, the environment and the process).

Figure 2.1: Gartner's model determined by situations

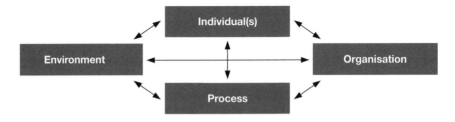

Source: Gartner (1985), p. 698.

Many other contingency theories with emphasis on the entrepreneurial individual
have been formulated – one by Timmon and Spinelli (2003). Their theory considers
the following components as crucial for entrepreneurship: opportunity, resources
and the entrepreneurial team.

Since contingency theories point at entrepreneurship as something that is created in a dynamic interaction between individuals and factors in the environment, it is implied that entrepreneurship is not something that you are born to. Instead, it is considered as something that is created by the situation, and therefore there is not only one way in which the entrepreneur can be created.

While contingency theories are effective tools to provide you with an overview of the mechanisms that are in play in entrepreneurship, they do not deal much with the entrepreneur as a person. In many ways, they remove the focus from the individual. Instead, they emphasise the interaction between some overall structures or system-components. *"The failure to find the centre of entrepreneurship in the subject of the entrepreneur has led entrepreneurship researchers towards an investigation of 'structural' factors outside the subjectivity of the entrepreneur"* (Jones & Spicer 2005: 235).

Exploration of the individual

However, during the last years, studies that take more direct starting points in studying the entrepreneurial individual have emerged. First of all through research that emphasises cognitive processes. Cognition represents the study of the way in which the mind and our thoughts are organised; how we understand and what we think about things taking place in our surroundings and inside of us. It is about the study of the brain that comes to terms with the impulses and the information which the human being receives from the environment. In the entrepreneurial research, the cognitive approach has for instance been used for the purpose of understanding why some individuals discover or create opportunities and go for these while others do not. Especially three cognitive characteristics that make entrepreneurs exploit opportunities have been emphasised (Shane 2003):

- ■ Entrepreneurs are more optimistic than others in their way of coming to terms with impulses.
- ■ Entrepreneurs are more willing than others to generalise on the basis of small tests. In that way, they have a tendency to take big decisions in spite of the fact that only little information is available.
- ■ Entrepreneurs use their intuition more than others. Thus entrepreneurs have a tendency to abstain from collecting information because they possess a feeling of or inner belief that the right thing is to exploit a given opportunity.

In addition to this, self-efficacy is often pinpointed as a crucial cognitive mechanism in the attempts towards explaining the entrepreneur's actions. Self-efficacy refs to the belief in one's own power of action and thereby the belief in one's own abilities to carry through a given action. It is a fact that: *"... people who have higher self efficacy are more likely to exploit entrepreneurial opportunities than people who have a lower self efficacy"* (Shane 2003: 111).

While cognitive research focuses on the identification of general regularities concerning the entrepreneurial individual, other types of research focus on gaining a thorough understanding of the peculiarities that attribute to the individual. Through the use of qualitative methods, this kind of research wants to use the entrepreneurial individual as its starting point for understanding how entrepreneurs perceive themselves and their environment. From this perspective, studies of the entrepreneurial identity have risen. Identity can be defined as *"... a person's sense of who he or she is in a setting"* (Weick 1995: 461). A person's perception of himself or herself is constantly changing depending on who the person interacts with and in what contexts he or she participates.

Identity is created through social processes. Additionally, it can be assumed that the individual can have multiple identities. The entrepreneurial individual is not only an entrepreneur. He or she is also a parent, a football player, a student, a part-time employee or a pensioner. These different identities affect the way in which he or she understands and carries out the entrepreneurial identity. We can for instance not expect that the individual is totally dedicated to the entrepreneurial identity. It is also possible to meet a person who is involved in the entrepreneurial process but who does not regard himself or herself as an entrepreneur. He or she perceives for instance primarily himself or herself as an engineer and the entrepreneurial process is just a means to unfold the identity as such. Entrepreneurial identity is not a list of specific qualities which are necessarily attached to the personality. Identity is a continuous process in which the entrepreneur tries to create meaning and build up an understanding of how the entrepreneurial process is running.

According to this research, all people are potentially able to develop an entrepreneurial self-perception. Creating an entrepreneurial self-perception depends on what social relations the individual is engaged in as well as his or her existing self-perception or wishes of certain future identities.

Because the creation of identity constantly takes place and is a part of everyday life, this way of thinking breaks with the perception of entrepreneurship as an extraordinary hero-phenomenon.

Internal versus external stimulation

In order to understand what starts the entrepreneurial process, it is always interesting to distinguish between the ways in which some individuals consciously chase the creation of an entrepreneurial identity – from the beginning they have an internal intention of becoming entrepreneurs – while others seem to end up as entrepreneurs as a result of external factors. We distinguish between internally and externally stimulated entrepreneurship.

Figure 2.2 illustrates how internally stimulated entrepreneurship is characterised by the fact that the intention of becoming an entrepreneur precedes discovering or creating an entrepreneurial opportunity. An individual who from childhood has had a dream of becoming an entrepreneur, usually intends to follow that way in his or her career. A realisation of the dream presupposes, however, an opportunity which the individual can be expected to consciously seek out.

Figure 2.2: Internally stimulated entrepreneurship

Intention of becoming an entrepreneur ▶	Discovery or creation of an opportunity

Theories such as Ajzen's theory about planned behaviour reflect the logic behind internally stimulated entrepreneurship. The theory suggests that action presupposes a conscious intention of carrying the action out. Intention is an indicator of how hard an individual will work in order to achieve something – for example entrepreneurship and *"… as a general rule, the stronger the intention to engage in a behaviour, the more likely should be its performance"* (Ajzen 1991: 181). Hence it follows that entrepreneurial actions are not coincidences or just a result of social stimuli. They are a result of an internal rational intention that attributes to the individual and his or her will to carry out an entrepreneurial action. Ajzen's theory provides us with some tools that help us explain and predict entrepreneurial intention because "intention" is referred to as a crystallisation of three variables:

- View of feasibility: how difficult the individual considers the entrepreneurial project – the extent of behavioural control.
- View of standards: to what extent the individual feels a social pressure in terms of carrying out the entrepreneurial action or not doing it.

■ View of desirability: to what extent the individual will choose the entrepreneurial action in favour of another action – view of the prosperity associated with the action (Ajzen 1991: 183).

The rule of thumb is that the more the individual experiences behavioural control, the more respect is gained from the surrounding world, and the more the individual experiences the action as favourable, the stronger the individual's intention of becoming an entrepreneur. An individual with a strong internal intention of becoming an entrepreneur therefore feels a strong need to discover or create an opportunity. But at times the entrepreneurial opportunity precedes the intention of becoming an entrepreneur. *"People can and will discover entrepreneurial opportunities without actively searching for them"* (Shane 2000: 451). Often, new opportunities are discovered or created as a result of our everyday actions with other people in different contexts – that is through activities that are externally orientated. Over time the entrepreneurial opportunity can give rise to the intention of becoming an entrepreneur, for instance when the individual is curious to explore the potential of the opportunity, when he or she has no other career options or if he or she is pushed into entrepreneurship by other people who find the opportunity attractive. Basically, it is a question of a more unconscious start-up of the entrepreneurial process. The logic behind externally stimulated entrepreneurship is illustrated in figure 2.3.

Figure 2.3: Externally stimulated entrepreneurship

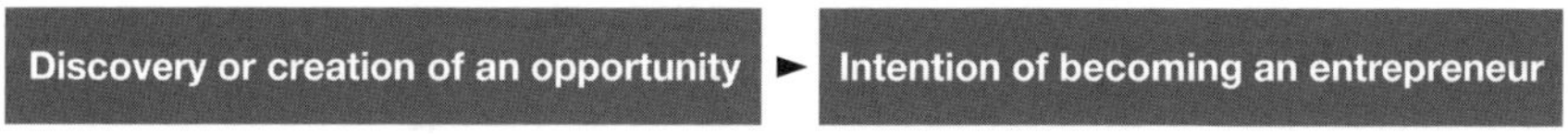

Discovery or creation of an opportunity ► Intention of becoming an entrepreneur

Externally stimulated entrepreneurship underpins how all of us have a potential for ending up as entrepreneurs without intending it from our starting point. But who will become entrepreneurs is hard to predict. It depends on the circumstances, who we meet, opportunities, coincidences, our needs and self-perception and much more than that.

Entrepreneurs: Born or Made?
Thus, from a theoretical perspective the entrepreneurial individual has had a rather turbulent existence. From being a character in disguise to being perceived as the core issue till after that being evaluated as a far from trendy research area, the individual has once again become interesting. Without much success, it has been

attempted to describe and identify fixed features concerning the entrepreneur's personality and character. Nevertheless, this research seems to influence the common understanding of entrepreneurs as heroes who are more or less born to this profession. An investigation among students at the University of Aalborg shows that about 1/3 of the students think that people to a high or very high degree are born to become entrepreneurs (Sørensen et al. 2005). However, a contradictory opinion is that an entrepreneur is not something you are, it is something you become. Life experiences, people you meet, self-perception, situations, knowledge and experiences etc. are all factors that contribute to the shaping of the entrepreneurial character. It is not predetermined who will become entrepreneurs and there are no general rules applying to the personality which determine that only a few of us have the entrepreneurial character inside of us. We are all potential entrepreneurs. The paradox born or made is summed up in table 2.1.

Table 2.1: The paradox: Born or Made?

	Born	Made
Who is the entrepreneur?	Special super individuals	All are potential entrepreneurs
Perception of the entrepreneur	Stable over time – Once entrepreneur, always entrepreneur	The entrepreneur is created through a process
Stimulation	Internal character features	Internal and external factors
Research emphasis	Character features attached to the entrepreneurial personality	The interacting individual and contextual factors that create individuals, cognitive processes and identity
Objectives	To be able to predict and point out the entrepreneur in the crowd	To understand the entrepreneur and how an entrepreneur is created

The table illustrates how the research of the entrepreneurial individual has been influenced by two perspectives. The one perspective emphasises that entrepreneurs are born. This means that entrepreneurs are special super individuals who, being born as entrepreneurs, stay entrepreneurs throughout their entire lifetime. It is presumed that internal character features stimulate some individuals to be entrepreneurs. Therefore, the entrepreneurial research focuses on the study of the stable character features that are attached to the entrepreneurial personality. The objective of the research is to be able to point out the special entrepreneurial person in the crowd.

The other perspective, seeing the entrepreneur as made, pinpoints that we are all potential entrepreneurs and that the emergence of this phenomenon is pro-cedural. It can emerge as a consequence of external as well as internal stimula-tion. Actually, it is often the interaction between internal and external factors that create entrepreneurs as emphasised in contemporary entrepreneurship research. The research includes, however, also considerations about cognitive and identity related processes that attribute to the entrepreneurial individual with the purpose of understanding the individual and how it is created.

■ A theoretical interpretation

Below, two possible interpretations of the two narratives which initiated this chap-ter are given. In the interpretation, the narratives are linked to the above mentioned paradox. At first, the two narratives are interpreted from the born-perspective and later on from the made-perspective.

The born-perspective

In many ways, Thomas's story is a classic. It is about an entrepreneur who through combinations of something existing (vitamin supplement to food, fitness wear and internet trade) creates a successful entrepreneurial process. And why does he create the process? The sociological tradition is helpful here. Thomas's own view is that it was the indirect backing and request for the entrepreneurial living from home that took him that way in life. Since childhood, Thomas wished to become an entrepreneur. His story also applies to a lot of the characteristics that in the psy-chological tradition are associated with the entrepreneur's personality. He is crea-tive, wants to be independent of authorities, inventive etc. In other words, Thomas is typical of the idea of the entrepreneur which the psychological and sociological traditions have contributed to point out.

Thomas's preliminary intention of becoming an entrepreneur is the beginning of the entrepreneurial process and this is in keeping with the idea of internally stimulated entrepreneurship which is illustrated in figure 2.2. In addition, this is emphasised by the fact that from the beginning Thomas does not have an opportunity on which to base the realisation of his intention. The result is that Thomas consciously looks for an opportunity which he can use for the implementation of the intention. This is manifested by the fact that Thomas and Kåre often discuss and look for various potential opportunities. The story illustrates that a conscious search for opportunities can lead to unforeseen opportunities. The opportunity associated with the vitamin supplement to food does not emerge as a result of conscious and planned acting of Thomas.

Mette's story is not a classic in the same sense as that of Thomas because Mette from the beginning is not conscious of the characteristics that shape her natural foundation of being an entrepreneur. As such it is tempting to interpret Mette's story as an example of the fact that she is not born to be an entrepreneur. But in spite of her own scepticism towards herself as being an entrepreneur she has the features that make it possible to characterise her as a born entrepreneur. Mette is creative, inventive and a promoter.

Her inventive nature is especially demonstrated by the fact that she, as a contrast to Thomas, actually creates a far more innovative product with considerable chances to break with existing ways of doing things in the off-shore industry. Mette focuses also on investigating to what extent there is a market for the innovative idea. The fact that the market does not yet know the product and its opportunities of making previous methods for inspection more effective, pinpoints the innovative nature of the idea. In Schumpeter's universe, Mette might be characterised as an innovative entrepreneur who breaks with existing structures in the economy.

Mette's obvious entrepreneurial character features are however undermined by her perception of herself as an engineer. But behind the perception the entrepreneur seems hidden. From a born perspective, Mette would never have ended up trying to become an entrepreneur had it not been for her deeper character features, although they were suppressed for some time. That she is and always will be a born entrepreneur is also clearly revealed by the fact that she becomes eager for a career as an entrepreneur in spite of her failure to convert the offshore opportunity to a commercial success.

The made-perspective

However, Mette's story can also be perceived from the made-perspective rather than the born-perspective because she, until the day when the opportunity emerges, has not spent much time thinking about the entrepreneurial career. And she does not identify herself with entrepreneurial characteristics. As she says, it is easy to find someone who is more entrepreneurial at heart than she is.

However, Mette's story can also be perceived from the made-perspective rather than the born-perspective because she, until the day when the opportunity emerges, has not spent much time thinking about the entrepreneurial career. And she does not identify herself with entrepreneurial characteristics. As she says, it is easy to find someone who is more entrepreneurial at heart than she is.

Instead, it makes sense to say that Mette, although she actually acts as an entrepreneur, does not understand herself as an entrepreneur from the outset. In the entrepreneurial context, she is an engineer in a foreign territory. It is through interaction with the environment, pointing to contingency theory as relevant, that Mette gets pushed by the instructor into entrepreneurship. She becomes "made" as an entrepreneur through her interaction with the environment in spite of her view of herself as a person who wishes the stability which can be gained by a job as a wage earner.

This suggests the situation illustrated in figure 2.3, where an individual starts by having an opportunity of becoming an entrepreneur but has not yet made up his or her mind about it. The intention of becoming an entrepreneur is not present, it must be externally stimulated. By acting as an entrepreneur, Mette seems however to consider to what extent she is a potential entrepreneur. In any case, Mette stresses that at the end of the entrepreneurial process she has greater entrepreneurial intentions than ever before. It is interesting to consider the question: If she had not finished the entrepreneurial process but continued the adventure, would Mette have ended up taking over the entrepreneurial identity and letting the engineer identity be secondary? Or would the two identities have existed side by side?

If we leave the born-entrepreneur thinking behind, it is also possible to understand Thomas's story from a perception that is determined by situations or the made-perspective. In the light of the focus on situations in Gartner's (1985) theory, it can be emphasised how it is the interaction between Thomas's special entrepreneurial characteristics and the environment in terms of the parents and Kåre that give rise to an entrepreneurial process. In the same way as in Mette's story, Thomas also develops his perception of himself as an entrepreneur by entering into a constant interaction of different components which leads to the creation of his and his partner's business bodyman.dk.

■ Practical tests of the theory

On the basis of the above thoughts and discussions you are ready to set up your own experiments in understanding the entrepreneurial individual and the factors that create him or her. The following are suggestions for exercises.

Exercise 1: Interview with an entrepreneur

Make a list of interview questions that seek to encapsulate some of the crucial discussions about who the entrepreneur is and how he or she is being developed. Get in contact with an entrepreneur and interview him or her with a view to testing the theory presented in this chapter. Based on this, you can create your definition of who the entrepreneur is.

Exercise 2: How the entrepreneur is presented in the media

Find newspaper articles conveying something about successful entrepreneurs. Make an analysis of what kinds of perceptions of the entrepreneurial individual are presented in the media. Discuss how these presentations can influence how many and who starts their own organisation in the Danish society.

Exercise 3: Are you the entrepreneurial type?

Make the personality test which is available on startvaekst.dk. Go through the different questions and find out what personality profile you have. How is your score for example on the four personality types (the producer, the administrator, the entrepreneur and the integrator) that the test goes through? In the light of your personality profile, what will you take into consideration if you are supposed to put together a team that is to take part in starting up a new company? Is it necessary that the team reflect all four types of personality?

Literature

Ajzen, I. (1991). The Theory of Planned Behaviour, Organizational and Human Decision Processes, 50, 179-211.

Begley, T. M. & Boyd, D. P. (1987). Psychological Characteristics Associated With Performance in Entrepreneurial Firms and Smaller Businesses, Journal of Business Venturing, 2, 79-93.

Gartner, W. B. (1985). Conceptual Framework for Describing the Phenomenon of New Venture Creation, The Academy of Management Review, 10(4), 696-706.

Gartner, W. B. (1988). Who is the Entrepreneur? Is the Wrong Question, American Journal of Small Business, 12(4), 11-32.

Hérbert, R. F. & Link, A. N. (1988). The Entrepreneur – Mainstream Views and Radical Critiques. New York: Praeger Publishers.

Hisrish, R. D. & Peters, M. P. (2001). Entrepreneurship. Boston: McGraw-Hill.

Jones, C. & Spicer, A. (2005). The Sublime Object of Entrepreneurship, Organization 12(2), 223-246.

Kilby, P. (1971). Hunting the Haffelump. In P. Kilby (Ed.), Entrepreneurship and Economic Development (pp. 1-42). New York, The Free Press.

Llewellyn, D. J. & Wilson, K. M. (2003). The Controversial Role of Personality Traits in Entrepreneurial Psychology, Education + Training, 45(6), 341-345.

Nicolaou, N., Shane, S., Cherkas, L., Hunkin, J. & Spector, T. D. (2005). Is the Tendency to Engage in Entrepreneurship Genetic, London, South Kensington Campus.

Schumpeter, J. A. (1934). The Theory of Economic Development. Cambride: Harvard University Press.

Schøtt, T. (2006). Entrepreneurship in the Regions in Denmark 2006: Studied via Global Entrepreneurship Monitor. Kolding: University of Southern Denmark.

Schøtt, T. (2007). Growth-entrepreneurship in Denmark 2007 – studied via Global Entrepreneurship Monitor. Kolding: University of Southern Denmark.

Shane, S. (2000). Prior Knowledge and the Discovery of Entrepreneurial Opportunities, Organization Science, 11 (4), 448-469.

Shane, S. (2003). A General Theory of Entrepreneurship: The Individual-opportunity Nexus. Cheltenham: Edward Elgar.

Sørensen, S., Ivang, R. & Sørensen, O. J. (2005). Iværksætterpulsen 2005 – Der er vilje... Er der vej? Institut for Erhvervsstudier, Aalborg University.

Timmons, J. A. & Spinelli, S. (2003). New Venture Creation: Entrepreneurship for the 21st Century, New York: McGraw-Hill.

Weick, K. E. (1995). Sensemaking in Organizations. Thousand Oaks: Saga.

Chapter 3

Emergence of opportunities

The entrepreneurial individual is crucial for the understanding of entrepreneurship. But the essence of entrepreneurial theory is by many considered as the discovery or the creation of opportunities. An opportunity is an idea which is judged as something that can create value for other people. Without opportunities, entrepreneurship cannot come into existence. In addition, many people think that an emphasis on opportunities is what makes theory of entrepreneurship unique. But what is an opportunity and where does it come from? That is the topic of this chapter.

In order to be able to discuss opportunities, we introduce another concept which is the concept of an idea. Ideas come before opportunities but not all ideas grow and become opportunities. Some ideas remain at the idea level because evaluation suggests that they cannot gain ground and be carried out. Thus, when we think of ideas and opportunities it is important to distinguish between two possibilities related to the market. If it is evaluated that sales at a market cannot be realised, the idea remains an idea. But if, on the other hand, it seems realistic that sales at a market can be realised, the entrepreneur can take the initiative to develop the idea into an opportunity.

In this chapter you will meet different suggestions for what characterises an opportunity. From our point of view, every opportunity which opens for something new is entrepreneurial because entrepreneurs expect the opportunity to create value for other people whether the value is economic, social or societal.

■ Meet practice

At this point, an entrepreneur will tell his story about how the opportunity on which he bases his entrepreneurial process comes into existence. If, having read his story, you wish to get better acquainted with him, you should visit the homepage: www.idea-textbook.dk. This page will supply you with video clips dealing with the entrepreneur concerned.

A brilliant idea

"We thought that we had a brilliant idea (...) One of the first things we did was to make some writing paper. And to this very day it is the finest writing paper we have ever had in the company." In this way, the story of the existence of a potential opportunity begins – an opportunity that soon gives rise to other opportunities. The story is told by David Madié. During his studies at the business college in Århus, he and two of his fellow students get a great idea. The three young men have

through their time at college taught companies the use of Excel and gained experience in using computer programs. By this means, they have developed an online cash management system which can be used for supporting the liquidity management of the companies. The year is 1995 and they are ready to begin because they believe in their idea.

But the idea becomes far from a success: *"We never had any customers at all."* The entrepreneurs fail in convincing the customers about the potential of the idea. Perhaps the reason is not that the idea is without potential in terms of creating value for the customers. The explanation is rather that the three young entrepreneurs lack credibility and that the companies have already been offered similar products by banks with a high degree of credibility. Thus, it is difficult for the young entrepreneurs to transform their idea into a real opportunity.

The market has a demand

But the three entrepreneurs keep going. An idea which turns out to be a real opportunity suddenly appears. *"One day, we were washing up after a party in a holiday cottage. Then my partner was complaining: Those classes we teach ... they have called asking if we could teach some more and we haven't got the time."* A conversation begins. How many IT-businesses need instructors? Is this demand only the tip of the iceberg?

A concept that is evaluated to correspond to the market demand begins to take shape. David and his partners try to figure out how they can collect a teaching team of fellow students who can teach Danish IT-businesses Excel and related programs. They use the opportunity. The demand for the teaching team is big from the beginning. The entrepreneurs are in the right place and they come up with the right solution at the right time. A new and better version of Windows has just been put on the market which makes the demand for the teaching team huge: *"We hit the bull's eye (...) Here the chance was to build up a business."* David and his partners have the advantage that they now know the customers on the market and in addition they have teaching experience.

Netguide.dk, which is what the opportunity is called, certainly becomes a success. During a period of eight years, the organisation grows from three to 100 employees. It establishes a number of joint venture companies in countries of the Third World where the demand for instruction in computer programs is at least as big as in Denmark. However, the organisation is sold to international investors in the year 2000. David continues as chairman of the board.

Growing pains

Due to the success, David and the others gain self-confidence: *"Now you have started something successful and then you can start something else."* They constantly seek new opportunities. For example, one day a man comes in from the street. He asks for a computer. Why not become suppliers of computers! A lot of initiatives are taken. After approximately four years, the organisation consists of a collection of products which are all available at Netguide.dk. The product portfolio is wide: advising, teaching, translation of cd-roms from English to Danish, internet school, websites, resale of games and language programs, development of games etc. What is to be done with so many products? The three entrepreneurs decide to keep them: *"We were enthusiastic about the ideas. We wanted it all."*

■ Your immediate interpretation

The story gives you an idea of the emergence of opportunities. How will you spontaneously interpret it? Here are some suggestions for what you might consider.

- ■ You are going to write a letter to the editor of the local newspaper about the importance of opportunities. Why do you find them important? In the light of David's story, how will you define an opportunity? Are both ideas and opportunities at play in the story and how?
- ■ A reader asks: Where do opportunities come from? With respect to the story, how do you answer the reader's question? Another question posed by the reader is: How can you explain that it is exactly these three entrepreneurs who create Netguide.dk? What are they capable of doing which other people are not? What distinguishes them from other people?
- ■ Think carefully: Have you ever had an idea which you think has the potential of getting transformed into an opportunity? If your answer is yes – describe how you got the idea.

■ Theories of entrepreneurship

From an overall perspective, theories of opportunities deal with what opportunities are, why and how they exist, what form they can take and what role the entrepreneur plays in the emergence processes. Now we come to the heart of the matter in the sense that we will provide you with one or more perceptions of the nature of opportunities. It is not an easy task.

Disagreement is not only prevalent to the discussions about who the entrepreneur is, it also applies to the question of what an opportunity is. Put very briefly, two perspectives pertain to this problem. One perspective emphasises that opportunities are around us all of the time. They only wait for us to *discover* them. On the contrary, another perspective focuses on a perception of opportunities as something belonging to the future – something that is created through the way the individual acts and interacts with other people and his or her ability to reflect upon these. Thus, opportunities depend on human activities and intervention. This chapter will present you with the two perspectives which create the paradox:

Created or discovered?

Opportunity versus idea

We initiated this chapter by stating that an opportunity is an idea that is evaluated to be able to create value for others. Criteria for the evaluation are to decide to what extent the idea is:

- Rooted: Bound up with a product, an output or an experience that creates value for others.
- Attractive: Others are willing to pay for the value which the idea represents.
- At the right time and in the right place: The environment is ready to meet the entrepreneur and his idea.
- It is possible: The opportunity can be realised in practice (Barringer & Ireland 2008).

The last-mentioned refers to the assumption that the entrepreneur must possess or be able to gain access to the resources, competences, legitimacy and knowledge that are required in order to make the idea valuable to others. The idea can only be judged as a real opportunity if it creates value to others (and not only to the entrepreneur himself) to a considerable extent so that others are willing to pay for the value and if it comes into existence at the right time and in the right place and if it can be realised. With respect to that, do you think that the following illustration in figure 3.1 is a picture of an opportunity?

Figure 3.1: Is this an opportunity?

From the illustration above, it appears how an opportunity is often differentiated from an ordinary idea – a thought. Ideas have the potential to become opportunities but they do not meet the above-mentioned criteria for an opportunity. You might have a really great idea but all your competitors also have the exact same idea and in addition, the market is perhaps not ready for your idea. As a result, your idea remains an idea and it will never be transformed into an opportunity. However, it is important to mention that it is often difficult to make a clear distinction between an idea and an opportunity. It is a fluid transition which will also mark the discussions in this book.

The extent of intentions and opportunities
If you talk about opportunities, you should at the same time discuss intentions. It is in a way unimportant to what extent the individuals have discovered or created opportunities if they do not intend to exploit them through organising. At the same time, it can be claimed that it is unimportant whether individuals intend to exploit an opportunity or not if they have not discovered or created one – that is if they do not possess an opportunity.

The discussion was taken forward by Bhave (1994). He identifies two different ways to entrepreneurship. The entrepreneurial process either begins with the fact that the individual has an intention of starting an organisation. Afterwards, he or she will be chasing an opportunity. Or the entrepreneurial process begins with the fact that the individual by accident discovers or creates an opportunity after which an intention of exploiting it is developed. We have already touched upon that way of thinking in chapter 2.

Bhave's (1994) reflections pinpoint that a society at a given time consists of a population where some people have an intention of taking the initiative concerning entrepreneurship, some possess an opportunity, some possess both an opportunity and an intention and others possess neither an opportunity nor an intention. In 2004 the Danish part of the Global Entrepreneurship Monitor (GEM) investigation (www.gemconsortium.org) collected some data which point to the extent to which opportunities and intentions are carried by Danes. GEM is an international research project with the objective to identify:

- Connections between the entrepreneurship activity and the economic growth of a country.
- How entrepreneurial activity varies across countries.
- Which national framework conditions promote the entrepreneurial activities of a country.

More than 50 countries have participated in GEM since the start-up of the project in the late nineties. Annually, data about entrepreneurship are collected in each of the participating countries. The most decisive collection of data is a population survey of randomly selected respondents consisting of at least 2,000 adults in each country. Table 3.1 shows the data collected in 2004 on the extent to which opportunities and intentions are carried by Danes.

Table 3.1: The extent to which opportunities and intentions are carried by Danes (% of the population)

		Opportunity	Opportunity
		Yes	No
Intention	Yes	Potential entrepreneur-ship 7 %	Waste of intention 3 %
Intention	No	Waste of opportunity 16 %	No entrepreneur-ship 74 %

Source: GEM Denmark (2004).

The table pinpoints that approximately 74 percent of the Danish population are not at all involved in entrepreneurship while 7 percent possess an opportunity and also have an intention of exploiting it. They are potential entrepreneurs. But the two exciting categories are waste of intentions and waste of opportunities. Out of the Danish population, 3 percent belong to the first-mentioned category. We are here dealing with persons intending to start an organisation, but they need an opportunity to exploit. From a social perspective, it is a waste of intentions. Actually, approximately 30 percent of the Danes (3/(3+7)) who at some point in time have an intention of starting an organisation need a concrete opportunity.

The other interesting category is waste of opportunity encompassing 16 percent of the Danish population. These people possess an opportunity but they do not have the ambition to exploit it through organising. 70 percent of those (16/(7+16)) who possess an opportunity do not intend to exploit it. Again, from the social perspective, we are dealing with a considerable waste. Thus, table 3.1 clearly demonstrates that the most considerable waste in the context of Danish entrepreneurship is the lacking intention to exploit the opportunities which the Danes actually possess.

Types of opportunities
In the various attempts towards defining what an opportunity is and how it emerges, especially two theorists are mentioned: Schumpeter (1934) and Kirzner (1976). As mentioned in chapter 1, the essence of Schumpeterian theory is the fact that opportunities come into existence through new combinations of something existing. In addition to this, they are characterised by the fact that they break with the existing perceptions and ways in which things are done. A funny example of how existing knowledge can be recombined is the story of an industrial designer who in the year 2000 claims to have a monopoly of a new type of bulletproof vest. The vest is based on knowledge about and studies of insects. Some insects are soft on the inside but have a sturdy and movable skeleton on the outside. The vest is designed in accordance with these principles and break in this way with existing constructions of bulletproof vests. The industrial designer got the idea for the vest when he was watching a programme about insects on Discovery Channel. Therefore, by combining the existing knowledge about bulletproof vests with knowledge about insects, the designer created a completely new, more flexible and comfortable vest.

On the other hand, Kirznerian opportunities are characterised by exploitation of existing information about the market by entrepreneurs in order to find "holes" in the market which can be exploited more effectively than at present. In other words: Is there a potential value in the market which is not yet exploited effectively by others? The entrepreneur focuses here on optimising and making the existing market effective. For example, the establishment of one more hairdresser's on one more street corner can be an example of a Kirznerian opportunity if the saloon fills a potential gap in the market – a potential that has not yet been exploited. Figure 3.2 is a simplified illustration of the differences between Schumpeterian and Kirznerian opportunities.

Figure 3.2: Schumpeterian versus Kirznerian opportunity

A Schumpeterian opportunity

= A new opportunity

A Kirznerian opportunity

= A new opportunity

Figure 3.3 goes more thoroughly into the difference between the two types of opportunities from a market perspective. Schumpeterian opportunities can be perceived as a break with the existing equilibrium that exists in the market because they break with existing ways of doing things. Effectively this means that a Schumpeterian opportunity does not have to exist because the market needs the new opportunity. The opportunity comes into existence because existing knowledge is recombined which creates development in the light of the known market. In some cases, the new opportunity can actually, as mentioned in chapter 1, reorganise entire businesses. In some cases, this causes annoyance to those who will have to rearrange for example existing methods of production, supplier relations or even have to invent new products that can cope with the value which the new opportunity represents.

Kirznerian opportunities, on the contrary, can be illustrated as an equalisation of lack of equilibrium. They contribute to create equilibrium in markets. Often, equilibrium will appear on markets when existing needs suddenly can be satisfied better by the means of new opportunities. An example might be that an entrepreneur discovers how a hitherto very expensive production can be remarkably cheaper or faster. Therefore, the Kirznerian opportunity will not be innovative in the same way as a Schumpeterian opportunity. Instead, it helps promoting equilibrium in the market. We can conclude that Kirznerian and Schumpeterian opportunities play different roles in the market. But they can also be encountered as complementary approaches to opportunities. While Schumpeterian opportunities create a lack of equilibrium in the market, the Kirznerian opportunities help bringing back equilibrium in the market. Therefore, figure 3.3 is designed like a ring.

Figure 3.3: Two perceptions of opportunities

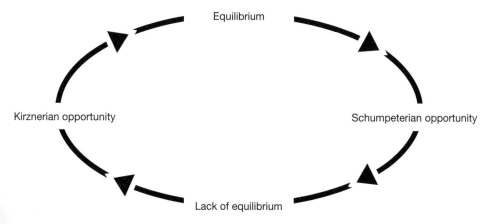

Discovery of opportunities

Now we are going to concentrate on the process which leads to a new opportunity. The Kirznerian opportunity is likely to be perceived as objective by nature. It is simply part of our environment (profit holes in the market) waiting to be discovered. The concept of objectivity refers to the fact that opportunities exist independently of human intervention, time and place. Effectively, this means that we can take it for granted that opportunities exist as part of our world in spite of the fact that we are not always aware of them. Shane and Venkataraman explain it in this way: *"... the opportunities themselves are objective phenomena that are not known to all parties at all times. For example, the discovery of the telephone created new opportunities for communication, whether or not people discovered those opportunities"* (Shane & Venkataraman 2000: 220).

But if the opportunities are objective, why does not everybody discover them? Why does the privilege of discovering opportunities only belong to some individuals in our society? The answer to this question is versatile. Some entrepreneurs pro-actively look for opportunities which we also referred to in chapter 2 as "internally stimulated entrepreneurship". But as also mentioned in chapter 2, many opportunities emerge because an entrepreneur discovers an opportunity without consciously looking for it. Kirzner introduces the concept "alertness" in order to encapsulate the new discovery. The concept refers to: *"... the ability to notice, without search, opportunities that have hitherto been overlooked"* (Kirzner 1979: 48). This means that "alertness" refers to the fact that the entrepreneur has a kind of embedded red alert which reacts to unforeseen opportunities on which he or she, more or less unconsciously and unintentionally concentrates his or her attention. In that way, the entrepreneur discovers new opportunities without looking for them actively, consciously.

But if we proceed with the discussion about "alertness", the question is still if all people have a constant red alert towards opportunities or if some people are more predisposed to discover opportunities in preference to others. As a comment on that, Shane and Venkataraman pinpoint: *"... recognition of entrepreneurial opportunities is a subjective process"* (Shane & Venkataraman 2000: 220). This means that even though the actual opportunity is objective, the discovery of the opportunity is attached to the individual. For example, the individual's information and experiences pertaining to a certain area will in most cases lead to a higher degree of awareness of solutions and new ways of handling the challenges. Shane (2000) investigates this by letting a group of entrepreneurs with different backgrounds look at the same technology. They end up suggesting different ways of looking at the technology as a potential opportunity depending on the information and experience, they possess.

Shane (2003), however, pinpoints that other factors than information and experience can affect who discovers which opportunities. This is illustrated in figure 3.4.

Figure 3.4: The individual and the opportunity discovery

| **Access to information** (including life experiences, social networks and search processes) | **Ability to discover opportunities** (including capacity to absorb, intelligence and cognitive processes) |

Source: Inspired by Shane (2003).

The figure emphasises that access to information is important and goes into detail with the fact that this access will depend on our life experiences, social networks and our efforts to look for opportunities. Research shows that the more people look for opportunities, the more likely it is that they will discover an opportunity. In addition to this, the figure points out that our ability to discover opportunities depends on our capacity to absorb (that is to say our ability to interpret information in a useful way, for example to be able to find solutions to the problems we meet), intelligence and cognitive processes. The last refers to the fact that we have different cognitive constructions which according to chapter 2 refers to how an entrepreneur understands and thinks about the things taking place in his or her surroundings and inside and outside of him or her. Depending on how the brain of an entrepreneur works, the perception of opportunities will appear differently. Typically, the entrepreneur will often perceive some opportunities as more optimistic than others and act faster than others on the opportunity in spite of lacking information because he or she possesses an inner belief in the potential of the opportunity.

Creation of opportunities

If you think that opportunities are not objective phenomena in our surroundings then there is nothing to discover. Many people seem to share this perception. Opportunities are not: *"... concrete realities waiting to be noticed, discovered, or observed by entrepreneurs"* (Gartner et al. 2003: 104). Instead, opportunities are something created by human beings: *"... opportunities and markets have to be invented, fabricated, constructed, made"* (Sarasvathy 2008: 181). Without an acting human being, no opportunities would exist. Opportunities are perceived as subjective realities. As we understand it, the Schumpeterian opportunities are examples of the fact that human action is crucial for the creation of opportunities. They do not take their starting point in the existing information about markets, prices, consumer preferences etc. Instead, the ability of human beings to act creatively through the creation of new combinations is crucial where creativity refers to the ability to think groundbreaking thoughts. In addition to this, the perspective accentuates that the interaction between people plays an important role for the creation of opportunities.

Consequently, we can conclude that if opportunities are not objective phenomena, they can instead be perceived as social constructions that depend on the individual and they are created in everyday life, in the interaction with others, ourselves and our contexts. Fletcher comments on this by saying: *"... entrepreneurial activities, features, and characteristics are not "objects" given a fixed or static ontological status as they come into being. Instead, they are dynamic and constantly emerging, being realized, shaped and constructed through social processes"* (Fletcher 2003: 127). Instead of perceiving opportunities as objective truths that are present at all times and potentially visible to all, they are a subjective phenomenon rooted in our daily lives: *"We need to recognize that the entrepreneurial activities of everyday life have a great capacity to move us in new and unexpected directions"* (Boutaiba 2004: 24). Figure 3.5 is an illustration of how opportunities come into existence in the interaction between the entrepreneur, other people and their contexts in everyday life.

Figure 3.5: A model of opportunity emergence

A new opportunity

Often, our daily interaction results in a reproduction of the existing. What is prevalent to human beings is that to a high degree they can be ruled by habits. But at times it happens that something new emerges, such as a new opportunity. Figure 3.5 also indirectly shows how opportunity creation is not only about discovering an optimal opportunity. Because of the fact that opportunity creation takes its starting point in everyday interactions, the pivotal point is instead: What comes into existence at this very moment? What is possible? What makes sense in the light of the existing situation? Is it possible? In other words, opportunity creation is a very pragmatic part of everyday life.

Listen for example to the story about how the opportunity attached to eBay came into existence. The entrepreneur behind eBay says, *"So people often say to me – "when you built the system, you must have known that making it self-sustainable was the only way eBay could grow to serve 40 million users a day." Well…nope. I made the system self-sustaining for one reason: Back when I launched eBay on Labor Day 1995, eBay was not my business – it was my hobby. I had to build a system that was self-sustaining… Because I had a real job to go to every morning, I was working as a software engineer from 10 to 7, and I wanted to have a life on the weekends. So I built a system that could keep working – catching complaints and capturing feedback – even when Pam and I were out mountain-biking, and the only one home was our cat."* (Sarasvathy 2008: 189). The story is an illustrative example of how the opportunity emerges as a result of everyday interactions. The entrepreneur attempts to create an opportunity that is possible in the light of the other people with whom he interacts (Pam) and his context (the work). From the beginning, he did not know that the opportunity would end up with eBay as we know it today. He just started in a small way by creating an opportunity and he chose everyday challenges as his point of departure.

Last but not least, the above-listed thoughts also emphasise that opportunities are constantly developing. Opportunities change all of the time because of the interaction. Opportunity creation is a process in which the entrepreneur cannot necessarily decide the development by himself. The entrepreneur is after all only one of many players who have the possibility to influence the process.

Opportunities: discovered or created?

The pivotal point of this chapter has been an examination of two opportunity perspectives. The one perspective argues that opportunities are discovered whereas the other perspective contemplates opportunities as created. Table 3.2 sums up the two perspectives which together make up the paradox: discovered or created.

Table 3.2: The paradox: discovered or created?

	Discovered	Created
Opportunity character	Objectively given unit in the environment	Dependent on the interactions of the individual
Opportunity emergence	Involves discovery	Involves creation
Opportunity source	The individual who is attentive towards existing market information	The individual who creates by means of his or her creativity
Opportunity status	The opportunity is stable	The opportunity is dynamic
Opportunity type	Kirznerian hole in the market	Schumpeterian market ruption

As it emerges from the table, according to the discovery perspective, opportunities are given objects in the environment. Their coming into existence here involves the individual's discovery of "holes" in the market in terms of unexploited resources. It can be explained by the fact that the opportunity depends on the individual's attention towards existing market information. It is assumed that the opportunity which is discovered remains the same over time – it is stable. In terms of type, the opportunity is Kirznerian.

On the contrary, the creation perspective emphasises that opportunities are closely bound up with a pro-active individual. The individual is again rooted in a social context which explains why he or she acts in relation to others and interacts with others and the environment. All these are contributing factors to the creation of op- portunities. It is emphasised that the emergence process of opportunities requires a creatively acting individual. Because of the fact that the process which creates opportunities is a result of interacting elements (such as the entrepreneur himself, other individuals and their contexts), the opportunity will constantly change – it is dynamic. The perspective partly refers to Schumpeter's thoughts about opportuni- ties as new combinations of the existing order.

If you do not think that it makes sense perceiving opportunities as either created or discovered, you may share the view of Sarasvathy et al. (2002). They emphasise that some opportunities: *"… lie buried in the soil waiting to be dug out by the alert individual. Yet, others require several stakeholders, including founding entrepre- neurs to act effectually to "create" them (or nurture them into being) in a dynamic and interactive process of contingency, design and negotiation"* (Sarasvathy et al. 2002: 2). In this way, opportunities are not necessarily either Kirznerian or Schum- peterian. Perhaps opportunities which require discovery and opportunities which require creation co-exist.

■ A theoretical interpretation

Below, an interpretation of the story which initiated this chapter is offered. At first, we will approach the story in the light of the discovery perspective after which it will be looked at from the creation perspective.

The discovery perspective

The story of the three young entrepreneurs who create an instruction team of students can easily be interpreted in the light of the discovery perspective. This perspective will focus on how the given opportunity emerges reactively as a result of a "hole" in the market. In other words, there is a potential in the market – a potential which has not yet been exploited optimally, effectively, namely instruction in the use of IT-programs. The market shows this by an increased demand for the competences of the students which the students discover. Thus, the opportunity related to the instruction team exists independently of the activities of the students.

As this opportunity improves existing market structures, it can be defined as a Kirznerian opportunity. By pursuing the opportunity, the students are contributing to creating a balance between supply and demand in the market for IT-instruction.

The above refers to the opportunity linked to the instruction team. But at first, the students pursued an opportunity about a cash management system. Whereas this opportunity reflects what the students are willing to sell, the instruction team represents to a higher degree an opportunity which the market is willing to buy. Actually, it can be questioned to what extent it is possible at all to see the opportunity of a cash management system as an opportunity and not just as an idea. According to Barringer & Ireland (2008), opportunities should be rooted, attractive at the proper time and place and possible to realise. The idea of a new cash management system turns out not to be considered attractive by the customers because they do not feel that the system creates further value for them. Furthermore, the cash management system is not practically possible to realise since the students do not possess the credibility that should give access to the necessary resources.

Last but not least, it can be questioned why it is exactly these three students who discover the opportunity of the instruction team. Because they are already interested in creating entrepreneurial processes, the students are very aware of opportunities – they are "alert". Finally, to a high degree they possess relevant information, social networks, competences, life experiences etc. which according to figure 3.4 raise the individual's chances of discovering opportunities. After all, they already have experience with supplying their lives as students with IT-instruction. The students discover the opportunity and immediately formulate a concept which can fill up the market demand by exploiting their existing knowledge about this market.

The creation perspective
However, the story of the three young entrepreneurs can also be seen as a story of creation. Thus, the essence of the story is how the three young entrepreneurs create an opportunity of an instruction team based on a vast number of interactions

with the IT-companies, fellow students, the university context and each other, own competences and experiences. Especially, the first idea about the cash management system which, however, remained an idea, seems to indicate a process of creation that pays little regard to whether the market is ready for the opportunity or not, whether it is attractive to relevant players, possible to realise or created at the right time and place. Emphasis is on the creation itself. But also the opportunity linked to the instruction team can possibly be encountered as an opportunity which would certainly not be a reality without the activities of the three young entrepreneurs. Actually, it is their efforts, creativity, experiences, knowledge of the market and the players of the market which create the opportunity.

Instead of regarding the opportunity as a solution to a "hole" in the existing market, it is possible to argue that the opportunity related to the instruction team is an innovation in a Schumpeterian sense. Effectively, this emphasises how the opportunity is a combination of a traditional IT-instruction and the students' spare time jobs. This opportunity is innovative in the sense that such a team at the given time was a completely new thought. Therefore, the opportunity is not only a reflection on familiar ways of doing things. Its creation required that new pieces were put together for the purpose of creating a product that is new to the market.

The students end up by launching many different opportunities. According to the creation perspective, the opportunities which the students create can be described as dynamic because they constantly build on the essence of previous opportunities. This suggests that an opportunity is not a final construction but a construction to be changed by further activities and interactions.

■ **Practical tests of the theory**
Now time has come for you to participate again. You must keep the above-mentioned theories and discussions in mind when you now do some field work – you are going to make your own experiments with opportunities and their emergence.

Exercise 1: Study of technological improvements and opportunities
Search the internet. Make a list of three crucial technological improvements that have taken place since you began your studies. Describe two opportunities which have come into existence in the light of these improvements. Are you capable of formulating further opportunities that have emerged as a result of the improvements concerned without yet being exploited?

Exercise 2: New cases: "Happy days" & "Cepa Mobility"
Look through the following video cases at www.idea-textbook.dk: "Happy days" and "Cepa Mobility". In the light of the above-mentioned theories and discussions, analyse how the opportunity comes into existence in each of these cases.

Exercise 3: Draw your opportunity library
From the chapter it appears that your attention towards new opportunities among other things depends on the information, you already possess. The information can be a result of your life experiences, education, your spare time job, your spare time hobbies or your time together with friends, fellow students, family etc. Take a piece of paper. Draw your brain. Imagine your brain as a library with a lot of books which contain the information that you possess. Now, write down names of the books. Are they about gardening, football or arithmetic? Now, evaluate through the combination of the books in the library what opportunities you have the potential to discover or create.

Literature

Barringer, B. R. & Ireland, R. D. (2008). Entrepreneurship: Successfully Launching New Ventures. Upper Saddle River: Prentice Hall.

Bhave, M. P. (1994). A Process Model of New Venture Creation, Journal of Business Venturing, 9, 223-242.

Boutaiba, S. (2004). A Moment in Time. In D. Hjort & C. Steyaert (Ed.), Narrative and Discursive Approaches in Entrepreneurship – A Second Movements in Entrepreneurship Book (pp. 22-57). Cheltenham: Edward Elgar.

Fletcher, D. E. (2003). Framing Organizational Emergence: Discourse, Identity, and Relationship. In D. Hjort & C. Steyaert (Ed.), New Movements in Entrepreneurship (pp. 9-46). Cheltenham: Edward Elgar.

Gartner, W. B., Carter, N. M. & Hills, G. E. (2003). The Language of Opportunity. In D. Hjort & C. Steyaert (Ed.), New Movements in Entrepreneurship (pp. 103-125). Cheltenham: Edward Elgar.

Kirzner, I. M. (1976). The Economic Point of View: An Essay in the History of Economic Thought. Kansas City: Sheed and Ward.

Sarasvathy, S. D. (2008). Effectuation: Elements of Entrepreneurial Expertise. Cornwall: MPG Books Ltd.

Sarasvathy, S. D., Dew, N., Velamuri, S. R. & Venkataraman, S. (2002). A Testable Typology of Entrepreneurial Opportunity: Extension of Shane & Venkataraman (2000), University of Maryland and University of Virginia.

Schumpeter, J. A. (1934). The Theory of Economic Development. Cambride: Harvard University Press.

Shane, S. (2000). Prior Knowledge and the Discovery of Entrepreneurial Opportunities, Organization Science, 11(4), 448-469.

Shane, S. (2003). A General Theory of Entrepreneurship: The Individual-opportunity Nexus. Cheltenham: Edward Elgar.

Shane, S. and Venkataraman, S. (2000). The Promise of Entrepreneurship as a Field of Research, Academy of Management Review, 25(1), 217-226.

Emergence of opportunities

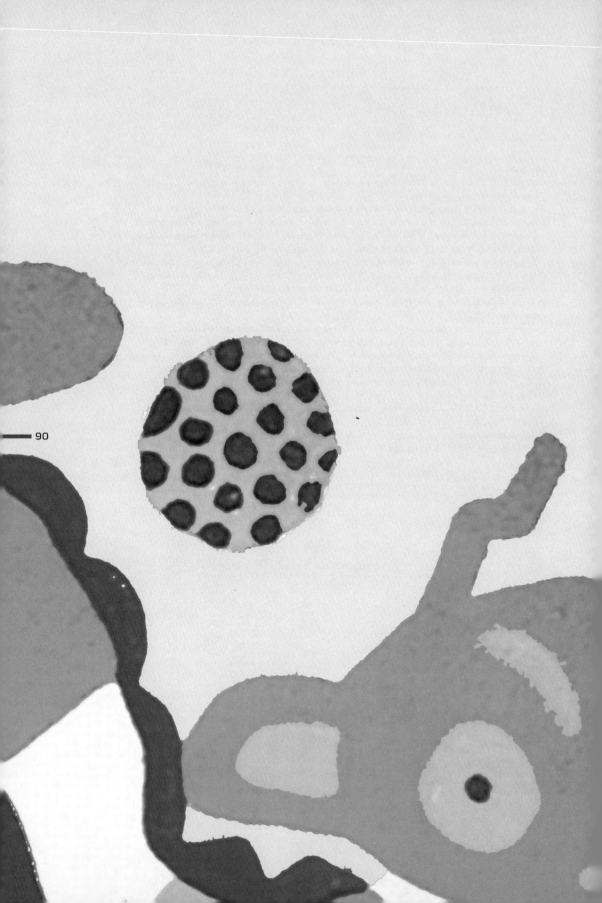

Chapter 4

Evaluation of opportunities

Opportunity evaluation is a crucial issue in entrepreneurship. An entrepreneur cannot summarily expect market players to experience the opportunity (and the organisational effort which the entrepreneur intends to display in order to take advantage of the opportunity) as attractive and at the right time and place. It is not certain that the market can or will honour the value which the opportunity and its organisational implementation represents.

Consequently, the entrepreneurial process involves the evaluation of the opportunity. Here, the entrepreneur seeks to assess whether the idea that he or she intends to pursue will create value in the eyes of the market and thus can be regarded as an actual opportunity. Seen in this light, opportunity evaluation covers the process in which an idea is assessed in relation to the opportunity with a view to its realisation. You could say that *"... evaluation is the key to differentiate an idea from an opportunity"* (Keh et al. 2002: 126). Especially, it is often interesting for the entrepreneur to assess whether the idea represents a cost-effective opportunity, at least in the long run.

As mentioned in chapter 3, conceptually, it can often be difficult to determine whether you are dealing with an idea or an opportunity. The transformation from an idea to an opportunity is characterised by a wide grey area. Consequently, there will be many situations where you may think that the wrong term has been used. For instance, some people might argue that this chapter should have been called "Evaluation of ideas" and not "Evaluation of opportunities". Therefore it is important to read the chapter flexibly with regard to these concepts and just bear in mind that evaluation is the very process where the entrepreneur seeks to assess whether the idea represents an opportunity or not.

■ Meet practice

You are about to meet the Danish fashion scene and an entrepreneur who, to a great extent, has taken part in defining the scene. The name of the entrepreneur is Naja Munthe and the company is called Munthe plus Simonsen. This is the tale of the start-up process. Especially, you should observe how Naja and her partner Karen evaluate the potential of their idea both in the beginning and in the making. How do they find out whether it is profitable? If you want to see and hear more about Naja and her story, visit www.idea-textbook.dk. Here you will find video clips of Naja.

"The sky is the limit"

The two students from Kolding Designskole (one of the Design Schools in Denmark), Naja and Karen, started their entrepreneurial journey successfully. More or less from the outset, their fashion collection was a great success. Customers wanted the luxury bohemian style that Naja and Karen delivered. Naja says, *"We rode the wave of success and generally speaking, we couldn't do anything wrong (…) Karen always said, 'The sky is the limit', and I thought that was kind of cool because then there are no limits. It became our motto."* But unfortunately the roller coaster went downwards in 2006. Munthe plus Simonsen was heading towards insolvency and had to suspend payments. Maybe Naja and Karen's idea did not have what it takes to make it in the market after all.

Photo: Naja Munthe and Karen Simonsen.

Next stop Copenhagen

Naja and Karen meet each other at Designskolen in Kolding where they become friends. After graduation, they have no plans. But one day in 1994, Karen, who has found a boyfriend in Copenhagen, says, *"Why don't we go to Copenhagen and start a business?"* Naja would like to come along, but as she says: *"… we didn't really think it through. We didn't have any definite and fine-tuned plans for what to do."* The organisation is set up, but it is not based on a clear idea. They fill their schedules with any jobs they are offered: *"We just started at one end and offered our services for all sorts of things."* The two girls perform as TV presenters, stylists, writers, guest speakers and much more.

A collection to be sold

Yet along with the many jobs, in 1995 Naja and Karen also manage to create their first collection. But who is to buy it? That is a question they have not considered: *"When we designed our first collection we didn't give much thought to the identity of our end customer. For many years, we were our own target group. We just worked with what we liked ourselves."*

Consequently, it is only natural for Naja and Karen to try to sell their first collection by phoning their own favourite clothes shop, namely "Nørgaard paa Strøget" situated on the main shopping street in Copenhagen. It is, however, necessary to call several times, since the shop managers do not seem particularly interested in what the two young designers have to offer. In the end, though, the shop managers become tired of the many phone calls, and they allow them a minute to present their clothes. They are not to expect anything, though. The owner and CEO of the shop, Mads Nørgaard, ends up buying their entire collection. From this experience, Naja learns: *"Never take no for an answer. Keep on going. You can rely on one thing out there in the real world, and that is that a lot of doors are closed."*

A couple of dressmakers?

The two young women experience more difficulties in opening the doors. At this time, the Danish fashion trade is still in its embryonic stage. This means that Naja and Karen are confronted with the challenge of participating in the creation of the trade as a whole. Furthermore, they have *"… no one to lean on. There are no role models or precursors"* who can guide them. Without a guide, they are left to find their first supplier in the yellow pages, which ends up in them accidently hiring a cushion factory that manufactures plastic cushions to produce their first collection. It is not easy to attract media attention either. Naja says, *"Also in connection with the media, which is how you make a living these days, it was extremely difficult to catch attention, particularly as a designer. We were just seen as a couple of blond dressmakers who sat around cobbling together dresses for ourselves."*

Owing to an enormous drive and fighter spirit, Naja and Karen succeed in catching on after all. They know how to draw attention to themselves and their products through a lifestyle where only the best is good enough and a promotion of their own expression rather than a commercial expression. *"We took pride in not being commercial (…) We didn't focus on an end customer or whether our business was profitable."* So when Magasin (a Danish department store) addresses them with a wish to promote their products, they turn down the offer. Magasin is too commercial.

During the first years, their lifestyle and "only the sky is the limit" mentality result in Naja and Karen buying a lot of expensive furniture, hiring 1,600 sq. metres of office space, opening new shops, establishing showrooms in key fashion cities and hiring expensive supermodels. For instance, they hire Cindy Crawford for one of their campaigns. These activities constitute a marketing success. They receive a lot of positive feedback in the form of high revenues and various awards, such as the branding award of the year and the Danish business woman of the year award. But unfortunately the success comes to an end.

Suspension of payments
"If you are employed as a checkout assistant at a supermarket and drink champagne every night, at some point in time your income will not be quite in proportion with your consumption. And it is the same thing that happened to us." In 2006, Naja and Karen face a suspension of payments. According to Naja, things go wrong for several reasons, such as inadequate business know-how, lack of consulting assistance and quite a few stupid mistakes. An example of the latter is that they forget to take into account an expense of a million Danish kroner (approximately 132,000 euro) for postage in connection with issuing a Cindy Crawford catalogue.

Naja and Karen use the insolvency situation as a time out to think about how to create a healthier business structure with balance between earnings and expenditure. Upon having received a capital injection, they work hard and trim the organisation in every respect imaginable. *"We shut down that one, we have to fire those people, we cut down here, and we cancel this showroom. Can we afford this? Yes, but only 50 percent."* Naja and Karen begin to think financially, commercially and strategically – how they can optimise the organisation through "lean business". *"No doubt there is greater focus on earnings now and running a profitable business (…) There is also more focus on not being so egoistic in our expression. We are still true to what we are, but we also incorporate others into it… thinking commercially and about the end customer."* However, they still do not make actual formal market analyses to grasp the identity of their customers. Information on the core customer is brought in through for instance distributors, employees and sales representatives. These stakeholders are also invited to contribute to redefining Munthe plus Simonsen's line of design.

Last but not least, organisationally Naja and Karen now make use of the franchise model rather than being owners of the shops. Hereby, they spread the risk and involve people with a local commercial knowledge about who buys their products, where and why.

■ Your immediate interpretation

Think about the narrative and present your interpretation of how Naja and Karen evaluate whether their idea creates value at the market and thus a real opportunity. Below you will find inspiration for reflections which can help you interpret the narrative.

■ You have been given the assignment to produce a description of the way Naja and Karen so far have evaluated whether their idea represents a profitable opportunity. Which aspects will you consider? Do they evaluate the idea at all? And if so, what characterises the evaluation process?

■ Your description is so convincing that Naja and Karen engage you as their personal consultant straight away. What advice will you give them as to how to streamline their evaluation of the idea in the future? Do you believe that Naja and Karen ought to have tackled the evaluation differently from the beginning? If so, how?

■ One day, Naja stops by your office. She is considering carrying out a market analysis of core customers and competitors. The analysis should substantiate an assessment of the cost-effectiveness of the idea. Make an estimate of possible evaluation advantages and disadvantages involved in carrying out such an analysis.

■ Theories of entrepreneurship

When reading the literature on entrepreneurship, you will soon experience that the emergence and organisation of opportunities are two truly central themes. Discussions about opportunity evaluation are less prominent. *"Little is known about how entrepreneurs actually evaluate opportunities."* (Keh et al. 2002: 125). The fact that we know so little about this subject is a mystery, considering the pivotal role of evaluation in the entrepreneurial process. After all, the evaluation tells the entrepreneur whether he or she can expect the idea to become a profitable opportunity or what the entrepreneur can do to achieve this. Finally, in many respects it is the evaluation that bridges the emergence and the organisation of opportunities, since it tells the entrepreneur whether it makes sense to spend resources pursuing the opportunity through organisational activities.

Based on the literature which, after all, exists on how opportunities are evaluated in the entrepreneurial process, we will point out two perspectives on opportunity evaluation. The first and most well-known perspective stresses how opportunity evaluation is a means to achieve a certain result or goal. As already mentioned, the goal will often be to create a profitable organisation which will be able to survive in the market. In this way, evaluation is seen as purposeful action and therefore belonging to an instrumental perspective. The actual evaluation process is characterised by the entrepreneur systematically pursuing fixed and predefined rules of analysis.

Contrary to this, we will find a perspective that stresses the creation of legitimacy as essential to the evaluation of opportunities. According to this perspective, the success of the entrepreneur is dependent on whether he or she can get other people to accept the opportunity – and the new organisation carrying it forward – as being valuable and attractive. If this proves successful, the entrepreneur can rightly assess that the idea represents an opportunity – the entrepreneur evaluates the opportunity positively.

Legitimacy is important because when a new idea arises, it typically suffers from low legitimacy because it is unknown. Consequently, the challenge of the entrepreneur is to find market players who will support the idea with resources and in other ways. This requires legitimacy – that other people accept the opportunity as being valid in a market context. Without legitimacy, the idea will not be considered a real opportunity, since it is not realisable. Fundamentally, the legitimisation process is a social process in which, through interaction with the market, the entrepreneur obtains a realisation of whether the idea represents an opportunity or not. Systematic analysis is not employed and the social interaction determines the unfolding and the result of the evaluation process. The paradox which will be explored in this chapter on opportunity evaluation is thus whether evaluation is carried out:

Instrumentally or legitimately?

What is evaluation?

Generally, evaluation can assume many forms (classical evaluation, effect evaluation, user evaluation etc.). An example of a familiar evaluation tool is the "Cost-Benefit analysis" in which the effects are evaluated seen in the light of expenditure. We often associate evaluation with a retrospective and systematic assessment of performances and processes attached to a certain activity, such as for example the evaluation of a public initiative which has been running for a number of years. Has the initiative been actualised in accordance with the established targets seen in the light of the direct and indirect resource consumption? So, evaluations are often carried out in connection with something which has taken place. Further-more, an evaluation typically requires clear goals that you want to achieve from the activity. However, the objectives of doing an evaluation are very diverse. Examples of objectives are control, documentation, legitimisation, strategic means or learning (Dahler-Larsen & Krogstrup 2001).

The process of evaluation of entrepreneurial opportunities differs from the typical evaluation process in crucial ways, though. The evaluation is concerned with the question whether the idea represents a future attractive opportunity in a market which may not even have come into existence yet. Thus, within entrepreneurship we are dealing with a forward-looking evaluation (ex ante) rather than a retrospec-tive evaluation (ex post). It is all about envisaging and predicting the future to find out whether the idea can form the basis of a cost-effective and viable organisation *"The entrepreneur must forecast future prices and goods and resources and use intuitive judgement to gauge market potential"* (Keh et al. 2002: 130).

Consequently, in entrepreneurship the purpose of evaluation is not to control or document something which has already taken place but to assess the future po-tential of an idea. This makes the evaluation process more uncertain, complex and risky. The decision to realise an opportunity is made in a situation where the entre-preneur does not know the future conditions (uncertainty), and he or she must take many circumstances into account (complexity). Uncertainty is closely connected with risk. The entrepreneur's conception of the risk involved in an entrepreneurial project is thus an important element in the evaluation process. If he or she believes that it involves a low risk, the probability that the project is attempted realised is strong and vice versa.

This reflects the fact that the assessment of the question whether an idea is valu-able to others and realisable is primarily a cognitive process taking place in the mind of the entrepreneur. The entrepreneur can seek other people's advice to sup-port the process or make use of various tools. But at the end of the day, it is his or her decision. Since cognition varies from person to person, two people with the same idea and placed in the same situation may very well end up in taking diffe-rent decisions. One can be more optimistic and willing to take a risk than the other and therefore seek to realise an opportunity which the other relinquishes.

The instrumental evaluation
As mentioned, the instrumental perspective is the most widespread in the litera-ture concerning evaluation of opportunities. Maybe because the perspective gives

some clear and simple guidelines concerning the way in which the entrepreneur can evaluate whether an idea is or might be profitable. Fundamentally, the instrumental perspective is composed by a series of tools and guidelines to gather knowledge which can support the evaluation process. The tools and guidelines are rational by nature. If the entrepreneur uses these, it is expected that he or she gains insight as regards whether the idea represents a real opportunity or not. In other words, the instrumental perspective aims at giving the entrepreneur control over the evaluation process. This makes it possible for the entrepreneur to assess beforehand whether he or she can achieve his/her goals before the actual organising of the opportunity is started. It also reflects how evaluation according to the instrumental perspective is something that takes place before the actual organisation process, i.e. before the entrepreneur seriously engages himself or herself in involving other players (such as investors), gets access to resources (such as capital) and establishes technology (such as machines).

The instrumental gathering of knowledge to support the evaluation happens as an analytic process, where the entrepreneur is recommended to divide the evaluation into areas. There is no consensus as to which areas are the central ones. But we find a good bet in Barringer and Ireland (2008). They suggest the entrepreneur to focus on especially four areas, namely:

- Product/service
- The market/industry
- Organisation
- Financing

Therefore, the central interest areas of the evaluation will be: Are the customers interested in the product/service of the entrepreneur? Is there room for such a product/service in the market in the light of competitors, the market development etc.? How is the entrepreneur to organise himself to reach the customers? What financial resources are necessary to realise the idea? Of these areas, the evaluation of the market/industry is by some researchers believed to be especially important: *"Unquestionably, the analysis of the industry and market in which the business will operate is the most important analysis of the entire feasibility study. Without customers – without an industry and market that are receptive to the business concept – there is no business"* (Allen 2006: 90).

Typically, the evaluation will follow some predefined phases. Based on Barringer and Ireland's division above, a process model might look as shown in figure 4.1.

Figure 4.1: A processual model for opportunity evaluation

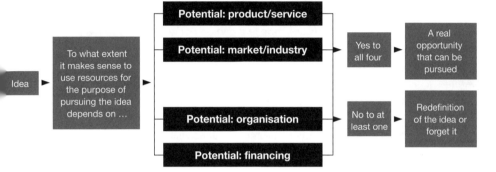

Source: Inspired by Barringer & Ireland (2008).

The model shows how the entrepreneur can assess whether he or she is to pursue the idea further through analysis of the four areas "product/service", "market/industry", "organisation" and "financing". To support the analysis of each area, the literature often refers to traditional management theories. This may for instance in connection with analysis of the market/industry be tools and models such as a "SWOT-analysis" and Porter's "Five Forces Model".

As mentioned, there is no universal agreement about the areas mentioned. Especially some researchers, among others Hindle et al. (2007) and Allen (2006), emphasise the importance of evaluating the human factor, i.e. qualities and competences in the entrepreneur or the entrepreneurial team. An engineer can for instance be a brilliant technician and inventor but incompetent as sales representative and manager. Many investors, especially venture capitalists and Business Angels who invest in high-risk projects with great news value, emphasise very much evaluation of the human factor when clarifying whether they are to invest in the new opportunity or not.

Thus, evaluation both comprises external circumstances like the market and internal circumstances like the human factor. It is structures and processes in these external and internal circumstances together that create a picture showing whether the idea of the entrepreneur may result in a product or a service which creates value for others and in this way is realisable – whether the idea has resulted in an opportunity.

Evaluation of opportunities

One of the means to obtain a general idea of the chances of the opportunity to be realised is the business plan, which will be discussed more deeply in chapter 8. Many researchers within the instrumental perspective consider it to be the key for evaluation: *"Some entrepreneurs are impatient and do not want to spend the time it takes to write a business plan. This approach is usually a mistake. Writing a business plan forces an entrepreneur to think carefully about all aspects of a business venture. It also helps a new venture to establish a set of milestones that can be used to guide the early phases of the business rollout"* (Barringer & Ireland 2006: 19-20). The business plan stresses how it should be possible from the beginning to predict the general destinations the entrepreneur has to visit during the entrepreneurial process. This leaves us with a linear and predictable understanding of the evaluation process.

Evaluation of opportunities with great potential
Opportunities have different extent and potential. Some are small and local, others great and global. But how do we evaluate in advance what potential a specific opportunity has? Which criteria can we use, and are there tools which make systematic evaluation possible ex ante?

Wickham (2004) points out three central criteria for evaluation of opportunities. He refers to the importance of assessing the potential of the opportunity in the light of "scale", "scope" and "span". "Scale" refers to the size of the opportunity and "scope" to the value it brings in the short and long run. "Span" refers to the validity of the opportunity over time – is it a one-day wonder or does it have a lasting potential? A successful opportunity could easily be a one-day wonder, as long as its "scale" is great. For instance the opportunity of selling Chinese joy bracelets in Denmark in 2008 might be expected to be a one-day wonder. The opportunity is especially impelled by the fact that two of the participants in the popular television singing-talent-show "X-Factor" wear the bracelet in question. When the "X-Factor-fever" of the year has blown over, we might expect that the same thing will happen with the success linked to the Chinese bracelets. However, this does not necessarily mean that the introduction of Chinese bracelets on the Danish market is not an attractive opportunity.

Hindle et al. (2007) build on slightly different, however, comparable criteria. Here, the "viability", "durability" and "credibility" of the opportunity are emphasised. The areas which they seek to evaluate resemble the ones we have described above, namely "product", "market", "industry", "people" and "money". A special thing about this evaluation model is that it takes place at three levels. First it is assessed whether the idea is viable, then its potential, and finally whether it can be implemented.

The model has been developed based on two PhD-theses about opportunity evaluation. Via tests the accuracy in evaluations of a large number of innovation ideas based on the model has turned out to be high. However, the model ought not to be considered as a sort of oracle, as it is based on evaluation of the various areas which, to a great extent, are subjective. What it gives is primarily a systematic approach to the evaluation process. Furthermore, it nourishes a possibility of dialogue for instance between investor and entrepreneur, between advisor and entrepreneur and between students among themselves, if they are asked to evaluate a specific opportunity.

Figure 4.2 shows the components of the model with five columns and three levels. The model is called Venture Intelligence Quotient (VIQ). In Denmark, the model and the software tools attached to it are called IDEA-VIQ™. The model is clarified below.

Figure 4.2: The VIQ-model

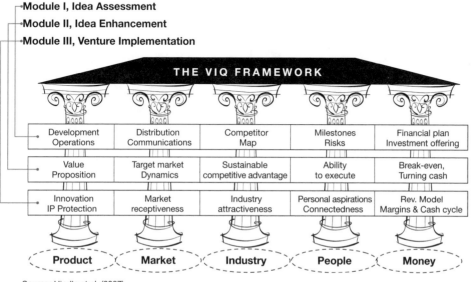

Source: Hindle et al. (2007).

The first module (Idea Assessment), which appears from the left side of the model, covers evaluation of whether the idea which is the basis of the entrepreneurial process is worth pursuing. The second module (Idea Enhancement) focuses on strengthening the idea. Can the elements that make up a successful opportunity be developed based on the idea? In other words, the potential of the idea is established and comprehended. The third module (Venture Implementation) concerns the actual implementation of the idea. This part offers suggestions for how the entrepreneur might actually build up a new organisation based on the idea. Here the VIQ-tool covers issues which this book will focus on in chapter 5.

The five columns cover, as mentioned, five areas: Product = The essence of the idea which can be a product, service, experience or process; Market = The group of customers and organisations which are interested in the idea and have resources for obtaining the product or the service which the idea represents; Industry = Organisations offering the same or substituting products, services, experiences or processes; People = The entrepreneur/the entrepreneurial team, and Money = The financial dimension.

If you want to further explore the VIQ-model and the software program, IDEA-VIQ™, you have access to this tool via the minidisk attached to the book. Access and descriptions of the tool can be found on www.idea-textbook.dk. The tool can be used to evaluate one of your own ideas or an existing organisation. You can also use it as an aid when you are to write a business plan.

As mentioned, the tool is a scientifically based decision tool which can teach you systematic competences for evaluation according to the instrumental perspective. Generally seen, the tool works as follows: You complete the upper part of a questionnaire with name and details about the idea you want to evaluate. Then you answer a series of questions about the idea (totally about 20 questions). In connection with all questions, you are to give an assessment on a scale. An algorithm which among other things takes trade variation into account will at last calculate strengths and weaknesses connected to the opportunity and organisation at which your idea aims. You will get a graphic illustration of strengths and weaknesses at the five areas as well as an estimation of the potential of the idea.

Evaluation through creation of legitimacy
However, evaluation does not always take place as an instrumental process where the evaluation criteria and areas are defined ahead of the entrepreneurial activity itself. Also, it is not always the case that evaluation is a systematic and analytic

process directed at a particular goal and based on some specific tools playing down the complexity of the situation. This stresses the perspective of legitimacy. Instrumental models might have built in an assessment of legitimacy cf. the dimension "credibility" in the VIQ-model, but the basic way of thinking is totally different from the perspective of legitimacy.

What is legitimacy? In brief, something is legitimate if it is in accordance with the norms, values, beliefs, practices and procedures accepted by a given social group (Johnson et al. 2006). According to a known definition, legitimacy is: "… *a generalized perception or assumption that the action of an entity is desirable, proper, appropriate, within some socially constructed system of norms, values, beliefs and definitions"* (Suchman 1995: 574).

It follows that the entrepreneur's idea can be assessed as being a legitimate opportunity, when the economic, social and political environments accept its existence as a valid part of the market. According to this way of thinking, the environment determines when there is "room" for a given entrepreneurial process, and when there is not. It is especially clear when a new type of organisation or a new trade is developing. *"Organization populations emerge when the goods and services they provide are seen as legitimate and desirable by the host society"* (Reynolds 1991: 57). Therefore, we can say that *"… certain kinds of organizations simply cannot be founded before their time"* (Aldrich 1999: 75).

The reason is that without the necessary legitimacy, it will be difficult for the entrepreneur to raise the necessary capital, recruit staff, get customers, etc. It is especially valid when new trades are developing and a series of innovative entrepreneurs try to establish new organisations at the same time. *"Among the many problems facing innovative entrepreneurs, their relative lack of legitimacy is especially critical"* (Aldrich & Fiol 1994: 645). An empirical investigation of a large number of innovative organisations in the first year of their life confirms that the ability to survive depends on the ability to obtain legitimacy (Delmar & Shane 2004). The investigation is based on two symbolic actions promoting the legitimacy, namely registration of a legal organisation and preparation of a business plan.

However, legitimacy cannot be obtained and evaluated at one's desk and via symbolic actions and planning. First and foremost, it is through interaction with other players including especially other players in the market that the entrepreneur can evaluate whether others regard the opportunity as legitimate. To stress it, Quinn (2004) tells a story about how he and a group of colleagues invite a consultant

Evaluation of opportunities

to support them in finding their core competence as foundation for an entrepreneurial project. He makes them write a list of their view on own core competences. However, they are to throw away the finished list. It is not useful. Instead, they now are to e-mail acquaintances and business partners to get them to identify their core competences. The moral is that our "best" self is when we create value in the opinion of others and not in the opinion of ourselves. Our "best" self is the self that is legitimate in the opinion of others, and this we can only find by interacting with others. As Quinn writes: *"Reading what these people have written, I felt approved and received"* (Quinn 2004: 128).

The process towards legitimacy
Johnson et al. (2006) estimate the process where new objects – such as a new idea – obtain legitimacy and in this way are evaluated as a real opportunity. The process consists of four phases: 1) innovation, 2) local validation, 3) spread and 4) general validation. First phase covers the creation of the opportunity. Next phase is characterised by local players being convinced that it is possible to relate to the new object and that it makes sense compared to existing norms, values, procedures, etc. Once accepted in the local environment – or other relation-tight contexts – a spread of the new object to other contexts can be started. *"As the new object spreads, its adoption in new situations often needs less explicit justification than it may have needed in the first local context"* (Johnson et al. 2006: 60). As a result of the spread, the new might over time be more generally accepted as a natural part of the environment. So the legitimacy process can be seen as ripples spreading on the water and at last they fade away totally and become an integrated part of a bigger sea. The spread is dependent on the social interaction and accept which direct the progress of the process.

The more innovative the idea of the entrepreneur is, the bigger problems he or she may get in convincing others of the relevance and legitimacy of the idea, as it may be difficult for the environment to understand the idea and for what they are to use it. Aldrich and Fiol express it as follows: *"The first organization of its kind faces a different set of challenges than the one which simply carries on the tradition pioneered by many predecessors"* (Aldrich & Fiol 1994: 663). Consequently, the innovative entrepreneur simply lacks the knowledge and confidence among other people, which are decisive for them engaging in the advancing opportunity. Another consequence of being an innovative entrepreneur on a growing market is that he or she lacks role models to lean on. Role models are seen as decisive for entrepreneurial success.

Strategies for building of legitimacy

Entrepreneurs can carry out different actions to convince the environment of the relevance of the idea. For instance, the entrepreneur can imitate other organisations which are already accepted in the environment, or they can try to obtain official certificates to stress that their idea actually makes sense in the light of the existing (Shane 2003). Furthermore, it might be desirable for the entrepreneurs to cooperate with others to obtain legitimacy in society, for instance via a new trade organisation or network, instead of seeking legitimacy individually. Another strategy for building of legitimacy is to focus on establishing trust among central interested parties who are to give the entrepreneur access to knowledge, resources, etc. Trust is important as it is fundamental for all types of interactions between people. The entrepreneur has different opportunities for the building of confidence. For instance he or she can convince others that the opportunity makes sense by behaving "as if" the opportunity were already a successful reality. *"Founders can behave "as if" the activity were a reality – producing and directing great theatre, as it were – may convince others of the tangible reality of the new activity"* (Aldrich & Fiol 1994: 651). Many other actions can be utilised to promote legitimacy, including practical/symbolic actions like getting a business card, stationery and a homepage.

However, according to the perspective of legitimacy, the entrepreneur seldom pursues a specific strategy related to creating legitimacy. Rather, the process of legitimacy takes an experimental and exploring starting point; through daily actions in the market, the entrepreneur seeks signals telling him or her whether the idea is regarded legitimate. Metaphorically, the entrepreneur carries his/her idea under the arm and goes into the field to test it by trying to convince others of its excellences, in this way evaluating the degree of legitimacy of the idea – is it worth pursuing further? Through the efforts to convince others of the excellences of the idea, the entrepreneur receives different sorts of feedback telling him or her whether the idea makes up the foundation for a realistic opportunity. Feedback may take the form of resources, knowledge, new opportunities, barriers, etc. which naturally can be used specifically as physical inputs to shape the idea to an opportunity and later on an organisation. But feedback also has a symbolic value as it tells the entrepreneur whether others regard his or her opportunity as legitimate. This leads to a clarification of whether the idea of the entrepreneur makes sense, and in this way whether it is relevant to pursue it further as an opportunity.

Thus, the idea is evaluated according to the perspective of legitimacy through exploration and experimental actions and social interactions, rather than via systematic and analytical tools which are taken into use ahead of the actual entrepreneurial process. Evaluation takes place in the process, and it is also here that the criteria for what ought to be evaluated are created. As a result, evaluation becomes a progressive and procedural journey where the entrepreneur over time creates an assessment of the potential of the idea as opportunity.

Different types of entrepreneurs experience different challenges concerning the creation of legitimacy. It is often relatively easy for the engineer who has created a physical prototype of his idea to create legitimacy around it, as the players in the market have something specific to relate to. Contrary to this, a person who wants to sell expert advice or a cultural performance is confronted with the challenge of creating legitimacy around a more intangible product which fundamentally is the person himself.

Evaluation: Instrumental or legitimate?

Now two different perspectives of the evaluation of opportunities have been presented to you, that is the perspectives of instrumentality and legitimacy. These are summarised in table 4.1.

Table 4.1: The paradox: instrumental or legitimate?

	Instrumental	Legitimate
Evaluation perception	Tool to achieve a certain objective	Legitimacy creation
Evaluation objective	To state the direction for action	To convince the actors of the market of the idea
Evaluation criteria	They should be formulated before the process	They emerge during the entrepreneurial process
Evaluation process	Rational, systematic og analytic	Social, interactive, experimental and exploring
Evaluation character	Evaluation and entrepreneurial action are two separate activities	Evaluation and entrepreneurial action are two inseparable activities

The instrumental perspective sees evaluation as a means to obtain a certain goal, where the goal is to indicate directions for action compared to how and if the idea is presumed to be the starting point for a profitable opportunity. The evaluation criteria are defined ahead of the actual evaluation process. The criteria appear from various analytical frameworks such as the VIQ tool or the business plan. These frameworks often indicate a linear and systematic chain of analytical evaluation activities, that the entrepreneur is to go through to obtain the goal. Thus, the evaluation process is characterised by systematic analysis which indicates the direction for the further entrepreneurial action. This also means that evaluation and the actual entrepreneurial action are two separate activities. First we evaluate and then we act based on the directions of the evaluation.

By contrast, the perspective of legitimacy stresses that creation of legitimacy is the focal point of the evaluation process. The goal of the evaluation is to convince the players in the market of the excellences of the idea. If the entrepreneur succeeds in doing just that, it is a positive evaluation. If he does not succeed, the has to consider redefining or dropping the idea. The exact criteria for the evaluation are not decided beforehand but in the legitimisation process itself where the interaction with the market will signal gradually which criteria are relevant. The evaluation process is social, interactive, experimental and explorative by nature. By confronting the social environment with the idea, the entrepreneur has an opportunity of creating trust, acceptance and understanding of it. The entrepreneur takes the idea to the market and tests it. This points out how the evaluation process and the entrepreneurial action according to the perspective of legitimacy run as two inseparable processes.

■ A theoretical interpretation

We now offer our interpretation of the story about Munthe plus Simonsen, which started the chapter, seen in the light of the theory presented. First, the story will be seen through the lenses of the instrumental perspective, after which we focus on the perspective of legitimacy.

The instrumental perspective

Only to a small extent does the story about Munthe plus Simonsen reflect the instrumental perspective. At the beginning of the entrepreneurial process, Naja and Karen, at any rate, have no certain idea or goal they aim at fulfilling through rational and analytical processes. But if we study the story over time, Naja and Karen seem to be more and more focused, goal-oriented and planning-oriented in their activities. Especially the suspension of payments gets them to pause in order to analyse and evaluate systematically what they can do to create a collection and business model which the market will find attractive. Evaluation has been an explorative and experimental process for them, but now Naja and Karen try to make their objective clear, and through analysis of the budget they find out which financial cost cuts are necessary to reach the goal. In other words, the business is really cut to the bone through a systematic financial evaluation. Now the objective is to create a modern and financially healthy organisation, and they know that all the time they have to look at how they can optimise the business and which financial consequences are linked to which activities. It is no longer sufficient for them to make some great clothes – it also has to be a viable business.

From refusing to be a commercial organisation, Naja and Karen start thinking commercially. This is also reflected partly by them moving focus away from what they like themselves and their own lifestyle to for instance involving thoughts about who the end-user is, and what should make her buy their clothes. As a part of this more commercial orientation, in their own way Naja and Karen make a systematic analysis of the client base and in this way an analysis of the potential of the product in the light of the market to be able to incorporate the needs and wishes of the market in their designs. This is realised by involving distributors, employees, sales representatives, etc. in the evaluation of Munthe plus Simonsen's target group and in the redefinition of the design line of the organisation. Last, but not least through franchising, Naja and Karen try to establish a more stable and profitable situation. This can be seen as a sort of organisational evaluation.

In other words, it is clear that the suspension of payments causes a more instrumental approach to evaluation where goals are fixed ahead of the evaluation process, and they start using systematic analytical tools.

The legitimacy perspective
Contrary to this, the beginning of the Munthe plus Simonsen tale is very much evidence of the perspective of legitimacy. It is a story about two young girls who meet big difficulties in convincing the outside world that they have an attractive product. Especially the fact that Naja and Karen start up within a line of business that is still not in itself an accepted part of the market creates legitimacy problems for the young entrepreneurs. Not only are they to convince the outside world of their own collection, but also of the value of a totally new line of business. As a result, at first they are rejected by media, sales channels etc., and they have no role models to lean on.

However, their organisation spreads in ever-widening circles and is increasingly regarded as legitimate. By pushing their way through to Nørgaard paa Strøget, their product is quickly accepted by the outside world as attractive, maybe because precisely this sales channel enjoys a wide-ranging social accept in the world of fashion. Naja and Karen open the door to the sales channel by daring to explore, to be persistent, not take no for an answer and by displaying their products. Drive, persistence and interaction with the "right" people are characteristic of Naja and Karen's creation of legitimacy. But it is also by acting "as if" they have a very precious product that they get others convinced. Acting "as if" is among other things reflected by their use of known supermodels, expensive office buildings and establishment of shops and showrooms in key fashion cities from an early stage of the entrepreneurial process. Through these actions, Naja and Karen also create legitimacy by being able to be different from the crowd, which is a central quality in a line of business like the fashion trade. It is clear that the evaluation process in the beginning very much is an integrated part of the entrepreneurial process. It is expressed by the fact that Naja and Karen do not seem to make a deliberate evaluation of their idea. Actually, in the beginning they take pride in not relating their designs to the market.

Naja and Karen's explorative and experimental approach to opportunity evaluation leads to a lot of positive feedback from the market – and apparently, they hit an upward market trend with their clothes. An important feedback is increasing earnings and another is awards, which might be understood as official certificates creating further legitimacy for Munthe plus Simonsen. Certainly, Naja and Karen have the upper hand. They have created an attractive opportunity that develops at a time when the bohemian style is desirable. Actually, a lot suggests that Naja and Karen's actions do not only create legitimacy for their own organisation, but that they also contribute to the fact that the Danish fashion scene as a whole over time is getting more legitimate. For many, Munthe plus Simonsen is synonymous with the tale of the success of Danish design.

■ Practical tests of the theory

The interpretations, thoughts and discussions of the chapter make you ready to outline your own tests to understand opportunity evaluation. Here are some exercises you can start with.

Exercise 1: Use the VIQ tool

Open the enclosed IDEA-VIQ™ mini-disk and read about its functions on www. idea-textbook.dk. Now it is your task to evaluate Munthe plus Simonsen by means of the tool according to the information in the case and by seeking additional information. Then make a print of the graphic illustration which shows the strengths, weaknesses and potential of the organisation. Assess whether Munthe plus Simonsen is an attractive organisation which you would be prepared to invest in yourself.

Exercise 2: Your own idea

Make the same test as described above. But this time you are to evaluate your own idea. If you do not have an idea already then make one up. Does your idea make sense in the light of the market?

Exercise 3: Learn from the customers

Learn more about whether your idea is attractive in the light of the market. Design an investigation which can give you knowledge of your customers and in which circumstances and where they would buy the product/service your idea covers. Make the analysis and evaluate the potential of the idea in the light of this.

Literature

Aldrich, H. & Fiol, M. C. (1994). Fools Rush in? The Institutional Context of Industry Creation, The Academy of Management Review, 19(4), 645-670.

Aldrich, H. E. (1999). Organizations evolving. London: Saga.

Allen, K. R. (2006). Launching New Ventures: An Entrepreneurial Approach. Boston: Houghton Mifflin Company.

Barringer, B. R. & Ireland, R. D. (2006). Entrepreneurship: Successfully Launching New Ventures. Upper Saddle River: Prentise Hall.

Barringer, B. R. & Ireland, R. D. (2008). Entrepreneurship: Successfully Launching New Ventures. Upper Saddle River: Prentice Hall.

Dahler-Larsen, P. & Krogstrup, H. K. (2001): Tendenser i evaluering. Odense: Syddansk Universitetsforlag.

Delmar, F. & Shane, S. (2004): Legitimating First: Organizing Activities and the Survival of New Ventures, Journal of Business Venturing, 19, 385-410.

Hindle, K., Mainprize, B. & Dorofeeva, N. (2007). Venture Intelligence: How Smart Investors and Entrepreneurs Evaluate New Ventures: Melbourne: Learnfast Press.

Johnson, C., Dow, T. J. & Ridgeway, C. L. (2006). Legitimacy as a Social Process, Annual Review Sociology, 32, 53-78.

Keh, H. T., Foo, M. D. & Lim, B. C. (2002). Opportunity Evaluation Under Risky Conditions: The Cognitive Processes of Entrepreneurs, 27(2), 125-148.

Quinn, R. E. (2004). Building the Bridge as You Walk on It: A Guide for Leading Change. San Francisco: Jossey-Bass.

Reynolds, P. D. (1991). Sociology and Entrepreneurship: Concepts and Contributions, Entrepreneurship Theory and Practice, 16(2), 47-70.

Shane, S. (2003). A General Theory of Entrepreneurship: The Individual-opportunity Nexus. Cheltenham: Edward Elgar.

Suchman, M. (1995). Managing Legitimacy: Strategic and Institutional Approaches, Academy of Management Review, 20(3), 571-610.

Wickham, P. A. (2004). Strategic Entrepreneurship, Harlow: Pearson Education Limited.

112

Chapter 5

The organising of opportunities

Let us assume that an opportunity has come into existence and has been positively evaluated in the light of the market. Time has come to exploit the opportunity, which then requires organising of the opportunity. Basically, organising is about developing some meaningful structures and systems which we call organisations. Organising is a process the entrepreneur can make use of in order to collect resources, coordinate activities, exchange and involve others so that the opportunity can be transformed into practice. In other words, organising is a tool to transfer the opportunity to the market through the creation of new and independent organisations or organisational entities in existing organisations. Organising *"... represents the infrastructure, processes, and systems by which the business will move from idea to reality"* (Allen 2006: 241). It is also possible to imagine that the entrepreneur exploits his or her opportunity by buying a franchise-unit or by selling the opportunity to an existing organisation. In this chapter, however, we will concentrate on what organising of opportunities through the creation of a new organisation involves.

■ Meet practice

Before we set out on a long account of opportunity exploitation through organising, time has once again come to meet an entrepreneur. Perhaps you already know him. His name is Claus Meyer; he is a chef and a famous person in the Danish media. Listen to his story about organising. If you would like to see some video clips with Claus, then visit www.idea-textbook.dk.

A famous chef: *"It just happened"*
"I never wanted to have a big company. I wanted big victories but I never wanted many employees or a huge turnover or having 7-8 companies...This is something that just happened. I never worked with plans; and until a few years ago, I never worked with budgets, and the idea of having a Board is only four years old. We never took loans in the bank. I have only tried that once and it was not a success (...). Thus, we started in the easiest way." This is how Claus describes his approach to entrepreneurship. In 2008, the Meyer Group (incl. subsidiaries) consisted of a number of food companies which altogether employed more than 300 people.

It all begins in the 60s and 70s with Claus growing up in the Danish food culture. It is at a time in history when many women have left the kitchen in favour of the labour market. Danish households are in those days increasingly filled with frozen vegetables, mince, margarine and other types of food products, which are supposed to make everyday life easier and keep the expenses down – often at the expense of the quality of the food and the food experience. As a young man, Claus has no specific interest in food until one day he finds himself working for a famous chef in the South of France. After that experience, his mission in life becomes evident for him. He will change and improve the Danish/Nordic food culture. The experience, the soul, the quality and the sincerity should be brought back in the food, but how? Claus has no plans about how to realise his mission.

Other people would perhaps have become a chef's apprentice but not Claus. He begins to study at Copenhagen Business School. In fact, Denmark's probably most famous chef never gets any chef training. Instead, Claus initiates his first entrepreneurial project at the same time as he studies at the business school: "take-away food" from his student's apartment. Later on, the principal offers him to take over the canteen. That is the beginning of a long and entrepreneurial journey. Many organisational projects get started (The Chocolate Company, Meyer and Tingstrøm staff restaurants, luxurious company trips/teambuilding, fruit growing, the top restaurant Noma, Meyer's Deli etc.). Figure 5.1 offers an overview of the companies belonging to the Meyer Group in 2008.

Figure 5.1: Organisation diagram – The Meyer Group

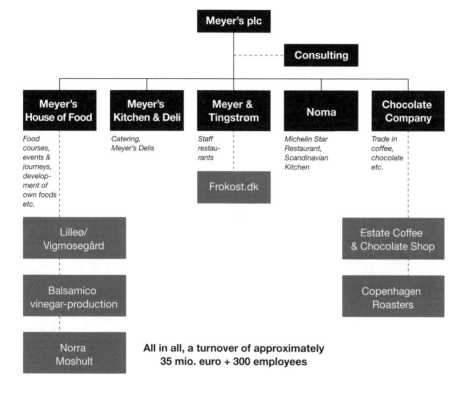

Meyer's plc

Consulting

Meyer's House of Food	Meyer's Kitchen & Deli	Meyer & Tingstrøm	Noma	Chocolate Company
Food courses, events & journeys, development of own foods etc.	Catering, Meyer's Delis	Staff restaurants	Michelin Star Restaurant, Scandinavian Kitchen	Trade in coffee, chocolate etc.

Frokost.dk

Lilleø/ Vigmosegård

Estate Coffee & Chocolate Shop

Balsamico vinegar-production

Copenhagen Roasters

Norra Moshult

All in all, a turnover of approximately 35 mio. euro + 300 employees

The mission comes into focus

"The best idea of my life came to me about four years ago. The idea synthesized the last fifteen years of my life. I did not intend to enter the restaurant business but I got an offer… a lovely place… an old warehouse in Christianshavn. My idea was to build a Nordic gourmet restaurant." The colleagues laugh. Nordic food is not exquisite – not worthy of a gourmet restaurant. The colleagues scoff at the restaurant and call it the "whale restaurant". But together with his partner Rene Redzepi who has experiences with the gourmet business, Claus establishes the restaurant Noma (an abbreviation of "Nordisk Mad" in Danish which translates to "Nordic Food" in English). They build the restaurant around the unique history, taste and origin of the Nordic kitchen. Nobody has considered that before. We all know the Thai, the French and the Indian kitchen. But what is a Nordic kitchen? None of the two entrepreneurs dream about creating an enormous financial success. Their dreams are about something bigger than that. Like Claus's mission in

life, their overall success criterion is to define the Nordic kitchen and to create a shared mission among Nordic farmers, small and big companies, citizens, politicians etc. towards promoting Nordic food of a high quality. Everything turns out to be an enormous success. In 2008, two Michelin-stars decorated Noma which is also ranked the fifteenth best restaurant in the world. The finest position a Nordic restaurant has ever achieved.

The start-up process
To a high degree the establishment of Noma involves a lot of different people. First of all the partner Rene Redzepi. Claus's role is primarily to back up Rene by using his experience as a serial entrepreneur: *"I nurtured him and helped with financial backing, building up a homepage, recruiting staff members, creating the first menus, choosing the graphic designer; I took care of contractual relations to the owners of the premises – and maybe the most important, I involved the entire Nordic food intelligence... ministers from Norway and Denmark etc. and leading people from the Nordic food industry in order to discuss how everybody could share our vision."* Claus simply chooses to invite ministers, top leaders from the Nordic food industry, journalists and famous chefs to a symposium in order to explain the idea about the Nordic kitchen. The participating chefs are asked to define a manifesto for the new Nordic kitchen – the manifesto is formulated as ten commandments.

The manifesto becomes the starting signal for a completely new movement – a movement with many different actors (chefs, consumers, politicians and business people from all the Nordic countries). The movement is gathered in order to promote Nordic food culture and the words of the manifesto. The Nordic ministers of food also become part of the movement since they on the basis of the manifesto formulate a "New Nordic Food Programme". This programme provides funding to develop, produce or market products in accordance with the manifesto.

Consequently, in reality a restaurant (and its business foundation) has turned into a movement. Through the movement, Claus succeeds in his mission of creating a platform for a Danish/Nordic food culture that is no longer about frozen vegetables, mince and margarine: a food culture which promotes the unique quality and roots of Nordic food.

To dance around
To the question about to what extent Claus sees a connection between how he cooks and creates his organisations, a very interesting picture emerges: *"How will I compare cooking with entrepreneurship? There are many similarities. The way I love*

to cook is without a recipe and without any fixed plan. I love to come to some place, to Hungary or wherever, and see which vegetables are growing in the garden, what meat is available and what is in the fridge. Then I dance a little, wondering what I can do and what I know. A kind of interfering with the surroundings and that is also the way in which I do business. I listen to people, I talk to my employees. If I have a table clearer who is good at flowers, then I should be dead if I did not ask him to do the flowers. If I meet someone in my life who wants to build a dairy, and if we did it together, it could be greater, then I would be attracted. So the way in which I build businesses is similar to the way in which I cook. I dance around; I see what happens and try to feel the energy."

A professional Board

So, over the years Claus creates his organisations without an overall plan for how they should look in the future. He acts and sees what happens. But in the course of time while the organisation grows, Claus experiences a need for professionalising and structuralising his organisation. He sets up a professional Board which, however, is mostly supposed to function as inspiration. He himself likes to have the control. *"The Board helps me in developing a well organised company with the right skills in the right positions in accordance with what we want to do. Who should be the leader of whom? (...) I do not have much experience in building up big organisations. I never aimed at a big organisation but now I have one (...). I just hope that I am a good 'priest' and visionary person and that all the employees want to follow my path. But I am not the classical CEO."*

■ Your immediate interpretation

How can we understand the process which Claus tells us about? Here are some questions that can help you reflect on the story in the light of organising.

- ■ You are a substitute teacher in the eighth class (pupils around 15 years old). In the light of Claus's story, you are to explain the class what an organisation is and how organisations come into existence. What do you tell the class?
- ■ You draw a chronology table on the blackboard and give the class a survey of Claus's progress. You get a reaction. One of the boys from the class asks you: *"When do you know that the entrepreneurial process has led to the establishment of a new organisation?"* What do you answer?
- ■ A girl in the class is also curious. She asks, *"Why does Claus not from the beginning establish Noma which is actually the opportunity that really realises his mission in life?"* Do you have an answer?

■ You should put yourself in Claus's place. He has become old and he is sitting in a rocking chair thinking back on his life. Especially, he considers to what extent his entrepreneurial organising activities have been planned and whether or not he would have been more successful if he had focused on planning to a larger degree. What do you think?

■ Theories of entrepreneurship

As you know, organising of opportunities is the topic of this chapter. The literature presents us with many different perceptions of what organising involves. Some think that it can be planned. Actually, it is widely believed that organising is a conscious phenomenon which to a certain extent can be rationally planned in order to achieve a certain goal – a successful organisation. In that way, the entrepreneur becomes an architect who is supposed to organise the opportunity most efficiently through planning. This perception reflects a planning perspective of organising.

However, an improvising perspective emphasises that entrepreneurial organising is about creating something new – a new organisation – and that the future cannot be predicted or planned. Consequently, there is much uncertainty associated with such processes, which tends to back up the perception that planning does not fully make sense. Instead, the entrepreneurial process is in practice characterised by entrepreneurs feeling their way, consulting other people and finding resources during the journey. Fundamentally, it is about improvising. Only through the many and unpredictable small steps does a new organisation get realised. In all, the planning and improvising perspective makes the paradox:

Planning or improvising?

What is an organisation?

Since organisations are the result of organising (organisations in emergence), it is interesting first to look more closely at what characterises an organisation before we consider what organising involves. Basically, an organisation is a wide and ambiguous concept. Perhaps because organisations in many ways are invisible although *"… most people in the world today are born, work, and die in organizations"* (Jones 2007: 2). From an overall perspective, organisations are likely to be defined as tools which we use for the purpose of coordinating our actions so that a desired output can be obtained. Entrepreneurs are examples of individuals who think that they possess the necessary competences to create an organisation – either a new and independent organisation or a new organisational entity in an existing organisation.

But how do we know when we are dealing with an organisation? Some people emphasise the formal structures, goals and processes that are prevalent to organisations. Others focus on informal and human dimensions like for example competences and culture. Berger and Kellner offer a definition of an organisation: *"Every human organization is, as it were, a crystallization of meanings or, to vary the image, a crystallization of meanings in objective form"* (Berger & Kellner 1981: 31). From this perspective, organisations are organised communities consisting of human actors, resources, knowledge etc. And the glue that glues together the entire thing is opinions and perceptions that are shared by the actors. This seems to emphasise how organisations basically are about group creation where the individuals are not only together as accidental passengers in a railway carriage. On the contrary, they interact in order to achieve a common aim. The organisational interaction is characterised by being:

- Formalised: It is defined by some common rules and physical conditions
- Complex: Emphasises the importance of administrative functions which connect the activities
- Goal oriented: Headed towards a certain and overall goal (Bakka & Fivelsdahl 2004).

Therefore, organisations can be perceived as the scopes of structured and coordinated human action. The basis of starting a new organisation involves only one or few entrepreneurs which also explain why it does not immediately remind you of group creation. But at the same time as the entrepreneur's opportunity is being organised (a logo is created, resources are collected, exchanges with customers are carried through) the entrepreneurial opportunity is developed from being attached to the entrepreneur to becoming a socially accepted organisation which also involves many other people. The aspect of involving other people can simply be seen as the goal of organising. *"People construct organizations to accomplish things they cannot do on their own"* (Aldrich 1999: 75). The many players who are involved make demands on further formalising, direction and thereby structure. So starting up a new organisation takes shape through the interactions between many different players. The more players who get involved in the process, the more complex it becomes and the demands made on how the emerging organisation should be formalised in correspondence with objective and administrative processes become bigger.

What does organising involve?
Organising is a process which is about creating a new organisation over time. By inspiration from Fayolle (2003), the development of a new organisation can be divided into five phases: The phases cover the aspects of getting an idea, evaluating it as a real opportunity, conceptualising the opportunity to an entrepreneurial project so that it can be exploited by materialising the opportunity to a new and emerging organisation which again over time will be shaped in a more and more stable way. This chapter is primarily about the fourth phase. The last phase is outside the interest area of this book. As you may remember from chapter 1, this book divides the entrepreneurial process into three phases which are: 1) opportunity emergence 2) opportunity evaluation and 3) opportunity organising. Basically, this distinction is in accordance with Fayolle's considerations. Figure 5.2 illustrates Fayolle's five phases.

Figure 5.2: The development of a new organisation

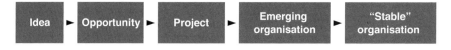

Source: Fayolle (2003), p. 41.

In the way that the five phases are described in this figure, the entrepreneurial process is seen as a linear and forward moving process. However, Fayolle's point about the phases is actually to show that relapse from later phases to earlier ones can occur. In addition, the phases do not necessarily develop in the outlined order. Some entrepreneurs for example formally establish an organisation before they have evaluated to what extent the idea represents a real opportunity. Finally, the process can stop at any given level. For example, a new organisation may never come into existence.

Fayolle's model shows that organising does not only consist of one single step – namely from a situation "without organisation" to a situation "with a new organisation". On the contrary, it is possible to talk about a number of organisational steps on the way towards a new and independent organisation or a new organisational unit in an existing organisation. Because of the fluid crossing between the situation "without organisation" and the situation "with a new organisation", it is in practice hard do decide when the organisation is created. Is it when the external financing is secured? Is it when the first bill has been paid? In accordance with this, one of the most widely accepted definitions of entrepreneurship, namely Shane's (2003) definition (compare chapter 1) does not use the word "organisation" but talks about "organising efforts".

While Fayolle's model offers an overall suggestion for how we may understand organising in the light of the entrepreneurial process as a whole, Jones (2007) is a great example of how we may more thoroughly understand the organising efforts the entrepreneur will have to go through in order to realise his opportunity in the market. Figure 5.3 is inspired by Jones (2007) and offers a survey of crucial components in organising.

Figure 5.3: The organising components

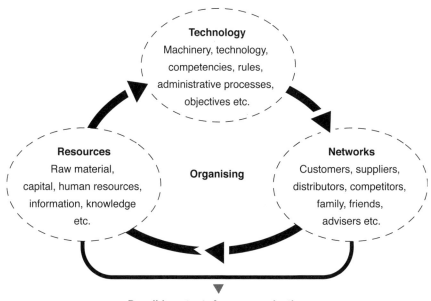

Source: Inspired by Jones (2007).

The figure illustrates that organising requires resources in terms of raw materials, human resources, information, knowledge, customers etc. As Bhave says, *"To proceed beyond the business concept identification, entrepreneurs require physical and other resources"* (Bhave 1994: 232). In chapter 6, we will go through the resource challenge more thoroughly.

Acquiring of resources presupposes that the entrepreneur acts and interacts with the environment because it is rare that he or she possesses the requisite resources. *"It is through the actions of entrepreneurs that organisations come into existence"* (Gartner et al. 2004: 285). It makes emergence and development of networks a critical factor. Like Aldrich proclaims: *"All nascent entrepreneurs draw upon their existing social networks and construct new ones in the process of obtaining knowledge and resources for their organizations"* (Aldrich 1999: 81). Relevant players are for example customers, shareholders, suppliers, distributors, competitors, advisers, family, friends etc. The network challenge is presented in chapter 7.

 A third and important factor in the creation of an organisation is the establishment of technology in a broad sense, so that inputs can be transformed into products and outputs by means of resources. Technology refers to machines, buildings, management systems etc.

In the final organisation, these three components are in place. A resource foundation, a technology and a network have been established. In the early phase, the task for the entrepreneur is to establish these conditions: to collect resources, establish the technology and develop the network. It is certainly not an easy task. Many different activities are supposed to unfold at the same time. Aldrich (1999) refers to an American investigation highlighting 17 key activities as relevant. These activities are illustrated in figure 5.4.

From an overall perspective, the activities illustrate the complexity of the process of establishment. It is also important to pinpoint that every process of organising is unique. Organising is not a generic route that will be marched over repeatedly by identical entrepreneurs. The processes (Bhave 1994: 224).

Figure 5.4: Crucial activities in the start-up process

✓ Serious thoughts about business

✓ Facilities/equipment: applied for, bought, leased and rented

Achieved positive monthly cash flow

✓ Initiated savings to invest

Devoted full time to new business

✓ Financial support: applied for and received

✓ Developed first prototype

Received money from sales

Hired employees

CREATED A NEW LEGAL ENTITY

✓ Organised startup team

✓ License or patent applied for

✓ Business plan: written

Source: Inspired by Aldrich (1999).

Organising is not always successful

Organising does not always lead to the establishment of a new organisation. Often, the entrepreneur will have to break off the process. Only half of the Danish companies that started in 2001 were running 4 years later (www.statistikbanken.dk). The dropout is visible especially in the very beginning of the start-up phase. The Global Entrepreneurship Monitor investigation indicates that only around a fourth of those who have the intention of starting up in fact make a start-up attempt and only around half of those who try succeed in establishing a new organisation.

Figure 5.5 shows the share of the Danish population in different phases of the entrepreneurial process at a given time. The numbers which are presented in the figure clearly suggest that a considerable drop-out exists. The figure is based on an interview with 10,000 adult Danes chosen at random in 2006 – people who have given answers as to whether they have an intention of starting a new organisation, have initiated the start-up process or already have established a new organisation. The investigation indicated that around 8.2 percent of the Danes in the early summer of 2006 had an intention of starting, approximately 3 percent had taken concrete steps towards starting up and less than 1 percent was running a new organisation less than one year old (Schøtt 2008).

Figure 5.5: Reduction in participation level across the entrepreneurial process (% of the Danish population)

Expecting to start within 3 years	In the process of starting up	Business owner, new company – maximum 1 year
8.2%	**2.9%**	**0.8%**

Time

Source: Inspired by Schøtt (2008).

Obviously, the figure poses the question: Why do so many fail in the entrepreneurial process? One of the important answers is that "trial-and-error" naturally must be prevalent in the start-up phase. Constantly, numerous new ideas emerge but on closer inspection and evaluation, a lot of the ideas cannot be characterised as real opportunities that are able to carry an organisation. In that way, it is a good thing that many give up on their way. Some also give up because something else occurs, as for instance a job offer. But this only partly explains the entire reduction of participants in the entrepreneurial process. There are many with good opportunities and intentions of starting up who do not take the plunge.

In order to explain this, literature points at different barriers, such as shortcomings concerning knowledge, opportunity identification, development of products and services and ability to develop systems and structures. In addition to this, legitimacy problems occur, i.e. barriers in terms of creating relevant networks and ability to identify and develop an attractive resource base. Finally, risk is emphasised as a crucial problem (Brush & Manolova 2004).

However, Wickham (2004) accentuates that it is important to understand success as subjectively determined. This means that whether entrepreneurs themselves experience success or failure in the entrepreneurial process should be seen in the light of the entrepreneur's expectations, motives and objectives. If they are not fulfilled, the entrepreneur will obviously experience the process as a failure. An entrepreneur can for example aim at more balance between his or her working life and family life. Therefore, success is when this balance is realised. Another entrepreneur is perhaps more motivated by economic growth. To him or her, it is not considered a success to create "the perfectly balanced life", but to create profit. In other words, failure and success are individual concepts.

Organising can be planned
Now we are going to consider how organising can be carried out. We will go into details with the two perspectives that were introduced earlier: the planning and improvising perspective. Let us start with the planning perspective.

As mentioned, the planning perspective dominates the literature of entrepreneurship. Actually, this perspective dominates the majority of literature on business economy. Originating from the classical management theory, organisations are presented as entities that are designed by the manager for the purpose of gaining predefined objectives. The manager is an architect who builds and operates the organisational machine by means of rational tools such as analysis and planning (Hatch 1997).

In entrepreneurship, the planning perspective especially finds its expression in the many textbooks that give a "how-to-do-it" insight into organisation creation. The perspective suggests that organising is intended, rational and considered thoroughly and that the process of organising can be approached by means of analysis and planning. In other words, the process can be managed towards a specific goal – a successful organisation. From the beginning, the entrepreneur has a clear idea of that organisation which he or she wishes to create. By pressing the right buttons and by making relevant adjustments, the entrepreneur can develop exactly this organisation. The perspective implies that a "best practice" exists for what buttons must be pressed and adjusted and how it can take place. Therefore, the process of organising is like a machine that the entrepreneur can make achieve predetermined goals; and there are recipes describing how the machine works.

Therefore, a key question that the entrepreneur has to ask himself or herself is: *"What must I do in order to achieve the desired effect – a successful organization?"* (Sarasvathy 2008). As mentioned, it is assumed that he or she is able to answer the question through the analysis of the situation, rational decision-making and by following the existing recipes. These activities will tell the entrepreneur what resources, networks etc. are necessary to identify in order to build up the desired organisation and what strategies the entrepreneur should pursue. In other words, they will give the entrepreneur a plan.

It is assumed that the entrepreneur has almost full information and an available and satisfactory resource base and that the entrepreneur makes a plan for the entire organising from the beginning. It is to be planned before it is carried out. This emphasises how the entrepreneur in the preparation of the organising process is separated from the concrete activities and problems that are bound up with the process. The fact that planning can be separated from action also pinpoints that it is presupposed that the environment is more or less stable and transparent. The reason is that the planned process is expected to be relevant in the light of the environment at the time of implementation.

Consequently, the planning perspective only makes sense if we presuppose that the future is predictable, the entrepreneur's objectives are clear and the environment is independent of the entrepreneur's actions.

Sarasvathy (2008) compares organising described in the planning perspective with a chef who is supposed to create a meal. The chef begins by choosing what menu he or she will make. Then the chef finds a recipe that he or she can follow to create the menu. The next step is shopping for the ingredients suggested in the recipe and after that, the menu can be prepared. The process *"… starts with selecting a menu as a goal and finding effective ways to achieve the goal"* (Sarasvathy 2008: 74).

Figure 5.6 illustrates the described process where the goal is given from the beginning. The entrepreneur can realise the goal through a number of rational steps are possible to predict from the beginning.

Figure 5.6: The planning perspective

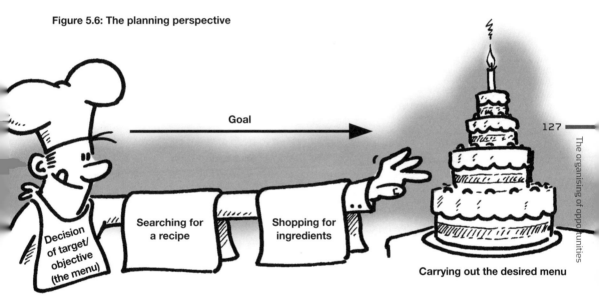

Source: Inspirered by Sarasvathy (2008).

The recipes which the entrepreneur can use to create a new organisation are many. The literature recommends that the entrepreneur start by answering questions such as: *"What is the objective of the organisation (vision, mission etc.)? How do you put it together, control it (number of employees, procedures, management, organisation structure etc.)? How do you unfold the organisation (strategy, growth, internationalisation etc.)?"*

Organising is about improvising

However, entrepreneurs are seldom met with predictable surroundings and they have far from full information about the future, clear preferences about objectives or unlimited resources at their disposal, which the planning perspective tends to assume. Therefore, the improvising perspective emphasises that beforehand the entrepreneur can neither formulate a clear objective of the organising process nor make a plan for how he or she can obtain the objective. Instead, the improvising perspective pinpoints that the entrepreneur takes his or her starting point in the often limited resources which he or she disposes of at that moment. It is these limited resources which frame the probability of having his or her opportunity transformed into a new and independent organisation or a new organisational unit inside an existing organisation. The perspective takes its starting point in the proverb "A bird in the hand is worth two in the bush." In other words, from this perspective, organising is about exploiting what you have instead of making the ultimate goal your starting point.

Instead of asking, *"What am I supposed to do in order to obtain the desired effect – a successful organisation?"* the entrepreneur must ask him- or herself, *"How can I make use of these resources?"* Again, Sarasvathy (2008) illustrates the view by relating organising to the preparation of a new meal. The chef begins the process of improvising by looking into the fridge in order to find the raw materials, ingredients and means he or she disposes of. After this, the chef designs possible meals which can be made from the ingredients. It is a process characterised by improvising where the chef will have to feel his way with different combinations. Actually, the meal is often developed at the same time as the chef is making it. The chef *"... starts with a given kitchen, and designs possible, sometimes unintended, even entirely original meals with its contents"* (Sarasvathy 2008: 74). Consequently, the process can have various outcomes – various different meals which were not possible to predict beforehand. It is the many small steps associated with looking into the fridge and feeling one's way by the means available that the menu is created. The result of the process is only possible to see when you are looking back at what actually happened. Figure 5.7 seeks to illustrate this process.

Figure 5.7: The improvising perspective

Source: Inspired by Sarasvathy (2008).

Sarasvathy (2008) elaborates on how the process of organising develops in the light of the improvising perspective. According to Sarasvathy (2008), entrepreneurs typically have three means at their disposal in the process of starting, namely insight into: 1) "Who am I?", 2) "What do I know?" and 3) "Whom do I know?" From these means, the entrepreneur estimates what possible actions he or she can carry through which, however, are often only realised through the interaction with others. At times, the interaction leads to the attachment of these other people to the emerging organisation, for example in the roles of investor, adviser, partner, customer etc. The many new players who become involved in the entrepreneurial process provide new means and goals to the process, which opens for new activities by the entrepreneur. Sarasvathy (2008) illustrates this by the model in figure 5.8.

Figure 5.8: Clarification of the improvising perspective?

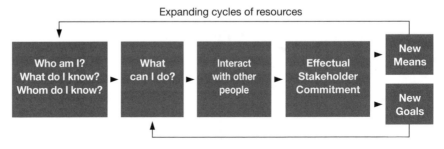

Source: Sarasvathy (2008), p. 101.

If we follow the logic of this model, it is apparent how the improvising perspective perceives organisation creation as a process which does not only involve the entrepreneur. Improvising is also shaped in the entrepreneur's interaction with other players, which makes the process even more complex and unpredictable since the process is constantly influenced by new means and a variety of objectives.

Organising: planning or improvising?
In this way, the paradox of this chapter is whether organising takes place as a planned process or whether it to a higher degree has an improvising character. The following table sums up the core of the paradox.

Table 5.1: The paradox: planning or improvising?

	Planning	Improvising
Starting point	The target is given	The means are given
Crucial question	"What can I do in order to achieve the desired effect?"	"What can I do with these means?"
The role of the entrepreneur	A rational architect	An improvising creator and social agent
Crucial activities	Analysis, planning	Small steps, interaction
Predictability of output	High	Low

In the planning perspective, the objective is given beforehand and the crucial question for the entrepreneur will be: *"What can I do in order to obtain the desired effect?"* It is assumed that the entrepreneur through rational decision making, analysis, generic recipes and planning can shape the process towards the desired objective. The predictability that attributes to the process is high since it is assumed that the environment is fairly stable and transparent and that the entrepreneur's preferences are clear and the objective is given.

Contrary to the planning perspective, the pivotal point of the improvising perspective is that the means are limited which explains why the entrepreneur must take his or her starting point in the question: *"What can I do with these means?"* What kind of organisation can he or she create? By feeling one's way and by interacting in an improvising way with the other players, the entrepreneur shapes an organisation based on the means and the additional means which are gradually supplied to the organising process as a result of the entrepreneur's interaction with other people. The predictability of the organising process is low since it is the available resources, the participating players and the many small steps and social interactions that shape the process.

■ **A theoretical interpretation**
In this section, an interpretation of Claus Meyer's story, which initiated this chapter, is offered. At first, we will deal with the story in the light of the planning perspective and secondly we will emphasise the improvising perspective.

The planning perspective
An interpretation of Claus' story based on planning is quite difficult since the story intuitively matches the improvising perspective better. However, on closer inspection, planning and calculation are in fact also present in the story.
First of all, Claus has a long-term mission and an overall objective. It is within this context he improvises. Consequently, there are business types and business areas that he will not deal with because they are not consistent with the mission. It indicates that Claus is partly rational in his organising process and that to some extent this is dictated by the question: *"What can I do in order to obtain the desired effect?"* As regards Noma, Claus identifies a relevant business partner who has insight in exquisite cooking and experience within the gourmet business in order to fulfil the objective that he has put up from the beginning. Together they create an output that fulfils the objective.

The story also gives rise to the question whether Claus in part exploits his image and brand as a "missionary" who, so to speak, is superior to down-to-earth and goal-oriented behaviour. In any case, it is a fact that he once chose to be educated at Copenhagen Business School where he must have learned a lot about rational models, economic management and the like. This education must have given him an understanding of business and analytical managerial tools that can be used goal-oriented to create new organisations. He says of course, *"I have never worked with plans"* but it can be perceived narrowly as not having prepared definite business plans before the start-up. Nevertheless, he has certainly been thinking strategically and thoroughly considered the steps that he takes.

Finally, it is worth noting that Claus at a given time chooses to make use of a professional Board. The Board supports him in the development of a structured and goal-oriented organisation: *"The Board helps me in developing a well organised company with the right skills in the right positions in accordance with what we want to do."* He is presumably aware that a traditional and rational organisation management is not his strong point and in order to compensate for that he establishes a board that can control his desire to improvise. This decision also indicates that Claus thinks and plans rationally in his organising activities.

The improvising perspective
Even though there are elements of planning in the story, it is predominantly told in the spirit of the improvising perspective. In his approach to entrepreneurship, Claus is oriented towards improvising. In many ways, he dissociates himself from planning or seeks to keep that side to a minimum.

The improvising perspective appears by the fact that from the beginning, Claus does not have a clear idea as to where his organising activities will take him. Instead, he takes his starting point in the means that he has brought from the time when he started his student company. A crucial motto seems to have been, *"We just started in the easiest way."* In this way, he has gradually managed to create a complex of food companies with emphasis on quality. Thus, we are dealing with an organising process without predefined objectives and strategies. Based on a lot of small actions and interactions, an output that nobody could predict is created, and some results are not intended at all. As Claus says, *"I never wanted a big company"* but in spite of that he has ended up having one. Claus is conscious of the unpredictable nature of organising. For instance when he says this about the Nordic kitchen, *"... how the new Nordic movement will end up is not something I can explain. We will know it in 10-20 years."*

In general, Claus's story perfectly shows how he is a social and interactive person and how it is by involving others, getting close to them and making them feel an attachment to his organising activities that Claus continuously creates new things. As he says, *"Rather gain a little victory with people you love than trying to catch a distant goal."* Claus seems, through interaction with others, to be a dab hand at mobilising resources to his organisations. But Claus also knows how to involve players in a broader sense such as ministers, top directors and other decision makers at the symposium he contributed to organise.

However, the improvising perspective is probably best illustrated by the way Claus compared the entrepreneurial process of organising with cooking. He dances around the food, he says, and he takes his starting point in the resources that are at his disposal when he cooks. He lives, so to speak, in accordance with Sarasvathy's (2008) theory of entrepreneurship as an improvising process where focus is on the available means.

Finally, we can ask the question, *"Why does Claus not start Noma from the beginning since it is that opportunity which ends up realising his mission in life?"* That can also be explained by the means of the improvising perspective. In the beginning, Claus hardly has the necessary competences and resources which are required to start Noma. He has not yet gained the entrepreneurial legitimacy in the environment, sufficient experience or cooking competences and first of all, he has not met the people who are taking part in the opportunity creation. Many small steps have to be taken before Claus is ready to realise his mission.

■ Practical tests of the theory

Think of what you have learned during this chapter and try to go through some of the exercises which appear below. In this way you will obtain an increased understanding of organising in the context of entrepreneurship.

Exercise 1: The connection between Claus's organisations

From an overall perspective, how will you describe the organisations which Claus has created in the course of time? Discuss whether there is a connection between the pivotal point for the different organisations and when they are created in his overall entrepreneurial process. Use for instance his website www.clausmeyer.dk.

Exercise 2: "Netguide"

Look through the video case "Netguide" on www.idea-textbook.dk. The case deals with David Madié whom you know already (Chapter 3). Analyse how David organises Netguide in the light of the theory that has been presented in this chapter.

Exercise 3: Bring yourself into focus

Think back at the process you went through when you were choosing your study. Draw a picture of the process and reflect on to what extent the planning perspective, the improvising perspective or a combination of those most effectively can explain the process.

Literature

Aldrich, H. E. (1999). Organizations Evolving. London: Saga.

Allen, K. R. (2006). Launching New Ventures: An Entrepreneurial Approach. Boston: Houghton Mifflin Company.

Bakka, J. F. & Fivelsdal, E. (2004). Organisationsteori: Struktur, kultur og processer. Copenhagen: Handelshøjskolens Forlag.

Berger, P. L. & Kellner, H. (1981). Sociology Interpreted: An Essay on Methods and Vocation. New York: Doubleday Anchor.

Bhave, M. P. (1994). A Process Model of New Venture Creation, Journal of Business Venturing, 9, 223-242.

Brush, C. G. & Manolova, T. S. (2004). Start-up Problems. In W. B. Gartner, K. G. Shaver, N. M. Carter & P. D. Reynolds (Ed.), Handbook of Entrepreneurial Dynamics – The Process of Business Creation (pp. 273-285). Thousand Oaks: Saga.

Fayolle, A. (2003). Research and Researchers at the Hearth of Entrepreneurial Situations New. In C. Steyaert & D. Hjorth (Ed.), Movements in Entrepreneurship (pp. 35-50). Cheltenham: Edward Elgar.

Gartner, W. B., Carter, N. M., & Reynolds, P. D. (2004). In W. B. Gartner, K. G. Shaver, N. M. Carter & P. D. Reynolds (Ed.), Handbook of Entrepreneurial Dynamics – The Process of Business Creation (pp. 285-310). Thousand Oaks: Saga.

Hatch, M. J. (1997). Organization Theory. Oxford: Oxford University Press.

Jones, G. R. (2007). Organizational Theory, Design and Change. Upper Saddle River: Prentice Hall.

Sarasvathy, S. D. (2008). Effectuation: Elements of Entrepreneurial Expertise. Cornwall: MPG Books Ltd.

Shane, S. (2003). A General Theory of Entrepreneurship: The Individual-opportunity Nexus. Cheltenham: Edward Elgar.

Wickham, P. A. (2004). Strategic Entrepreneurship. Boston: Pearson Education Limited.

The organising of opportunities

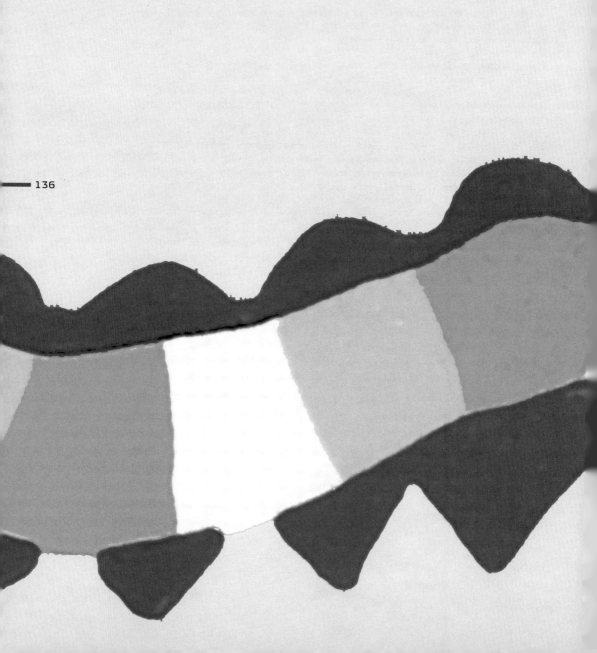

Chapter 6

Resources

In order to carry through the entrepreneurial process it is necessary to have access to a number of different resources. The entrepreneur needs money, knowledge, energy, enthusiasm, motivation, employees, help from friends and family etc. The list of resources needed to carry through an entrepreneurial process is almost inexhaustible. But the necessary resources in the specific case depend on the situation. We will now go into more detail with the way all these types of resources can be categorised.

Many have asserted that the acquisition of resources is among the important factors that distinguishes management behaviour from entrepreneurial behaviour (Evald 2006). Managers have often already established access to the necessary resources. Thus, their behaviour is characterised by their attempts towards optimising and making effective the use of the resources. On the other hand, entrepreneurs often have no or only a few resources at their disposal. But instead of accepting these resource restrictions, entrepreneurs are characterised by their ability to exploit opportunities independent of their resource access. Stevenson and Jarillo express it in this way: *"... entrepreneurship is a process by which individuals – either on their own or inside organisations – pursue opportunities without regard to the resources they currently control"* (Stevenson & Jarillo 1990: 23). Consequently, entrepreneurs act in spite of the fact that they might need important resources. So while leaders act with what they actually have, entrepreneurs act in spite of the limited resources they have. In this chapter we will present you with the entrepreneur's identification and use of resources.

■ Meet practice

A story of entrepreneurship and resources initiates this chapter. The chapter aims at stimulating your insight and learning about resources in entrepreneurship. The story deals with the organisation Logopaint which was started in 1997. In 2007, the organisation reached a turnover of 13.5 million Danish kroner (about 2 million euro). In 2008, the company had 24 employees and sales offices in several places in the world.

An idea about 3D-carpets

Logopaint sustains itself by optimising commercials and by sponsoring in sports. On their homepage, they write: *"The company's general goal was and still is to optimize advertising in sports and sponsoring"* (www.logopaint.com). They want to be the best in their niche and they try to achieve that aim via increased product value, security of delivery, experience and professionalism. They try to differentiate themselves primarily by taking responsibility for their products from the beginning to the end. On their homepage, they write: *"We want to make it easy and efficient to work with us. We take responsibility for our products, and ensure quality before, during and after delivery, so the client experiences that we see our products through to the end."*

The organisation produces primarily two different products: 3D-carpets and 3D-barrier boards. The most unique product is the first. Figure 6.1 shows an example of 3D-carpets. They are placed just behind the goal line next to the goal on a football ground. The writing on the carpet seems to stand up at a camera angle without this being the case.

Figure 6.1: Logopaint's 3D-carpets.

Source: www.logopaint.com.

There are several different stories about how the idea of the 3D-carpets emerged and nobody knows ten years after the start-up what story is actually the right one – perhaps a combination of several. A story focuses on the emergence of the idea as a coincidence in the sense that one of the persons from the start-up team from the top of a ladder discovers that the writing on carpets are conceived differently and look differently from different perspectives, especially at a high altitude. *"It is almost like the writing is standing"*, was the statement then.

This surprise makes the team look more systematically on how the writing on carpets (parallel with the ground) looks from different angels. Several in the start-up team have an educational and experimental background required to work with computer science and mathematics at a high level. That knowledge becomes crucial to the development. Ultimately, they end up having invented a formula that can calculate how different types of writing look from different perspectives. Their thought is that the formula can be used for the purpose of making commercials effective and for sponsoring in sports. By laying carpets in different places in a stadium (for example behind the goal in football as illustrated in figure 6.1) they will be able to calculate how the writing is to be designed in accordance with the cameras at a stadium so that the writing in the television is suddenly vertical from the perspective of the viewer.

The opportunity has quite striking advantages in comparison to what is allowed to do in the football stadiums at that time. For example, there are rules for how close to the goal line signs, barrier boards and the like can be placed due to the athletes' security. With these carpets, the security distance is no longer a limitation. The athletes can just cross the carpets. Suddenly, it is possible for the various stadiums to have an extra row of barrier boards besides the one or two rows of barrier boards which most of the bigger stadiums have. In addition, and perhaps most importantly, the new row of barrier boards represents by far the best place since it is placed just behind the back line. The potential is big. They know that. But how big? And how can they make sure that other competitors do not imitate their products at lightning speed? These are just some of the thoughts which the start-up team discusses persistently in the start-up process.

Taking out a patent: arguments for and against
Already during the development of the idea, they understand that the most secure way to avoid that competitors imitate is by claiming to have a monopoly to the idea. They also quickly realise that the costs – measured in money and time – are overwhelmingly big in terms of application for a patent. And after all, you are not even sure of getting the patent when you apply for it. You cannot just apply for a patent that is valid all over the world either. Different countries and different continents have their own patent system. Therefore, it is quite costly if you wish to take out a patent covering most of the world.

One of the reasons why applications for a patent are so costly for the start-up team is that they are obliged to buy assistance. None in their family or circle of friends have sufficient knowledge of or experience with patent application. There-

fore, they contact different lawyers, specialists and patent offices that are specialised in patent applications. And they are expensive.

Economically, they are faced with a dilemma. On the one hand, they believe in the
idea and the importance of the patent. This speaks in favour of their applying for
a patent in as many places in the world as possible. On the other hand, they do
not have the economic resources themselves which applying for patents all over
the world or just in a few countries requires. Therefore, they have to obtain extra
financial means if they want to carry through a broad patent application. In that
way, they will run a considerable risk if it all fails. If they do not obtain the patent
for the idea or if the idea simply has no value on the market, all financial means will
go to waste and the entrepreneurs will be left with a financial smack in the eye. At
the same time, they run a risk by applying for a patent in the sense that it will take
much more time before they will be ready to enter the market. In that time, possible competitors could overtake them or find other attractive technical solutions.

A golden middle course
The start-up team behind Logopaint chooses a middle course and takes out a patent in many countries all over the world but with crucial exceptions. They do not
take out a patent in China, Japan, Portugal, Eastern Europe and the Gulf countries
and others. Their criteria for selecting countries are first of all that the country concerned has a famous and exposed football league and secondly that the patent
system in the country is not simply a jungle. On their way, they are confronted with
different kinds of problems. Especially they are in a legal fight with a South African
company that has a similar patent already, but however, not identical. Gradually,
many of these legal problems are solved by the means of royalty agreements, and
in 2008, the South African company including the monopoly rights are bought by
Logopaint.

In spite of Logopaint not having a patent in every country they are market leaders
in all the markets where they operate. In the countries where they have a patent,
they have 100 percent of the market whereas they are content with 80 percent
in the markets where they do not have a patent. In Logopaint they have often
discussed the importance of these patents since they now have 80 percent in
the markets where they do not have patents. The business-development director
of Logopaint says about this: *"We would not have been in the position we are in
today if we did not have our patents – they gave us access to the market."* In 2008,
Logopaint sold their 3D-carpets to more than 30 countries and covered many different sport events, such as football, handball, volleyball, motorsport, basketball

and ice hockey. The 3D-products made by Logopaint are especially famous in the context of international football and they cover almost every large international football league, as for instance the Spanish, the French, the Italian and the German. Bayern Munich from the German league is for instance among their oldest and best customers.

■ Your immediate interpretation

What does the story tell you about resources? How will you interpret it off the cuff? The exercises below can support you in creating your understanding of the story.

- ■ You are the main speaker at a conference. The topic is entrepreneurship and resources. Take your starting point in the Logopaint story and explain to the audience what resources are important for the story and in what ways the resources play a role for the entrepreneurial process.
- ■ Your speech gives rise to a discussion as to how the type of resource that is at play in the story can be categorised. What categories are relevant in your opinion?
- ■ When you return from the conference, you simply cannot stop thinking about the discussions that day. In general, you consider what resources you think are crucial for starting a new and independent organisation. Make a list of all these resources.
- ■ You meet one of your friends who has already started an independent organisation. You discuss the significance of resources to entrepreneurs. He claims that it is always the idea that is crucial to the entrepreneur's success. If the idea is good, it is easy to attract the necessary resources. What do you think about this argument?

■ Theories of entrepreneurship

The story that we have just presented illustrates how entrepreneurs get confronted with resource questions. They are constantly in a situation where they must decide whether they should continue working with the resources that they have at their disposal at a given time. Alternatively, should they spend their time and limited resources on procuring or developing new and bigger resources in order to pursue the opportunity? In other words, should the entrepreneur focus on exploiting existing resources or exploring new resources in the entrepreneurial process?

By exploiting existing resources, the entrepreneur focuses on effective implementation of his or her existing resource base to evaluate and organise the opportunity. The advantage is that the entrepreneur has control over his or her resources and in that way, the risk involved with resource exploitation is relatively low. The problem can be that the development of the opportunity is limited through an emphasis on existing resources because the existing resources determine what is possible. On the other hand, if the entrepreneur chooses to explore new resources, the advantage is that new resources and combinations of resources can function as a catalyst for creative development of the opportunity. A problem attached to this perspective is that in this case, the entrepreneur does not possess the same control over the resource situation. Thus, the chapter deals with the choice between exploiting existing resources and exploring new resources, reflecting the paradox:

> **Exploiting or exploring?**

A change in focus – from market to resource focus
Before we elaborate on the paradox, we will have to determine how we perceive a resource. But first some history. Theories of resources and their importance originate from the strategy literature. It became famous for real in the mid-80s and the beginning of the 90s even though for example Penrose's (1959) groundbreaking book "The Theory of the Growth of the Firm" had introduced the discussion much earlier.

The discussion in the strategy literature was how organisations create long-termed competitive advantages. Even though the debate of course holds many different nuances, it can primarily be divided into two types of arguments: "the inside-out argument" and "the outside-in argument". According to the last mentioned argument, continuous competitive advantages are created most effectively by positioning in the market and differentiation from competitors. On the other hand, the inside-out argument pinpoints that continuous advantages as regards competition are created most effectively internally in the organisation via its unique combination of resources. Consequently, the outside-in argument takes its starting point in the market and then looks at the organisation (from this outside-in) while the inside-out argument takes its starting point internally in the resources of the organisation and after that looks at the market (from this inside-out). Thus, the discussion is whether continuous competitive advantages should be created outside the organisation on the market or internally in the organisation through its resources and competences.

However, in fact everybody agrees that both outside-in positioning and possession of unique resource combinations are decisive for the creation of competitive advantages. The disagreement concerns whether one should choose to focus on the unique resource combination in the long term and adjust in the short term through market positioning or whether market positioning is decisive in the long term, which effectively means that in the short term one should acquire the necessary resources and competences. In the literature of entrepreneurship, it is especially the inside-out argument that inspires when resources are discussed. Typically, the argument is also compared with the so-called resource-based theory which we will go through in the following.

Resource-based theory
According to the resource-based theory, entrepreneurs as well as existing organisations most effectively gain continuous competitive advantages through control over valuable resources. Even though the resource-based theory was originally developed with bigger established organisations in mind, it has also had a great influence on the theory of entrepreneurship. Big established organisations may have ownership over several resources compared with what independent entrepreneurs will usually have. However, it is not necessarily decisive what resources the entrepreneur owns from the outset. What seems to matter is what resources he or she has control over (or has the opportunity to gain control over). Thus, it is unimportant whether somebody else owns a certain resource, which the entrepreneur needs, if he or she controls it and decides how it is brought into play related to the opportunity. In the following, we will solely focus on the entrepreneur despite the fact that the resource-based theory often refers to the established organisation.

In addition to this, the resource-based theory is built on two basic assumptions. Firstly, it is assumed that the players in an industry are heterogeneous and in that way different from each other with regard to their control over strategic resources (Barney 1991). They simply have no access to and control over the same resources. The other assumption is that resources are not perfectly mobile between the players (Barney 1991). Hence, resources cannot as a matter of course be transferred from one entrepreneur to another because the value of the resources depends on the holder and the ability of the holder to exploit them.

Based on these assumptions, it is Barney's point that entrepreneurs gain continuous competitive advantages by having access to and control over resources that are both heterogeneous and immobile – more about this later on.

The resource concept

Before we begin the discussion of what characterises valuable resources in terms of creating competitive advantages we should discuss what it meant by "resource". There are many different definitions as to what a resource is. What applies to the resource-based theory is that resources are broadly defined. Wernerfelt defines a resource in the following way: *"By a resource is meant anything which could be thought of as a strength or weakness of a given firm. More formally, a firm's resources at a given time could be defined as those (tangible and intangible) assets which are tied semi-permanently to the firm"* (Wernerfelt 1984: 172). A similar focus on defining resources as something that helps entrepreneurs in their attempts to perform is found in Barney's definition: *"… firm resources include all assets, capabilities, organizational processes, firm attributes, information, knowledge, etc. controlled by a firm that enable the firm to conceive of and implement strategies that improve its efficiency and effectiveness"* (Barney 1991: 101). In this way, resources are to be perceived in a wide sense. The resource concept includes a vast number of resources which share the fact that they support entrepreneurs in pursuing opportunities through organising.

Valuable resources

The next question is, "What makes a resource valuable?" Barney (1991) argues that resources must be heterogeneous and immobile in order to create continuous competitive advantages. Wernerfelt argues that valuable resources help keeping competitors at a distance: *"What a firm wants is to create a situation where its own resource position directly or indirectly makes it more difficult for others to catch up"* (Wernerfelt 1984: 173). Here he introduces the concept of "resource position" which is crucial. An entrepreneur's resource position is made of the combination of resources, over which he or she has control. Access to and control over the new resources of course change the resource position.

However, access to and control over new resources, which immediately seem to strengthen the resource position, is not sufficient to make a resource attractive. The attractive resources are those able to contribute to creating a barrier seen in the light of the competitors' resource position. In other words, a barrier helps to keep existing and future competitors away from the game. Wernerfelt writes the following about this: *"The general attractiveness of a resource, understood as its capacity to support resource position barrier, is only a necessary, not a sufficient, condition for a given firm to be interested in it. If everyone goes for the potentially attractive resources and only a few can "win" in each, firms will lose unless they pick their fights well. So firms need to find those resources which can sustain a re-*

source position barrier, but in which no one currently has one, and where they have a good chance of being among the few who succeed in building one" (Wernerfelt 1984: 174-175).

Barney (1991) has developed some criteria that can be used to evaluate whether a resource contributes to such a barrier. He writes as follows: *"... a firm resource must have four attributes: (a) it must be valuable, in the sense that it exploits opportunities and/or neutralizes threats in the firm's environment, (b) it must be rare among a firm's current and potential competitors, (c) it must be imperfectly imitable, and (d) there cannot be strategically equivalent substitutes for this resource that are valuable but neither rare or imperfectly imitable"* (Barney 1991: 105-106). By using these criteria, it is possible to build up the model shown in table 6.1. The table can be used for evaluating an entrepreneur's resource position with respect to its competitive consequences. Thus, its primary function is to evaluate the combination of resources attributing to the entrepreneur. However, it can also be used for evaluating one single resource.

Table 6.1: Evaluation of resources

Caracterisation of the resource position				Consequences	
Valuable	Rare	Printable	Substitutable	Competitive	Economic performance
No	-	-	-	Disadvantage	Less than medium
Yes	No	-	-	Same	Normal
Yes	Yes	Yes	-	Temporary advantage	Above medium
Yes	Yes	Yes	No	Temporary advantage	Above medium
Yes	Yes	No	No	Permanent advantage	At the top/ high

Source: Inspired by Barney (1991).

When the resource position is not valuable, the model predicts that the entrepreneur will have a competitive disadvantage, that he will achieve less than normal and in that way in the course of time die out. When the resource position is valuable but not rare, competitive likeness and a normal performance are gained. In two different ways the entrepreneur can achieve a better situation with temporary competitive advantages where his or her achievement is above medium. When the resource position is valuable and rare but may be copied or when the resource position is valuable, rare and may be copied but not substitutable. Finally, yet importantly, permanent competitive advantages and a potential for economic top-performance are achieved when the resource position is valuable, rare, cannot be copied and is not substitutable.

Tripartition of resources
We have now discussed the resource-based theory and what is required for resources to be valuable and able to supply entrepreneurs with continuous competitive advantages through the establishment of a barrier by means of the resource position. In addition, we have defined what a resource is. However, so far, we have operated with resources as a broad concept. This we will now try to remedy. We will not reduce the definition, but divide resources into some different categories.

There are many different ways to categorise resources. One way could be to divide resources into hardware (start-up capital, machines, building etc.) and software (knowledge, social relations, rumour, reputation etc.). Sometimes, a distinction is also made between physical resources and intangible resources. In this book, we use a third way of categorising, inspired by Coleman (1988), namely a division into:

- financial resources
- human resources
- social resources

A little simplified, it could be said that financial resources correspond to the money that the entrepreneur has in his or her pocket whether they are borrowed or not. Human resources correspond to the knowledge and the competences which the entrepreneur (or the team of entrepreneurs) possesses. Social resources are the means the entrepreneur benefits from through his or her personal contacts and acquaintances.

In the discussion about the division into three parts, it should be mentioned that the concept "capital" is often used synonymously with resources in the literature. Thus, some talk about financial capital (corresponding to financial resources), human capital (corresponding to human resources) and social capital (corresponding to social resources). This terminology follows a supply-logic in the sense that supply should be perceived as the resources which a person owns or over which a person has temporary control (Stevenson & Jarillo 1990). Financial capital is a concept that represents the supply of financial resources at an entrepreneur's disposal. In the same way, human capital is a concept for the supply of human resources, at an entrepreneur's disposal. Finally, social capital is a concept for the supply of social resources that the entrepreneur has at his disposal via his contacts. In this book, we use the resource concept in preference to the capital concept. Table 6.2 gives some specific examples of financial, human and social resources.

Table 6.2: Three categories of resources

	Financial resources	Human resources	Social resources
Definition	Financial resources which are either supplied by the owners of organisations or other external players	Intangible resources such as knowledge and experience, inherent in human beings	Resources provided by the entrepreneur's personal contacts
Examples	Own capital (own money) Foreign capital (borrowed money)	Education and training Experiences (business, start-up, management experiences etc.) Engagement, motivation and enterprise	Entrepreneurial role models A large network Diverse networks Supportive circle of friends

Financial resources
Even though there are many different types of financial resources, in terms of the purpose of this book, it makes sense only to operate with two overall types: own capital and foreign capital. Own capital refers to the financial resources that are placed at the disposal of the owner of an organisation in expectation of participation in the decisions and profits in the future. Supply of own capital can either take place via the owners' investment of cash or other assets or when the owners retain part of the profit in the organisation. Foreign capital is the capital that is not

granted by the owners of the organisation. Examples of foreign capital could be mortgage loans, bank loans, supplier credits, etc. Foreign capital is often divided into what can be characterised as short-term debt and long-term debt.

Human resources
The list containing examples of human resources is almost endless. Therefore, we will only concentrate on a few. A human resource is inherent in people. Formal education can for example enable individuals to discover opportunities and carry through entrepreneurial processes more easily, just as more focused training – for example via entrepreneur courses – should contribute positively to the entrepreneurial process. Experience also seems to play a crucial role although it is possible to talk about many types of experience. The necessary experience depends of course on the type of entrepreneurial process you face as an entrepreneur. Typically, relevant working experience and previous start-up and management experience are seen as crucial to carry through entrepreneurial processes successfully. In cognitive psychology, many cognitive qualities, which seem to influence the entrepreneurial process positively and which can be perceived as human resources, have been identified. Several of these have already been pinpointed in chapter 2.

Social resources
Social resources are somewhat different from the two others. It is not a resource which one single person can possess in contrast to financial and human resources. Social resources are something created in interaction between people. They belong to the relation between these people but not the human being itself. In this way, social resources become something that entrepreneurs have access to via their personal relations. Chapter 7 goes more thoroughly into examples of social resources and how they can be established.

Differences and connections between resource categories
What is interesting about the division into three types of resources is, however, not the division in itself but the fundamental differences between the three types of resources. Some of the resources are being reduced when they are used whereas others actually multiply by increased use. Financial resources, for example, are being reduced when they are used. Money can only be used once – unfortunately. However, that is not necessarily the case with human and social resources. When the entrepreneur makes use of the knowledge from his or her education, a revival of knowledge takes place because it is being reproduced and eventually strengthened. Usually, it must be assumed that new knowledge is created when existing knowledge is used in new connections. Use of educational knowledge can for

example contribute to the creation of new knowledge and thus, the human resource increases by the use of it. That is also the case with social resources. When we interact with our surroundings and our personal contacts in the efforts to provide valuable resources to carry through the entrepreneurial process, new knowledge is generated in the relation. One could, perhaps pushed somewhat to its extreme, say that persons who never talk to someone and do not know anyone will have difficulties finding resources in their environment in comparison with persons who often interact. Therefore, at this point, it is possible to conclude that an increased use of the social resources can contribute to a further build-up of the resource. The last thing to be discussed about the division of resources is the connection between the three types of resources. It is interesting that the different resources can be transformed from one type to another. Social resources are often considered as a resource type that activates the two others (Burt 1992). For example, it is possible to use one's personal network (social resources) to recruit new and qualified employees (human resources) or to procure financial resources. Actually, several investigations point at personal contacts such as friends and family as the most frequent investor in the entrepreneur's start-up processes. Nevertheless, there are many other ways that can make the three types interact. For example, it is possible to buy advisory services about marketing (human resources) via one's own financial resources. Or it is possible to use one's own knowledge about business plans (human resources) to convince a bank adviser to raise the existing credit limit (financial resources).

Exploitation of resources

As previously mentioned, the entrepreneur is faced with a dilemma in relation to identification and use of resources. The entrepreneur must decide whether to continue working with and exploiting the existing resources at his or her disposal or whether to use existing resources to explore new resources. We are talking about the paradox: resource exploitation versus resource exploration.

According to March, the exploitation activities cover: *"... efficiency, selection, implementation, execution"* (March 1991: 71). This means that the entrepreneur exploits the existing resource position through rational and systematic considerations over how he or she can most effectively select and implement the existing resources so that they back up the opportunity in the best possible way.

In this way, resource identification and use are about strengthening an already given direction (Van de Ven et al. 1999). It takes for granted that the entrepreneur beforehand has an idea of the direction in which he or she wants to move. In other words, the entrepreneur has a clearly defined objective with the resource use. The challenge is to make the use of existing resources effective to achieve the objective. Furthermore, the perspective presupposes that the entrepreneur knows the value of a given resource in the light of the entrepreneurial process beforehand. Only in this way, can the entrepreneur point out from the beginning what resources he or she must identify and use in order to realise the objective.

Because of the fact that the starting point is optimisation of existing resources, we must assume that the entrepreneur has the management and control over the use of resources in the entrepreneurial process. It reduces the complexity and risk associated with the process. However, we cannot expect from the entrepreneur that he or she moves the opportunity in radically new and unexpected directions since existing resources limit the opportunity and its realisation. Thus, this approach to resources brings about a relatively stable entrepreneurial process.

Since the exploitation perspective in many ways excludes identification and use of radically new resources and resource combinations and in that way new ways to exploit opportunities, the perspective reflects a short-term approach to resources. The reason is that the entrepreneur focuses on how he or she can create effectiveness based on the existing resource position. In this way, thoughts are not made about how he or she can keep up with the continuous processes of change in the future markets where products, services and processes constantly become obsolete and must leave room for new ones.

Exploration of resources
However, the entrepreneur does not often control all the resources required to realise the opportunity. Likewise, the core of entrepreneurship is often – in any case if we follow Schumpeter's reasoning – seen as the pursuit of opportunities which break with the existing. This implies that the realisation of these opportunities requires alternative resources or new combinations of resources that are not yet known. Finally yet importantly, the entrepreneurial process is often characterised by risk, complexity and dynamics, which explain why the entrepreneur cannot as a matter of course assume that existing resources are sufficient or that he or she can estimate beforehand the value of resources needed during the entrepreneurial process. For these reasons, starting with a limited resource position, the entrepreneur has to explore new resources.

According to March, the exploration perspective includes "... *search, variation, risk taking, experimentation, play, flexibility, discovery, innovation*" (March 1991:

71). Contrary to the exploitation perspective, exploration is thus about expansion, flexibility, experimentation and development which can result in the creation or discovery of new opportunities and countless new ways to evaluate and organise. From this perspective, the entrepreneur is not limited by and focused on the existing resource position and its optimisation. Instead, through playful, proactive and open interaction with the environment he or she attempts to create resources that can take him or her in new and exciting directions in the light of the unfolding entrepreneurial process. We are dealing with resource behaviour where new borders are constantly tested.

The fact that new borders are constantly tested means of course also a more risky and unpredictable entrepreneurial process. The entrepreneur can simply not predict where he or she will end up. As previously mentioned, the unpredictable resource identification and use makes it difficult for the entrepreneur to gain control over the entrepreneurial process. Especially because the entrepreneur must acquire the resources before the real value of the opportunity is known because it is in the interaction with the environment that the value of the resource is created. This means that the value is a result of the way in which the entrepreneur actually uses the resource in the entrepreneurial process.

The exploration perspective shows a dynamic approach to identification and use of resources. In addition, it implies a forward-looking and long-term perspective. The reason is that an exploring entrepreneur is continuously open towards unexpected resources, which can result in radically new opportunities or ways to exploit these. In that way, on the face of it, the entrepreneur is also more prepared to survive in the long term in the light of demands for continuous change on the future markets.

As mentioned in chapter 5, Sarasvathy (2008) sees the entrepreneurial process as having its starting point in limited resources. At the point of departure, typical entrepreneurs possess only knowledge of who they are, what they know and whom they know. It is through interaction with and exploration of the environment that they acquire control over the resources that they do not immediately control and develop old resources. Through exploration, new resources are constantly added – resources that support the entrepreneurial process by being transformed into opportunities and new organisations. In other words, Sarasvathy's (2008) theory can be seen as an example of the way in which the exploration perspective presents the resource question.

Resources: to exploit or explore?

Above, we have discussed two different perspectives on how entrepreneurs can relate to resource identification and use. The discussion is summarised in table 6.3.

Table 6.3: The paradox: exploit or explore?

	Exploit	Explore
Resources	Existing resources	New resources
The entrepreneur's role	To use existing resources efficiently	To find and gain control of the new resources
Focus	To improve efficiency	To move
Changeability	Stability	Dynamics
Perspective	Short term	Long term

The exploitation perspective argues that the entrepreneur should make effective use of the available resources, while the exploration perspective argues that the entrepreneur should pursue new resources based on the limited resources he or she controls. Emphasis in the exploitation perspective is to "make effective where you are" and therefore, this perspective is very much about stability and the short-termed. The exploration perspective is more about "moving" constantly in the sense that through interaction with the environment, the entrepreneur creates new resources and resource combinations. Therefore, the exploration perspective is directed at something with a much longer perspective and represents a more dynamic approach to resources in entrepreneurship.

However, it is important to pinpoint that a trade-off between the two perspectives does not necessarily exist. Entrepreneurs cannot do both – exploring and exploiting – at the same time. They have to prioritise. Therefore, March (1991) also mentions that the discussion about exploitation and exploration is not a matter of "either or" but rather a matter of balance. March writes, *"… maintaining an appropriate balance between exploration and exploitation is a primary factor in system survival and prosperity"* (March 1991: 71).

■ A theoretical interpretation

We now provide two different interpretations of the Logopaint story that initiated this chapter. In the interpretations, the story is linked to the above theory and is interpreted from each of the perspectives of the paradox.

The exploitation perspective

If one chooses to approach the Logopaint story from an exploration perspective, focus will primarily be on the way in which Logopaint tried to optimise the use of their existing resources. The story is about the schism between financial resources and the application for patents. The first question that comes up is what type of resource a patent is. Is it an example of a monopolised human resource or a locked-up financial resource? The immediate impression is that a patent is associated with what we denote as a human resource. The patent departs from knowledge in terms of the formula that is developed. Later on, it becomes a patent. However, the patent is actually just a temporary monopolisation of the Logopaint entrepreneurs' inherent knowledge that they had from the beginning. Therefore, it is possible to argue that the patent most effectively can be denoted as a human resource. Thus, in the light of the exploitation perspective, the patent represents a crystallisation of existing resources which the Logopaint entrepreneurs own from the beginning of the entrepreneurial process.

Moreover, the exploitation perspective emerges because the purpose of borrowing capital is to optimise existing resources through a patent and not to develop new ones. The very concept of a patent is in itself an expression of a desire to optimise what one already has and does well. Through this focus, Logopaint does not develop because the story does not indicate that Logopaint at the same time creates capital to create new opportunities which can create competitive advantages in the long term in the light of the future markets.

In addition, when the story is interpreted from the exploitation perspective, we can argue that the Logopaint entrepreneurs in spite of the fact that they obtain new capital to finance applications for patents still feel that they only work with resources over which they have considerable control. First, they only apply for patents in markets where they think that the chances of success are best and not in markets where they think that the risk of refusal of the patent application is big. In that way, the financial resources that are used are fairly under control. Secondly, they are careful about using loan capital – they avoid running too big risks that could suddenly take over the control of them for example through loan conditions. Thus, it could be argued that Logopaint primarily optimises the resources they control.

They restrict themselves to applying for patents for money that they can control in spite of the fact that some of this money is borrowed.

The exploration perspective
Nevertheless, the story of Logopaint can also be perceived completely differently, that is from an exploration perspective. As is often the case in entrepreneurship, Logopaint has at its starting point no control over all the resources that are necessary to realise their opportunity. In other words, they are left to explore the environment with a view to creating further financial resources. In connection with that exploration, the company focuses on finding and increasing the control over as many new resources as possible. It is quite conceivable that Logopaint in one way or another has a risk profile that has prevented them from borrowing certain types of capital. It is very probable. However, the story can still be interpreted in the way that they want a patent protected position in as many markets as possible.

What puts restrictions on Logopaint is first of all their ability to obtain the economic resources which are required for the design and treatment of applications for patents. Therefore, when they do not apply for a patent on for example the Chinese market, it is primarily because they simply cannot finance the application. It is not because they choose to limit themselves and keep to the resources that they already control. Thus, it is the different markets, their risk profile and the related possible injection of capital that put the limitations on the number of applications for patents. The strategy of Logopaint is in other words to achieve as many patents as possible by borrowing money to be able to finance the applications for patents. By gaining many patents, they can explore opportunities within a bigger geographical area and simultaneously open up several new opportunities. It will increase their possibilities to develop and create advantages in terms of competition in the long term.

The end of the story pinpoints how, as mentioned in the exploration perspective, the value of resources cannot always be predicted beforehand. Logopaint is in any case in doubt whether the acquired patents create the intended value because the company also ends up with big market shares in the markets where it has not acquired a patent protection of its product.

■ Practical tests of the theory
On the basis of the above thoughts and discussions, you are ready to draw up your own experiments concerning your understanding of resources and how they take part in the entrepreneurial process. The following are suggestions for exercises.

Exercise 1: Interview with an entrepreneur

Make a list of interview questions that seek to encapsulate some of the most crucial discussions about the role of resources in entrepreneurship. Contact an entrepreneur and interview him or her with a view to testing the theory that has been introduced in this chapter.

Exercise 2: Balance between exploitation and exploration

See the video case with Munthe plus Simonsen at www.idea-textbook.dk (Chapter 4). Interpret the case in the light of the paradox of resources: exploitation or exploration. Come up with some suggestions for the way Naja Munthe and Karen Simonsen have emphasised exploitation and exploration in their entrepreneurial process and evaluate whether they have succeeded in creating a balance between the two perspectives.

Exercise 3: Give a piece of good advice to a friend

One of your friends who is a trained electrician and has always had an interest in design, tells you that he is working on an opportunity. He wants to design lamps in the high price bracket. You have confidence in his abilities to put together electronics, light and design so that it will be unique. Then he asks you how he is supposed to go about it in terms of finance. He has saved 25,000 euro, and he is willing to put up more. However, according to him, this amount is not enough at all. What should he do? What opportunities does he have? What is important to consider?

Literature

Barney, J. B. (1991). Firm resources and sustained competitive advantage, Journal of Management, 17, 99-120.

Burt, R. S. (1992). Structural holes – The social structure of competition. London: Harvard University Press.

Coleman, J. S. (1988). Social capital in the creation of human capital, American Journal of Sociology, 94, 95-120.

Evald, M. R. (2006). Brugen og betydningen af personlige netværk i udviklingen af højteknologiske virksomheder inden for en koncern inkubator, Syddansk Universitetsforlag.

March, J. G. (1991). Exploration and exploitation in organizational learning, Organization Science, 2, 71-87.

Penrose, E. T. (1959). The Theory of the Growth of the Firm. New York: John Wiley.

Sarasvathy, S. D. (2008). Effectuation: Elements of Entrepreneurial Expertise. Cornwall: MPG Books Ltd.

Stevenson, H. H & Jarillo, J. C. (1990). A Paradigm of Entrepreneurship: Entrepreneurial Management, Strategic Management Journal, 11, 17-27.

Van de Ven, A. H., Polley, D., Garud, R. & Venkataraman, S. (1999). The Innovation Journey, Oxford: Oxford University Press.

Wernerfelt, B. (1984). A resource-based view of the firm, Strategic Management Journal, 5, 171-180.

156

Chapter 7

Network

An entrepreneur without a network is like an angler without a fishing rod. In the entrepreneurial process, others than the entrepreneur himself must necessarily get involved. Otherwise, the process cannot be carried through successfully. Entrepreneurs involve a number of different persons through the entrepreneurial process. It could for instance be persons closely connected with the organisation such as customers, suppliers, investors, accountants etc. However, it could also be persons with a less noticeable role. Their role could be just as important to the entrepreneur's success. Some examples of the last category could be the importance of receiving free help and advice from experienced friends and family members and the importance of getting emotional support and having the right "backing on the home front".

Thus, entrepreneurs are influenced by the social environments they are embedded in as for instance in terms of the network they possess. Entrepreneurial decisions are not made in a vacuum but rather in social contexts. In a groundbreaking article from 1986, Aldrich and Zimmer wrote the following: *"The approach we take, by contrast, focuses on entrepreneurship as embedded in a social context, channelled and facilitated or constrained and inhibited by people's position in a social network"* (Aldrich & Zimmer 1986: 4).

■ **Meet practice**
"I'm your porn star Baby, Baby, Baby, PornStar ..." An entrepreneur and musician sings these lyrics. Over many years, this person succeeds in developing from being an underground hip-hopper to a commercial dance musician. That is the story of Miké Simonsen who, together with the two well-known and respected Danish DJs, producer Ronnie NME Veiler and producer, Kenn "The Killer", started the dance group Cargo. Cargo's most famous hit is probably "PornStar". In this connection, it is important to pinpoint that it is the story of the entrepreneur Miké and not the group we focus on in this context.

The underground culture of hip-hop in Vejle
As a teenager, Miké – an ordinary boy from the provincial town Vejle in Denmark – becomes interested in hip-hop music and the underground culture that applies to it. At that time hip-hop is an underground culture which is not yet noticed by most of the Danish teenagers. It is long before Danish hip-hop groups such as MC Einar and Rockers By Choice have captured the Danish charts in the late 80s.

Before the commercial breakthrough of hip-hop, we are dealing with a limited flock of young Danes who are strongly inspired by the American hip-hop culture. They make hip-hop music, "scrazz" the record player and draw illegal graffiti in their local areas at night. Many of them are committed and live for the hip-hop. To a high extent, we are talking about an underground culture in which only few are involved. However, at the same time, the young people who are involved know each other. Later on, many of the inveterate hip-hoppers of the past become DJs at discos and nightclubs all over the country. In the course of time, the hip-hop culture grows much bigger, exactly in the footsteps of the commercial successes such as MC Einar and Rockers By Choice.

Then it gets serious
Eventually, as Miké gets older, he is determined to have a career as a musician. In his youth, he tries many different things but everything applies to his interest and passion for the hip-hop culture. When he is 22 years old, he starts a studio together with a good friend and hip-hop/DJ-colleague. To sit in their own studio is a dream come true, which at the same time is also the ambition of having a record contract and having their hip-hop music on the air. It is difficult but they fight persistently for several years. The costs of the studio are financed through different ad hoc-jobs such as production of radio commercials and DJ-jobs.

At a time, they realise that they are stuck and do not develop further. They decide to close the studio and split. They want to experience new adventures and explore other opportunities in order to break through. At this time, Miké's ambitions have changed. From looking at himself as a hip-hopper, he now looks at himself in a broader perspective. He now sees himself as an artist and rapper. Consequently, this means that he has opened up for other styles of music and the commercial part of the music business. Miké's ambitions are now about becoming a successful musician in a way that resembles "pop stars" or "rock stars" of today, but without breaking the connection to the past and the hip-hop.

An opportunity emerges
Some months before Miké and his partner close their studio, Miké contacts two former acquaintances from the early period of hip-hop – Ronnie NME and Kenn "The killer". At that time both Ronnie and Kenn are recognised and respected DJs and producers who have had commercial success for a long time. For many years, Miké has not been in contact with Ronnie or Kenn but he remembers them from the early days of hip-hop. The same goes for Ronnie and Kenn – they also remember Miké.

Miké wants them to make a remix of his and his partner's newest attempt to break through – a song called "What's the Matter in Paradise?" If these famous people consent to remix their song, it will be easier to break through. But this never happens. Therefore, they decide to close the studio and give up the song.

Instead, Ronnie and Kenn persuade Miké to rap to a song they are making. As often when competences meet by chance, creativity emerges. This time in the shape of a piece of music called "The Horn" which is a dance track in keeping with the dance music of the nineties. They choose to call the group Cargo. Due to primarily Ronnie and Kenn's reputation, they relatively easily get the single "The Horn" released at Scandinavian Record. However, the record company requires that their next single must become a great success if they are to continue releasing Cargo's records. Cargo's second single called "Loaded with power" should at least be placed on top five on the "Dance chart".

New strategy

As a reaction to the demands of the record company, they change the strategy of the group. They are all DJs with a relatively big network of colleagues. They also know that the "Dance chart" is decisive for many of the decisions the record company makes. The "Dance chart" is a list of the dance hits that DJs all over the country each week consider as most successful. Thus, DJs with all their half-secret and non-commercial releases decide what should be on the "Dance chart". In that way, the "Dance chart" is not like other charts reflecting which singles are selling best commercially. However, a good sale can be the result of the weekly list of the "Dance chart". The different DJs' votes are prioritised in agreement with how many persons are at the dance floor when the different songs are playing. Consequently, the DJs who are playing at the big places have an enormous power in terms of which numbers are voted in.

The three musicians in Cargo burn approximately 20 CDs with their new track "Loaded with Power" and send the CDs to the most powerful of their DJ-colleagues encouraging them to vote in the number on the "Dance chart". The following week, they are at top ten and the following week, they are at top two. Later on, the single becomes Grammy nominated.

With the placing of the single "Loaded with power" on the "Dance chart", Cargo gets a record contract for a complete album. The album gets the title "The Movie" and is sold in 2,500 copies.

An opportunity is organised

However, it is not enough for Miké and Cargo. They do not think that they have utilised the musical material enough. Most of all, they are annoyed by the fact that the record company has not prioritised them in their budget in comparison with other nascent groups. The commercial success is therefore not satisfying even though the group, in the wake of the release, is on a long tour, primarily with club jobs.

At a time, the manager of the record company, who of course has an influence on how new growing groups are prioritised, is replaced. By chance, the new manager listens to his young daughter singing *"I'm your porn star Baby, Baby, Baby, Porn-Star ..."* – the most famous track from the album "The Movie".

The dance group Cargo.

The manager asks his daughter whom she is listening to and she answers that it is obviously Cargo. According to Miké, especially that incident is decisive for the fact that the manager, as regards Cargo, changes the strategy of the company and their way of prioritising. Among other things, Cargo is supplied with a bigger budget. In addition, the first album is being reintroduced but this time with a new cover and a new female front figure. Everything else is just as before. The title of the new album is, however, "The Movie goes Party". The bigger budget for commercials among other things brings about commercials for the new album on the Danish TV channel TV3.

The new album makes its début with a placing as number thirteen on the Danish list of the most sold albums. The week after, the album is placed as number six and in the third week, they are number seven. All in all, the album is on top twenty of the most sold albums for six weeks and achieves gold platinum (25,000 sold albums) within a month.

■ **Your immediate interpretation**

What does the story of Miké and Cargo tell you about the significance of networks? How will your immediate interpretation of the story be? The exercises listed below can support you in creating your understanding.

> ■ Do networks play a role in the story? Make a list of the meanings attributed to network and networking as they find expression in the story. Discuss these meanings.
> ■ How has Miké created his network? How does he use his network and what is characteristic of his way of using it?
> ■ What does Miké's network look like? Does his network consist of many or few people? Are the persons in his network identical or different? What other factors can contribute to describe Mike's network?
> ■ You have decided to start your own organisation and want to make sure that you profit as much as possible from your network. What will you take into account in your attempts at networking and creating the perfect net of contacts? Who should your network consist of and how will you get into contact with them?
> ■ You meet one of your friends. She is a successful entrepreneur. You discuss the significance of a network to entrepreneurs. She claims that she very consciously and calculatedly makes use of networking and that is the reason why she is successful. What do you think of this argument?

■ **Theories of entrepreneurship**

The story of Carco has many relations to the topic of this chapter, namely the theory of entrepreneurship and network. The theory is about how networks influence the entrepreneur's decisions and behaviour. However, having said that, the agreement ends. Because there is considerable disagreement about the significance of networking and the way in which entrepreneurs should be networking. In particular, two fundamentally different perspectives on what significance networks have and how networking can be approached are prevalent. The two perspectives are encapsulated in the paradox: rational or embedded?

The first perspective discusses to what extent network can be perceived as a rational tool that consciously and calculatedly is used by entrepreneurs in order to obtain success in their efforts to discover or create, evaluate and organise new ventures. In this way, emphasis is put on the way networks can be changed and optimised depending on what resources the entrepreneur needs.

The second perspective, on the contrary, perceives networks as a result of the entrepreneur's past. Thus, networks are a consequence of the life that has been lived and in that way something in which persons are deeply embedded with little possibility to manage and use the networks rationally. In other words, networks are ungovernable conditions, that the entrepreneur cannot change at pleasure. Put in another way, the chapter deals with the paradox to what extent network is a rational tool or ungovernable conditions in which the entrepreneur is embedded. In short, the paradox is:

> **Rational or embedded?**

Theory of entrepreneurship and networks

Theory of entrepreneurship and networks is based on and originated from the traditional social network theory. The traditional theory is originally developed in sociology but has since expanded to a number of disciplines in the social sciences including organisation theory and entrepreneurship theory. The crucial argument in social network theory is that networks influence the behaviour of individuals. Lin (2001) mentions four fundamental ways in which networks influence the behaviour of individuals. Networks can help:

- ... provide persons with information that can be used in relation to the situations which they face.
- ... influence other persons in the network. Network relations have so to speak influence on the decisions and actions that are to be made.
- ... create social legitimacy for persons within a network structure. Persons can so to speak get access to resources by the fact that other persons in the network vouch for them.
- ... develop and strengthen the identities of the persons. Persons can strengthen their identity by associating with others who want to maintain the identity.

The theory of entrepreneurship and network has primarily focused on the resources that can be provided through networks. Hoang and Antoncic write: *"Interpersonal and interorganizational relationships are viewed as the media through which actors gain access to a variety of resources held by other actors. With the exception of work on the role of networks to access capital (...), most research has focused on the entrepreneur's access to intangible resources. ... A key benefit of networks for the entrepreneurial process is the access they provide to information and advice"* (Hoang & Antoncic 2003: 169). The resources which can be provided through social networks are often referred to as social capital. Social capital refers to the means and resources that the entrepreneur benefits by through his or her personal contacts and acquaintances (chapter 6 provides more information about social resources).

Even though social network theory has a long history, the interest for network within entrepreneurship is somewhat younger. Birley (1985), Aldrich & Zimmer (1986) and Johannisson (1988) made the first contributions. These contributions can be seen as a backlash to the research dominating for instance the psychological tradition where the entrepreneur was treated as an individual without consideration for the environments that the individual was part of. On the contrary, as mentioned, in the theory of entrepreneurship and networks, an entrepreneur's network is considered a medium through which the entrepreneur can gain access to different resources. The individual and his or her environments are in this way in play at the same time in entrepreneurial network theory. Moreover, the importance of the network is not only related to the start-up of a new organisation but is valid throughout the entire life cycle of the organisation (Hoang & Antoncic 2003).

The heterogeneity argument
However, before we discuss the paradox, we will take a closer look at different types of network arguments influencing both sides of the paradox. Because although there is agreement on the fact that networks play a crucial role to the entrepreneurs, there is disagreement on what a good and effective network should look like. The dissimilarity or heterogeneity argument suggests that dissimilarity among the entrepreneur's persons in the network and weak ties between these create the most effective network. This should be seen in contrast to the argument about homogeneity which emphasises that a network consisting of homogeneous and strongly connected persons is the most effective – an argument presented in the next section.

The basis of the argumentation concerning heterogeneity is that entrepreneurs achieve access to valuable market information that they can use through the entrepreneurial process by having networks that consist of different persons with regard to their opinions, values, jobs, experiences, competences, etc. Through these differences among the persons in the network, the entrepreneur becomes, so to speak, the centre and the bridge for information, implying that the opportunity to discover and create, evaluate and organise new opportunities increases.

The argumentation takes place at two different levels: (1) The relationship level which focuses on the relation between the entrepreneur and his or her contacts. The relationship level is illustrated in figure 7.1 through the dotted box between the entrepreneur and his or her colleague. (2) The network level, on the contrary, includes the various contacts which the entrepreneur has in his or her complete network. The network level is illustrated in figure 7.1 through the squared frame around all persons in the network. All in all, figure 7.1 illustrates the heterogeneity argument.

Figure 7.1: Weak relations and a heterogeneous network

The relationship level

At the relationship level, the heterogeneity argument is strongly inspired by – or perhaps it even originates from – Granovetter's groundbreaking article from 1973 about the strength of weak ties. Granovetter defines the strength of relations in the following way: *"... the strength of a tie is a (probably linear) combination of the amount of time, the emotional intensity, the intimacy (mutual confiding), and the reciprocal services which characterize the tie"* (Granovetter 1973: 1361). Therefore, the less time, emotional attachment, confidence and reciprocity that are present between an entrepreneur and his contact, the weaker the relationship. In figure 7.1, dotted arrows between the entrepreneur and his or her contacts (friend, customer, family member or colleague) indicate a weak tie.

Granovetter argues that the strength of the relation influences the type and value of the information that the entrepreneur can get from his contacts. According to him, the entrepreneur is more inclined to receive valuable information from weak ties since these relations fundamentally act in other social networks than the entrepreneur himself or herself and therefore possess different information. Thus, he thinks that entrepreneurs with relatively many weak ties and relatively few strong ties have better access to valuable information and a better opportunity to spread information about their opportunities than the entrepreneurs with relatively few weak ties and relatively many strong ties.

The network level
Burt (1992) backs up Granovetter's argumentation for weak ties. He argues that the typical disadvantage associated with strong ties is that they are often closely related to each other – many of them simply know each other and therefore possess the same information. In that way, many strong ties become unimportant because you already, through the existing network, have access to the information these contacts possess. The information which you can receive from a strong tie you can certainly also receive from other strong ties in the network. For example, it is not necessary or profitable to have two uncles with experience from the advisory service area if you wanted to establish yourself in that field. The advice given by the two uncles would probably not differ much from each other and advice given by only one uncle and the contact to him would probably be enough.

Burt (1992), however, at the same time lifted the argument for heterogeneity to the network level where focus is on the entrepreneur's entire network, which effectively means all of his or her contacts. In this connection, Burt emphasises the importance of so-called structural holes in the entire network and the opportunity for entrepreneurs to be able to function as a bridge between different parts of the entire network. Structural holes in a network appear when certain persons in the entrepreneur's network are not mutually connected which means that they do not know each other. The more persons who do not know each other, the more structural holes does the entrepreneur's network have. In case some people do not know each other mutually, there will be persons in the network who become key figures and bridge builders between different parts of the entire network. They get access to what Burt labels non-redundant information which is absolutely decisive in order to discover or create, evaluate and organise opportunities. This means information that no other contacts in the network possess. Figure 7.1 demonstrates a network with structural holes since only the entrepreneur's friend and customer know each other.

The homogeneity argument

The argument about homogeneity is almost the opposite of the heterogeneity argument. The homogeneity argument is that the best is dense networks where as many people as possible in the network know each other and where the relation between the entrepreneur and these persons is strong. Weak contacts and heterogeneous networks consisting of many bridges do not play a role in this argument. How can that be?

What distinguishes the homogeneity argument and the heterogeneity argument is broadly speaking what types of resources are seen as most important. The heterogeneity argument focuses on information and especially market information primarily in connection with the process of discovery or creation, evaluation and organising of opportunities. On the contrary, the homogeneity argument focuses on resources such as emotional support, sensitive market information and access to financial resources. Thus, from this perspective it is about gaining access to the types of resources which are only exchanged if two parties trust each other, spend much time together, have an emotional attachment to each other and where reciprocity exists between the two parties. That is Granovetter's definition of what creates a strong tie. The homogeneity argument is strongly inspired by Coleman (1988) who is interested in the connection between social and human capital. As was the case for the heterogeneity argument, the homogeneity argument can be explained on a relationship level as well as a network level (see figure 7.2).

Network

Figure 7.2: Strong relations and a homogeneous network

The relationship level

On the relationship level, the point of the homogeneity argument is that the entrepreneur needs contacts to which he or she has strong and close ties. In such strong ties, trust and reciprocal commitments between the contacts are more often established. In this way, the probability that the entrepreneur receives the necessary emotional support required during the otherwise, at times, chaotic and complicated entrepreneurial process, increases. Persons who are not closely connected to the entrepreneur will probably not spend their time and energy on emotional support. The same goes for resource sensitive market information. Information about markets is only shared with people they trust. And exactly sensitive market information such as information about conflicts or research efforts in another organisation can be crucial for discovering or creating, evaluating and organising opportunities successfully.

As regards access to financial capital, the homogeneity argument can also be used. Bygrave et al. (2003) investigated the relation between entrepreneurs and their private investors across 29 countries. The investigation revealed that 40 percent of the entrepreneurs' investors were close family members and a another 8 percent were other family relations. Only 8 percent of the entrepreneurs who obtained private investors received capital from a stranger. These results attracted great attention when published. Focus changed away from the access to venture capital which can be characterised as professional and risk capital, in addition to being unattainable for the majority of the entrepreneurs. In figure 7.2, the fat arrow between the entrepreneur and the entrepreneur's contacts (friend, customer, family member or colleague) indicates a strong relationship.

The network level

At the network level, there is also an argument for homogeneity. In their groundbreaking article from 1986, Aldrich & Zimmer wrote that entrepreneurs embedded in the dense network where many people in the network know each other reciprocally have an increased probability – on the basis of the reciprocal trust – to act together. When persons are strongly connected in close networks, the probability that they act as a whole with a common objective in mind is increased. Such a collective energy can be quite decisive for the implementation of the entrepreneurial process.

People in close networks are also generally more alike in terms of attitudes, values, jobs, experiences, competences, etc. than people in networks where few know each other. Therefore, it is possible to imagine that the entrepreneur's contacts share the same passion for a certain leisure-time interest, which means that they know each other on a personal level. Because of the personal dimension in the network and the common interests, exchange of emotional support and exchange of sensitive market information is, in addition, more probable in close networks than in less close networks. In figure 7.2, the squared frame around the complete network indicates the network level.

Effective networks depend on the situation

We have now discussed two opposite arguments about how effective networks should look like when the entrepreneur fights his or her way through the entrepreneurial process, namely the heterogeneity argument and the homogeneity argument.

Immediately, both arguments seem to be watertight. Sense applies to both of them. Also empirically, both of them seem to prove correct. A number of investigations have supported respectively the heterogeneity argument and the homogeneity argument. The reason why each of these opposite arguments makes sense, and both are empirically supported, is that social networks are dynamic (Larson & Starr 1993). The entrepreneurs meet and are confronted with different challenges through the entrepreneurial process and each of these requires access to specific resources. Some resources are obtained most effectively through diverse social networks with many structural holes and weak ties to persons while other resources are obtained most effectively through close networks where there are strong ties between the persons.

Therefore, the effective networks depend on the situation of the entrepreneur. The challenges determine the demand for resources and what network the entrepreneur should aim at. Lin (2001) expresses this synthesis between the heterogeneity argument and the homogeneity argument in the following way: *"For preserving or maintaining resources (e.g., expressive actions), denser networks may have a relative advantage (...) On the other hand, searching for and obtaining resources not presently possessed (e.g., instrumental actions), such as looking for a job or a better job, accessing and extending bridges in the network should be more useful"* (Lin 2001: 27).

Several models, primarily life-cycle models, attempt to describe how the entrepreneur's network develops during the entrepreneurial process. In the very early stadium when the entrepreneur looks for an opportunity, the entrepreneur needs non-redundant market information in order to be able to create or discover a new opportunity. Therefore, the entrepreneur is interested in a network consisting of many different persons – a network with many structural holes and in which the entrepreneur has weak ties to other persons (Klyver & Hindle 2007). When the entrepreneur has identified an opportunity and is about to start the organisation, there is suddenly a need for other resources. In this stage, there is a demand for advice and support to be able to make the final decision about starting, and there might be a need for supply of capital. For that reason, the aim is at a closer network consisting of many strong ties including many family members (Evald et al. 2006).

After the organisation is started and the entrepreneur moves forward in the life cycle of the organisation, some of the persons in the network are being replaced. At this stage, it is crucial to the entrepreneur to be established in the market and consequently, the entrepreneur needs access to market information again. There-fore, the network will once again change to a network consisting of many different persons – a network with structural holes and a network with more weak ties, for instance to new acquaintances (Evald et al. 2006).

It appears that the network changes during the entrepreneurial process and that these changes can be related to the problems the entrepreneur is confronted with and thus the resources the entrepreneur needs. Figure 7.3 illustrates this graphi-cally.

Figure 7.3: Heterogeneous and homogeneous networks across the life cycle of the organisation

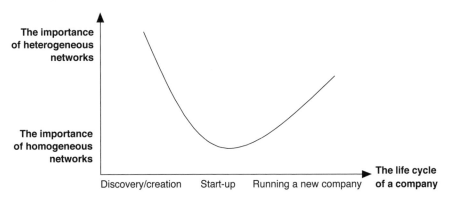

Source: Klyver & Hindle (2007), p. 26.

Network as a rational tool
So far, we have discussed two different types of network – heterogeneous and homogeneous which have different justifications depending on the different chal-lenges the entrepreneur meets through the entrepreneurial process. However, so far we have not discussed to what extent entrepreneurs rationally and calculatedly can use and employ their network or whether the network is rather something that structures and limits the opportunities of the entrepreneur. Thus, we are dealing with the paradox concerning to what extent a network is a rational tool or whether entrepreneurs are embedded in their network for better or worse.

From a rational perspective, the entrepreneur is perceived as a determined player who chooses his persons in the network based on who he expects will contribute with the best and most important resources in the process of carrying through the entrepreneurial process. We are dealing with a rational calculation of who it will be worth the trouble to get involved with. Thus, the persons in the entrepreneur's network become "supporters" who will each bring resources into the process such as advice, financing or intangible resources such as legitimacy.

From the rational perspective, the tie between the entrepreneurs and the persons who get involved will often be concrete (namely supportive), emotionally neutral, contractual and short-termed. Persons are chosen carefully but are also dropped again carefully when they do no longer support the process in the best possible way.

The rational approach to networks is very widespread –among researchers as well as politicians, advisers, and entrepreneurs. In the introduction to their anthology on entrepreneurs and networks, Bager & Klyver (2007) write, *"Networks and "networking" are today considered as being of decisive importance to entrepreneurs and their companies. The ability to establish a company and later on make it grow and obtain growth is affected by the entrepreneurs' network-ties"* (Bager & Klyver 2007: 7). In this anthology, there are several practical examples of how different persons rationally and by means of calculation attempt to create effective networks. Sørensen (2007) describes how the Confederation of Danish Industry (the premier lobbying organisation for Danish business on national and international issues) works to create networks for new business owners. The network is an offer for growth-oriented new business owners. In a similar way, Poulsen (2007) from Innovation Center Denmark talks about the inspiration they gain from networks from Silicon Valley where networking for many years has been one of the secrets behind the success. Among other things, she explains about the Americans' very rational and calculative way of joining network arrangements. Ways that are somewhat different from the way in which most Danes would act. Before joining, the participants check the programme of the network arrangement and who the other participants are, and they set themselves goals as to who they want to talk to during the arrangement. Secondly, an elevator-pitch (which was mentioned in the introduction of this textbook) is prepared and trained). The elevator-pitch refers to a short presentation of yourself which you use every time you meet a new person. Poulsen (2007) writes about how to behave at various network arrangements: *"You introduce yourself to the first person you meet and you deliver your 20 seconds elevator-pitch and ask what he or she is working with professionally. If it is an interesting contact that you would like to check up on, you exchange business cards and enter into an agreement with him or her about calling or meeting again. After that, you immediately end the talk and walk on to the next person. In about 30 minutes, you are likely to meet 10-15 persons of whom 3-5 end up becoming a part of your own network"* (Poulsen 2007: 14). That way of thinking network and network arrangements is an illustrative example of the rational approach to social networks and an example of the fact that networks are considered and treated as a tool which you can choose to use or not.

Besides the various attempts made by organisations to improve the entrepreneurs' network, many books and courses dealing with networking exist, and today many top executives and entrepreneurs have already participated in one or several of these. The consultant company Gugin, for instance, is willing to give advice about how entrepreneurs network in the best possible way. Under the overall title "Learn to network – effectively", several different types of courses are offered by Gugin. This is the description of one of them called "the entrepreneur's network": *"As an entrepreneur you depend on a good and varied network. You are a fiery soul but need many different competences in order to be successful. At this goal-oriented course, you learn to establish, maintain and extend your network as an entrepreneur, and you get good advice and experiences from people who have been entrepreneurs"* (www.gugin-networking.dk). This was just another example of the fact that network is considered as a tool which the entrepreneur can use rationally and calculatedly in his or her efforts to carry through the entrepreneurial process.

Embedded in network
As already mentioned, another perspective is the embeddedness perspective. The rational perspective acknowledges influence from the social environments but remains convinced that people rule themselves and decide what these social environments look like. That is not the case with the embeddedness perspective. This perspective takes social embedment and socialisation of human behaviour a little further and is more sceptical of the ability of people and entrepreneurs to choose the network that suits them in a rational and calculating manner.

Whereas the rational perspective emphasises the entrepreneur's opportunity to choose, the embeddedness perspective focuses on the fact that networks are brought from the past. According to this perspective, the entrepreneur cannot actively without consequences choose a network in relation to the problems he or she is confronted with. Rather than something that can be chosen or not chosen, the network is given from the past. For example, to many entrepreneurs it is necessary to discuss and involve their husband or wife in the important decisions that are to be made through the entrepreneurial process. Many of these decisions can have crucial influence on the future family life including for instance economy, spare time and working hours. Therefore, the entrepreneurial decisions cannot be considered and made isolated. Thus, regardless of whether they are supportive or not to the entrepreneurial process, the wife or husband will is most likely to get involved and have crucial influence.

In the embeddedness perspective, network is considered as something that is created and maintained through every activity in life and it cannot be limited and isolated to certain challenges as for instance the start-up of an organisation. Social networks are created holistically through activities performed by a person. In the same way, a network is a result of activities that a person has carried through in the past. A person's network is therefore a result of the life he or she has lived and therefore some people have big and varied networks. Others, on the contrary, have smaller and dense, homogeneous networks. Not because they have chosen it but because the life they have lived has brought it along.

The embeddedness perspective looks at relationships in a different way than the rational perspective. From the rational perspective, relationships were described as concrete (namely supportive), emotionally neutral, contractual and short-termed. From the embeddedness perspective, they if anything described as diffuse (both supportive and the opposite), emotional, trusting, reciprocally binding and long-termed.

The embeddedness perspective is thus something that is more sceptical of the positive influence of the network on the entrepreneurial process. It is not denied that it can be the case – not at all. But at the same time, it is emphasised that the network can also function as an impediment to entrepreneurs' path through the entrepreneurial process. In their famous article Aldrich and Zimmer expressed it this way: *"The embedded nature of social behaviour refers to the way in which action is constrained or facilitated because of its social context"* (Aldrich & Zimmer 1986: 4).

The consequence of dedicating oneself to the embeddedness perspective is that you can no longer consider network as a tool that can be used on its own in rela-tion to certain activities. On the contrary, network constitutes some structures that define and constrain the networking opportunities. We cannot control the network – instead, the network controls us, and therefore it makes sense to say that for better or worse entrepreneurs are embedded in their network.

Network: rational or embedded?

By now, the two different perspectives on what entrepreneurial networks are have been discussed. They are illustrated in table 7.1.

Table 7.1: The paradox: rational or embedded?

	Rational	Embedded
View of the entrepreneur	Goal-oriented, rational player	A socially embedded player
View of the networks	A rational tool	Ungovernable condition
View of the relation	Concrete, emotionally neutral, contract like and short-termed	Diffuse, emotional, trusting, reciprocally binding and long-termed
Focus	Effective networks	The facilitating and restricting qualities of the network
The importance of social contexts	Low	High

The rational perspective describes the entrepreneur as a purposeful and rational player who considers the network as a tool. The relationships between the entrepreneur and the persons in the network are concrete, emotionally neutral, contract like and short-termed. The research within this perspective aims at finding out and deciding what the most effective network looks like for the entrepreneurs. The rational perspective prioritises the importance of the social context in the low end in comparison to the embeddedness perspective. The criticism that applies to the rational perspective, exactly as it is presented from the embeddedness perspective, is that the entrepreneur is being under-socialised. That means that too little importance is attributed to the role of the social context in describing the entrepreneur's actions. On the contrary, the entrepreneur is seen as having more control over his own behaviour and decisions than what is perhaps realistic.

Whereas the rational perspective can be criticised for being under-socialised, the embeddedness perspective can be criticised for the opposite, namely to over-socialise. That means that the embeddedness perspective does not subscribe sufficient decision and action oriented power to the entrepreneur but primarily focuses on how decisions are determined externally, namely by the social context. Consequently, this means that the embeddedness perspective, to a higher degree, prioritises the importance of the social context.

The over-socialisation means that the embeddedness perspective perceives the entrepreneur as a socially embedded person who, with his or her network, is dealing with ungovernable conditions. The relationships between the entrepreneur and the persons in the network are diffuse, emotional, trusting, reciprocally binding and long-termed. The role of research related to the embeddedness perspective is to clarify how networks facilitate and/or restrict entrepreneurs.

■ A theoretical interpretation

We now give two different interpretations of Miké's story that initiated this chapter. In the interpretations, the story is attached to the theory above with emphasis on the paradox: rational or embedded?

The rational perspective

If you choose a rational interpretation of Miké's story, focus will be on how Miké consciously, rationally and by means of calculation uses his network in his efforts to become a successful musician. From this perspective, there are many facets to deal with. First of all, it is possible to argue that Miké and his partner in the music studio choose each other as partners in the hope of achieving some advantages. To begin with, it can be about reducing or perhaps sharing the economical costs and risks. However, another advantage that might also have played a crucial role is that they possess different competences and therefore are able to offer a better product. "Together" they think that they are something special. Thus, both of them have very clear motives for joining forces with each other. They choose each other. Nevertheless, as time goes by and each of them gradually realises that they have not achieved what they wanted, they begin to doubt whether the team and the partnership is the right thing for them. Therefore, they choose unanimously to split. This can be described as a conscious way of not choosing each other any longer.

Another situation that illustrates the rational network approach is the way in which Miké to begin with chooses Ronnie and Kenn to remix their "What's the Matter in Paradise" and subsequently how Ronnie and Kenn wish that Miké raps to their song "The Horn". Most likely, they have discussed who they knew who would be able to help them with this rap thing. They have screened the market for rappers and contacted those who they think are most likely to give them what they need.

However, the clearest rational choice situation is the way in which Cargo as a group uses their network to get a recording contract in the bag. They have a product/an album but are not sure of getting a record contract unless they have a great success with their other single. Thus, they change their strategy consciously in a calculated and smart way and use their network to legitimise and profile their product. By getting the single "Loaded with Power" on the "Dance chart" by means of their network to Danish DJs, they convince the recording company of the value of their group, and consequently they get a contract for a complete album. We are here dealing with a definite instrumental approach to networking where the network is used to gain the objectives that the entrepreneurs aim at.

The embeddedness perspective

Miké's story can, however, also be understood completely different namely from an embeddedness perspective where focus is on networks as ungovernable conditions. It is likely that in some situations he has consciously used his network as a tool to promote his own interests, but basically they are his existing networks – a result of his life. The contacts he uses on his way in his career are as regards the main part contacts or persons who he got acquainted with many years ago in his early period of hip-hop. Thus, they are persons who he created ties to without, at that time, having any kind of calculating intentions. For that exact reason, these contacts turn out to be of great importance many years later in his life. The common past (and the trust that was built in the wake of this) means that those people have a soft spot for each other later in life. Therefore, they wish to help each other – not in order to gain something in return or because they owe each other anything, but simply because they want to pay tribute to the relationship and the past.

For many years, Miké has not seen many of the persons who surrounded him in the early days of hip-hop. When he met them a long time ago, focus was on hip-hop and love for the underground culture. No one at that time thought about whom, from a rational point of view, it would be good to know in the future if you wanted to make a record. Anyway, if somebody had thought like that, it was probably impossible to make predictions about who ended up in powerful positions. Thus, it makes sense to argue that the network that turns out to facilitate Miké's career as a musician is created with reference to a completely different agenda and with completely different intentions.

Perhaps one cannot argue that Miké's network has limited his career as it is presented in this chapter. But one may well argue that Miké's past and life and the network which it has resulted in, have shaped and defined the limits and the opportunities for him as a dance musician. A question one may ask is whether he would have been just as successful with the same talent without a past as a hip-hopper.

■ Practical tests of the theory

Based on the above thoughts and discussions, you should now be ready to set up your own attempts towards understanding the entrepreneurial network and how it affects the entrepreneurial process. The following are suggestions for experiments.

Exercise 1: Interviewing an entrepreneur

Make a list of interview questions that try to encapsulate some of the most crucial discussions about how networks function. Contact an entrepreneur and interview him or her with a view to testing the theory presented in this chapter about entrepreneurial networks. On the basis of this, you should create your opinion about the paradox: rational or embedded?

Exercise 2: The Danish Learning Centre for Network

Visit the Danish Learning Centre for Network's homepage (www.laeringscenter.dk). Find one or several articles in their database (the articles are only available in Danish). Make an analysis of the articles. What implications do networks have to entrepreneurs according to the articles? Do you agree with the conclusions of the articles?

Exercise 3: Describe your own network

What does your network look like? Is it small, big, heterogeneous, homogeneous etc.? How many relationships originate from your childhood, youth, adulthood, etc.? How strongly are you connected to these people? Do people in your network know each other reciprocally? Why do you think that your network looks the way it does?

Literature

Aldrich, H. E. & Zimmer, C. (1986). Entrepreneurship through social networks, In Sexton, D. L. & Smilor, R. W. (Ed.), The art and science of entrepreneurship (pp. 3-23), New York: Ballinger.

Bager, T. & Klyver, K. (2007). Iværksættere og deres netværke. Copenhagen: Børsens Forlag.

Birley, S. (1985). The role of networks in the entrepreneurial process, Journal of Business Venturing, 1, 107-117.

Burt, R. S. (1992). Structural holes – The social structure of competition. London: Harvard University Press.

Bygrave, W. D., Hay, M. & Reynolds, P. D. (2003). Executive forum: a study of informal investing in 29 nations composing the Global Entrepreneurship Monitor, Venture Capital, 5, 101-116.

Coleman, J. S. (1988). Social capital in the creation of human capital, American Journal of Sociology, 94, 95-120.

Evald, M. R., Klyver, K. & Svendsen, S. G. (2006). The changing importance of the strength of ties throughout the entrepreneurial process, Journal of Enterprising Culture, 14, 1-26.

Granovetter, M. S. (1973). The strength of weak ties, American Journal of Sociology, 78, 1360-1380.

Hoang, H. & Antoncic, B. (2003). Network-based research in entrepreneurship – A critical review, Journal of Business Venturing, 18, 165-187.

Johannisson, B. (1988). Business formation – A network approach, Scandinavian journal of management, 4, 83-99.

Klyver, K. & Hindle, K. (2007). The role of social networks at different stages of business formation, Small Enterprise Research – The Journal of SEAANZ, 15, 22-38.

Larson, A. & Starr, J. A. (1993). A network model of organization formation, Entrepreneurship Theory & Practice, 17, 5-15.

Lin, N. (2001). Social capital – A theory of social structure and action. New York: Cambridge University Press.

Poulsen, M. F. (2007). Fysiske og virtuelle netværk i Silicon Valley. In Bager, T. & Klyver, K. (Ed.), Iværksætterne og deres netværk (pp. 13-22), Copenhagen: Børsens Forlag.

Sørensen, T. M. (2007). DIs IværksætterNetværk – et tilbud til vækst-iværksættere. In Bager, T. & Klyver, K. (Ed.), Iværksætterne og deres netværk (pp. 23-32), Copenhagen: Børsens Forlag.

180

Chapter 8

The business plan

Many entrepreneurs need a business plan and many have also written one. However, some entrepreneurs have also written a business plan without actually needing it and without having used it actively. The business plan has become the big pivotal point in many textbooks dealing with entrepreneurship, and in many of the courses applying to the field the value of a business plan has been emphasised to the entrepreneurs. However, a lot seems to suggest that the role and the importance of the business plan are much more complicated.

The business plan can play a crucial role in connection with the planning of the entrepreneurial process, both at an internal level in relation to the entrepreneur him- or herself and at an external level in relation to a third party as for instance investors. The business plan also plays other crucial roles which are more symbolic and legitimising as regards the environments. At the same time, some claim that the business plan can actually turn out to impede the entrepreneur's creativity. You will meet these topics and discussions in this chapter.

■ Meet practice

This is the story of two previous colleagues from Gumlink (a Danish company producing chewing gum), Jesper and Peter who in 2001 started a company called Back11Basics. Both have management skills before they start up the company and they have been posted in other countries through their jobs. It is the story of an organisation with no sales in 2001 and a turnover of 60 million Danish kroner in 2006. If you visit www.idea-textbook.dk, you can listen to Jesper telling about this development in a video case.

The four Fs as the foundation stone

Both Jesper and Peter would like another type of working day – a way of working that would give them more control over their day. Therefore, they choose the four Fs to be the founding stones of their organisation: "Freedom", "Financial reasons", "Fun" and "Flexible lifestyle". The idea is that these four Fs should characterise the way they run the organisation. However, it is not always as easy to comply with these founding ideas. Jesper says about "Fun", *"We wanted to have a funnier daily life and run things in our own way and in our own style. I still think that we are struggling with Fun! Things turn out to become humdrum and you often seem to forget remembering that element"* (quote from video case).

Economic set-up and being willing to run a risk
In connection with the start-up, they both choose to contribute 500,000 Danish

kroner (about 65,000 euro) – neither more nor less: *"Each of us could contribute 500,000 kroner, and that was the amount of money which we were willing to risk. We thought of it as a kind of casino game. We only brought this money into the game and that means that we left our credit cards at home because we did not want to get tempted to spend more."* Because of the limited means, they try persistently to keep down the costs.

Many opportunities and products to test
The starting point for the start-up is not a concrete idea. On the contrary, Jesper and Peter have several ideas they want to test – mostly ideas related to their previous experiences from Gumlink. Especially two ideas are tested before they decide for real which to pursue as an opportunity. Both ideas are related to the product "sugar-free fresh-breath products". The ideas are the following:

- They attempt to offer joint ownership to distributors in Eastern Europe about a fresh-breath product.
- They attempt to develop "private label"-products for Western Europe and the USA.

Ultimately, it is the "private label"-opportunity which they go for. At first, however, they experience several unsuccessful attempts in Eastern Europe because the region, according to Jesper, is not ready for their new way of thinking business.

The strategy process
In the start-up process, Peter and Jesper create a 5-year strategy plan – or business plan – which they use for presenting their idea to banks and suppliers. In order to fill out the business plan, they make use of different models, as for instance SWOT, to describe their present situation. Jesper says about the strategy process, *"… at that point, we made a big strategy presentation which we used for ourselves but also for external use, namely to banks, partners and suppliers."* Jesper continues: *"We always initiate with a quotation from Alice in Wonderland where the cat sits in the tree and Alice asks for help to find out where she is going; and the cat says, 'where are you going?' Then she answers that she actually doesn't know. The cat's conclusion is that it doesn't matter which way you go … And the same rule applies to companies in the sense that if you do not know in which direction to go, your plan is unimportant."*

Back11Basics follows the plan that has been made quite well in spite of the fact that the content is rather loose: *"And we must conclude that we were good at following this plan ... actually, when we started, many people told us that it was completely crazy. You are only two persons to start a company without products; without customers and then you make budgets that predict a turnover of 40 millions ... where did that number derive from? ... but we have followed our plan fantastically well as far as the budget is concerned."*

The strategy content
Back2basics constantly wants to challenge the market by searching for new customers and products. In this process, Peter and Jesper actively use their strategy. The entire idea of the organisation is to create success. Jesper declares, *"Our mission is that we do it for a certain reason and that is to become successful. And we do that for ourselves, for our employees, for our suppliers and perhaps, most importantly, for our customers."* It is the philosophy of Back11Basics that they are only capable of maintaining their own success if their customers have success. Originally, their mission is: "We challenge to create success" but for instance at trade fairs they often use the following motto instead: "Your refreshing partner in private label."

■ Your immediate interpretation
What does the story about Back11Basics tell you about the importance of business plans? How do you immediately understand the perspectives of the story? Here are some exercises that can support your understanding of the story.

- ■ How does Back11Basics use the business plan during the start-up of their organisation? What role applies to the business plan? Do you have the impression that they give very high priority to a business plan that has been written down?
- ■ Do they have a business plan that is written down or are they dealing with loose ideas and thoughts that are not necessarily written down? Do you think that it is important that the business plan be written down instead of just being ideas and thoughts?
- ■ You have decided to start your own organisation and you have been advised to write a business plan before you start up. What is such a plan supposed to contain, how long should it be and how do you work it out?
- ■ You meet one of your old friends from primary and lower secondary school. She has just got her title as Master in international business development. She considers starting her own company where, together with her partner, she would like to advise small companies that wish to start up export to

China. During their time at the university, both your old friend and her partner have dealt much with China. They have been on several field trips to China and they have had a semester in China and written their Masters thesis about export to China. They claim that they have a good knowledge of the topic and that, at the same time, they have the necessary contacts to start up. Consequently, they think that it is a waste of time to write a business plan. What is your opinion?

■ Theories of entrepreneurship

The story, which we have dealt with, is associated with the topic of this chapter which is the business plan. In many ways, discussions about business plans are about how entrepreneurs describe and communicate their recognitions and plans that ex ante and ex post are attached to the emergence, the evaluation and the organising of a new opportunity. Thus, it is about describing, in a structured way, the entrepreneur's recognitions and plans in relation to chapter 3 about opportunity emergence, chapter 4 about opportunity evaluation and chapter 5 about organising of opportunities.

There are many definitions of what a business plan is. According to Connect Denmark – an organisation helping technology oriented entrepreneurs with advisory services and financing – a business plan is supposed to *"… describe the business idea, how the company is considered to run, what the company plans to do, the objectives of the company and how to achieve them"* (www.connectdenmark.com).

Those who promote the importance of a business plan are often believers in the planning perspective in contrast to the improvising perspective (which was discussed in chapter 5 about organising opportunities). They believe that organising processes can be controlled and they see the business plan as an important management tool which helps to carry through an entrepreneurial process as painlessly as possible. On the contrary, there are others who are more critical towards the business plan – they see it as a curb of creativity. They argue that entrepreneurs are forced into a certain way of thinking through the structure of the business plan and that their, otherwise decisive creativity, is reduced. Therefore, the paradox applying to this chapter is to what extent the business plan is a:

Management tool or creativity curb?

The business plan: context, content and process

Before we go into a discussion about the paradox, we will concentrate on some other basic factors relating to the business plan. The discussion about the business plan is often compared with the concept of planning. "The plan" is the content or the output of a "planning process" which is called "planning". Planning is conducted within settings and conditions that are called "the context". This division into three parts is illustrated in figure 8.1 (De Witt & Meyer 1998).

Figure 8.1: The context, content and process of the business plan

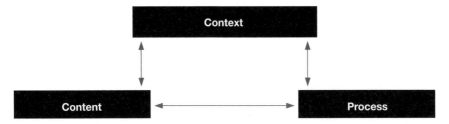

Source: Inspired by De Witt & Meyer (1998).

As the figure illustrates, the three dimensions are connected and they influence each other. For example, it is possible to imagine that in some industries (contexts), the demands made on the business plan and the planning process are bigger than in other sectors. An investigation made by Honig & Karlsson (2004) revealed for example that entrepreneurs who operate in the production sector are more inclined to make a business plan than entrepreneurs in other sectors. They explain that tendency with the fact that this sector has a planning approach. It increases the willingness of new entrepreneurs to imitate the tradition in order to obtain legitimacy and to make the other players understand them.

It is also possible to imagine that the need for much risk capital (context) requires another content of the business plan than if you are able to fund your start-up process yourself. An example of this is the business plan suggested by Connect Denmark to innovative and growth-oriented entrepreneurs. This plan demonstrates how some topics are dealt with more thoroughly such as the financial aspect in order to consider the target group for the plan: the investors (www.connectdenmark.com). Another imagined situation could be that some persons (contexts) have different needs for business plans. For example, to some persons with a long education (such as engineers, business economists or production planners), planning plays an important role, whereas creative processes are more important to persons educated as designers, chaos pilots or music teachers. Presumably, these persons will have different needs as regards planning and for writing things into specific business plan structures. Consequently, there are many different contexts that can influence both the demands to the content of the business plan and how the planning process can take place.

However, the process is also likely to influence the content, just as the content can influence the process. It is possible to imagine that a given way to go about it can result in some delimitation as far as the content is concerned. If the entrepreneur from the beginning decides not to consider comments from a public adviser about involving different decisive interested parties in the planning work – as for example players such as local community, financial advisers, family members – it is easy to imagine that some potential comments will be totally overlooked and not appear from the final written plan (content).

It is also possible to imagine that if the entrepreneur takes his starting point in a predefined table of contents to the business plan, it will influence the process that will be carried through. Some will claim that the starting point in a table of contents will require a structured analytical approach (process).

A written document or a mental process
It has also been discussed whether it is the business plan as a written document that is the decisive factor, or whether it is the thought and planning process that is essential. The arguments for the plan as a written document are that the entrepreneur realises what decisions are to be made in keeping with the supply of products, on which markets to act and what the competitive advantages of the organisation are. In addition, the plan as a written document can be important as regards communication with an external third party such as a bank, investors, customers or suppliers. Also as far as internal communication and reflection are concerned, the written document often plays a role. The business plan can be used in relation to communication with new employees as a foundation for inducing the desired behaviour and communication of the objectives of the organisation, but the plan can also in many ways contribute to maintaining and perhaps strengthening the entrepreneur's motivation.

However, other people argue that the process of writing down the plan is unnecessary and that the important process is to get through the right process of thinking. It is the process of thinking that contributes to clearness of the objectives of the organisation and how they can be fulfilled. Finally, it is the process that motivates. It is not the plan that is written down. Today, market conditions, the technological opportunities, legislation and many other factors related to the environment influence the organisational change process so much that the written business plan gets outdated almost before the writing of it is finished. Therefore, a continuous reflection is crucial.

There is an additional argument against the written business plan, an argument that is especially relevant during the start-up process of an organisation. People who are exploiting an opportunity are often short of time and resources. What matters to them is to have the opportunity realised through the process of organising as fast as possible so that a cash flow can begin and the organisation can begin to earn money and pay out wages. The longer the process takes, the bigger economic risk does the entrepreneur run and the bigger the need for funding for the start-up. Therefore, they are busier getting the organisation operationally and functionally started than speculating about long-term strategic plans. In the words of David Madié who is co-founder of Startup Company and presented as a case in chapter 3, *"Spokesmen for writing a business plan will object: 'It will never do any harm to have a good plan.' Actually, it can harm. Because the big problem concerning the business plan is all the time that is spent on it – perhaps 100 hours or more which correspond to the work of several weeks. ... However, the worst is not the time and energy that is spent on writing worthless business plans. The worst is thinking about what the time could otherwise have been spent on, something which could increase the chances of the company of surviving, growing and getting funds from either banks or investors"* (Madié 2007: 34-35).

Thus, there is a lively debate about whether it is the plan in a written form or it is the process of thinking that is decisive to the carrying out of the entrepreneurial process, a debate in which rational arguments apply to both sides. It is not all entrepreneurs who write down a business plan. An investigation of the Danish population that was done by the Danish Entrepreneurship Global Monitor team in 2003 shows that around 35 percent of the Danes which have an intention of starting a new organisation within the next three years or who are already in the process of starting have written a business plan. In other words, about 65 percent of the entrepreneurs may not have written a business plan. In addition, it is interesting that 25 percent of the entrepreneurs, who have written a business plan, write the plan at the request from their environment. The remaining 75 percent have taken the initiative themselves to make a plan.

Planning

Before we jump into the discussion about the content of the business plan and its attached paradox, we will briefly discuss some issues related to the close connection between planning as a process and the business plan as output. Therefore, as further indicated, in this section there will be parallels to the discussions which you dealt with in chapter 5 about the organising of opportunities.

During a planning process, there are some critical factors you have to be conscious about in connection with the working out of the business plan. These critical factors are crucial for making the business plan function as intended. Kuratko & Hodgetts (2004) synthesise these factors in four overall factors:

- The objectives should be realistic
- The plan should create obligation and engagement
- The plan should contain milestones
- The plan should be flexible

It is crucial that the objectives are realistic both externally as regards partners as for example possible investors or lenders and internally as regards your own motivation. If the objectives are not realistic and not well thought out, it is difficult to attract investors or lenders. At the same time, it is difficult to maintain the motivation for getting through the entrepreneurial process if you can see that the objectives are not realistic and cannot be achieved. It is also important that the plan contain some milestones that indicate when different activities should be finished and how these activities are reciprocally connected. In this way, it becomes possible to control whether you run on time and are moving in the right direction or not. Last but not least, it is crucial that the plan is flexible. This, however, can be inconsistent with the milestones of the plan. To carry through the entrepreneurial process is a rather complicated and very unpredictable process and therefore it can be necessary to open up for changes in the process.

The content of the business plan

There are many suggestions regarding what a business plan should contain. Often, these suggestions are shown as the table of contents that is structuring the business plan. But in spite of these vast numbers of suggestions regarding the content of the business plan, which are often presented as universal principles, the only reliable and universal advice is that the business plan needs to be adjusted to the opportunity, the situation and the target group of the plan. There is, of course, a difference between the ways different types of opportunities are described most

effectively in a business plan. The concrete situation attached to the opportunity has a great influence on the way the business plan should be made. It is possible to imagine that entrepreneurs with ambitions of export and growth would have to structure their business plan in a different way than an entrepreneur who only wants to establish locally. Finally, it is natural that different target groups (as for instance bank employees, investors, customers, suppliers, accountants, etc.) have completely different requirements to the information in the business plan.
Table 8.1 shows three examples of what the contents of a business plan could look like.

Table 8.1: Three examples of the contents of a business plan

Kuratko & Hodgetts (2004)	Schilit (1987)	Start-up & growth (www.startvaekst.dk)
Summing up	Summing up	Background inforrmation
Business description	Background and purpose	Summary
Marketing plan	Aim	Business idea(s)
Examination, design and development	Market analysis	Personal resources and aim
Production	Development and production	The product/service
Management/management group	Marketing	Market description
Critical risks	Financial plans	Sales and marketing
Financing	Organisation & management	Organisation of the company
Implementation plan	Ownership	Development of the company
	Critical risks and problems	Budgets
	Summary and conclusion	Financing
		Possible enclosures

The three different suggestions should be considered as different suggestions for a solution to the same problem. However, there is not immediately something that speaks in favour of the one rather than the other, unless the opportunity, the situation and the target group of the business plan are taken into account.

As you can see, there are different suggestions as to what the contents of the business plan should be. The crucial thing in terms of deciding a given plan is to think through what type of information is crucial in the specific situation. Henceforth, there are some recommendations that can assist in the making of the plan. The recommendations are one of the suggestions that Kuratko & Hodgetts (2004) come up with. The business plan should:

- ■ ... not be too long
- ■ ... be future oriented
- ■ ... avoid exaggerations
- ■ ... specify critical risk factors
- ■ ... identify the target group
- ■ ... be written professionally (in the third person)
- ■ ... catch the reader's attention and interests

The business plan as a management tool
We will now look at the paradox and discuss the two, apparently opposite perspectives. The one perspective perceives the business plan as a management tool and the other perspective perceives the business plan as curb of creativity. We start with discussing the business plan as a management tool.

By far, this view of the business plan is most commonly applied. This perception follows a rational logic that perceives the business plan as a tool to manage and plan the future of an organisation. Wickham (2004) characterises the business plan as an entrepreneurial tool for the purpose of goal-oriented exploitation of opportunities, and Delmar and Shane write about planning: *"We argue that business planning helps firm founders to undertake venture development activities because planning facilitates goal attainment in many domains of human actions ... Specifically, we argue that planning helps firm founders to make decisions more quickly than with trial-and-error learning; and to turn abstract goals into concrete operational activities more efficiently"* (Delmar & Shane 2003: 1166).

According to Delmar & Shane (2003), the use of the business plan has three overall advantages: 1) The business plan and the planning process can be used for making decision-making processes more effective by identifying lack of information before (financial) resources are tightened. 2) The business plan is a tool to control supply and demand of resources in a way that avoids emergence of bottlenecks. 3) The business plan is a way to identify the activities that should be initiated in order to maintain the targets that are set within the time framework.

Schilit considers the business plan as a management tool and describes it like this: *"What is a business plan? Essentially, it is a vehicle to: 1) Assess the current and future state of an organization and its environment; 2) Delineate long-range and short-range objectives based on this assessment; and 3) Develop appropriate action guidelines to achieve these objectives. It is clearly the results of diligent market research and sound financial projections"* (Schilit 1987: 13).

When you perceive the business plan as a management tool, it is associated with a conviction that the future can be predicted. March (1995) talks about some preconditions that should be present in order to make the planning, in a completely rational sense, possible:

■ Knowledge of the alternatives of the future
■ Knowledge of the consequences of these alternatives
■ Presence of a consistent number of preferences
■ A decision criterium/the best solution

Thus, the perception of the business plan as a management tool is built on some preconditions about the entrepreneur knowing the different alternatives applying to the future, as for instance in which ways the market is likely to develop. Effectively this means that an entrepreneur is capable of seeing through the consequences of the alternative – what does it mean to the entrepreneur if the market develops in accordance with the various alternatives? And later on, while moving through time and place, the entrepreneur maintains a consistent set of preferences in relation to these alternatives and is therefore able to make a rational decision. Even though some are very critical towards these preconditions, the people advocating the business plan as a management instrument are often convinced that even though the preconditions are only valid to a certain extent, it always makes sense to stay in control through the entrepreneurial process instead of losing one's way in the process because of lack of planning.

Thus, the advocates of the business plan as a management tool are not necessarily unshakable in their confidence in the above-listed preconditions. They are simply more interested in management than accidental behaviour. Actually, many of them are critical in their approach in comparison to the previously mentioned preconditions put forward by March (1995). Those who advocate the business plan often profess to bounded rationality (Simon 1947) where people (including entrepreneurs) are considered as individuals who are not capable of collecting and treating the necessary information to predict and control their future completely rationally. People try to act rationally but their behaviour remains rationally bounded, partly because they cannot handle the information which is present and partly because they cannot analyse and treat it sufficiently rationally. The advocates of the business plan also acknowledge that it is not possible to determine the consequences of the different alternatives completely. Finally, they acknowledge that people do not have consistent preferences through time and place. What an entrepreneur wants at a certain time can easily change over time.

Consequently, advocates of the business plan as a management tool are not naive as regards the preconditions on which their conviction is based. They are conscious of the fact that people are only capable of acting in a bounded rational way. However, they still acknowledge the importance of planning and the importance of the business plan as a tool to control this process.

The business plan as a curb of creativity
Empirical investigations illustrate that planning does not have any positive influence on entrepreneurs' achievements. Honig and Karlsson write for instance, *"We found that those who wrote business plans were no more likely to persist in nascent activity as compared to non-planners"* (Honig & Karlsson 2004: 43). These investigations have given rise to the discussion of other logics pertaining to human behaviour. The logic that characterises the planning approach and the perception of the business plan as a management tool is what can be referred to as logic of consequentiality. It is about prediction and prioritising from the perspective of the entrepreneur's preferences compared with the alternatives with the most profitable consequences in the future. However, something seems to indicate that other logics can also be in play.

It is likely that some entrepreneurs use experiences from the past (experience-based logic). They simply use experiences to carry through the entrepreneurial process once more. In such situations, it is likely that the knowledge from the experiences that come into play in many ways is intangible and difficult to describe. Nevertheless, it can still be of crucial value to the entrepreneur. Several empirical investigations show that entrepreneurs who have previous start-up experience are more likely to become successful than entrepreneurs who start an organisation for the first time. It might be because efficiency in the experience-based logic can compensate for the advantages associated with the logic of consequentiality.

It is also likely that some entrepreneurs simply imitate what other entrepreneurs have done previously, hoping that this behaviour once again will turn out to be effective. Or it is done because the surroundings expect it from you. Honig and Karlsson write about these expectations from the surroundings that almost force the entrepreneur into a planning approach: *"It appears that new organizations do not write business plans to improve performance, rather, they do so in order to conform to institutionalized rules and to mimic the behaviour of other ... In sum, we propose that new organizations plan because they are reacting to how they are expected to plan, because they imitate other successful organizations in their fields that plan, or because they are told to plan"* (Honig & Karlsson 2004: 43).

Thus, there are a number of things that speak against the advantages associated with the business plan as a management tool, but we have not yet touched upon the most serious problem. We have discussed some reasons for writing a business plan and some logics that drive entrepreneurs, but we have maintained a certain amount of optimism as regards the business plan. Even if the plan is considered as something that is written in order to take into account the requirements of the surroundings, the plan nevertheless plays a crucial role in the entrepreneurial process.

However, some actually think that the business plan has a restricting effect on the entrepreneur's creativity. They claim that when entrepreneurs begin to work with business plans, they are forced into a structural way of thinking – a way of thinking that spoils their creativity. The important dimension in the planning process is strategic thinking and it requires creativity to a bigger extent than is the case with consequential and rational logic.

Successful planning requires that the entrepreneur thinks "out of the box" and breaks with the existing and dominating paradigms on the market. It requires creativity – and creativity and structure do not fit together. Thus, creativity is spoiled if you begin to work with business plans which exactly try to structure the process. The famous painter Picasso once wrote: *"Every act of creation is first of all an act of destruction."* This quotation illustrates the importance of breaking with existing and dominating paradigms in order to create new opportunities instead of filling out some existing structures which planning basically is about. Another quotation by the philosopher Søren Kierkegaard also illustrates the importance of creativity and breaking with the existing: *"The one who follows in others' footsteps, never gets in front."*

Opponents of perceiving the business plan as a management tool are exactly opponents because they prioritise creativity in favour of the logic of consequentiality in the entrepreneurial process. It is not because they ignore and fail to appreciate logic and rationality. They just think that creativity is more important. They consider entrepreneurship as art where opportunities to a greater extent are created and exploited as a result of a creative and intuitive process than of a logical and rational process. Ohmae, who is one of Japan's most famous writers within strategic thinking, writes, *"My message, as you will have guessed by now, is that successful business strategy results not from rigorous analysis but from a particular state of mind. In what I call the mind of the strategist, insight and a consequent drive for achievement, often amounting to a sense of mission, fuel a thought process which is basically creative and intuitive rather than rational"* (Ohmae 1982).

The business plan: a management tool or a curb of creativity?

Until now, the context, the contents and the process of the business plan have been discussed, and in addition, we have discussed a paradox concerning what role the business plan plays to the entrepreneur, namely: The business plan as a management tool or the business plan as a curb of creativity. The discussion is summarised in table 8.2.

Table 8.2: The paradox: management tool or creativity curb?

	Management tool	Creativity curb
What is the business plan?	Tool for planning	Creativity curb
Logic	Logic of consequentiality	Other types of logic (experience logic; imitation logic)
The importance of business development	Rationality over creativity	Creativity over rationality
Focus	Consistency	Break with the existing
Metaphor	Science	Art

The first perspective, which is the business plan as a management tool, perceives the business plan as a tool to plan the entrepreneurial process. This approach follows the logic of consequentiality which is prioritised over creativity in terms of its importance for the business development. Focus is on consistence in the analyses that are carried through and the recommendations that are suggested, so planning is considered a science.

The second perspective perceives, on the contrary, the business plan as a curb of creativity for the entrepreneur's chance to carry through the entrepreneurial process. The argument that attributes to this perspective is that planning often takes place from the perspective of other logics and there can be other reasons for writing a business plan than to follow traditional consequentiality logic. This approach prioritises creativity more than rational reasoning. It is about breaking with the existing and thinking beyond how players in the markets already think. It is about thinking "out of the box". Therefore, planning is considered more like an art than a science and the business plan is considered an impediment more than a help to carry through the entrepreneurial process.

■ A theoretical interpretation

Below, two different interpretations of the Back11Basics-story, which began this chapter, are outlined. In the interpretations, the story is linked to the theory above.

The management perspective

The immediate interpretation of the Back11Basics-story can easily follow the idea of the business plan as a management tool. This perception resembles the idea of the business plan and planning which Jesper in the case expresses. Both Jesper and Peter come from Gumlink which is a large organisation where they have probably been used to planning. By virtue of their concrete work at Gumlink, they have probably written many business plans. Thus, the business plan comes naturally to them also when they are going to start their own organisation. It is also clearly demonstrated in the entrepreneurs' story of Alice in Wonderland because in that story plans emerge as the only way ahead. As the entrepreneurs emphasise: Without any plans, it does not matter which way you move.

Therefore, they have defined vision, mission and goals and they have made an analysis of themselves and the market in order to evaluate their potential and opportunities. The plan has functioned as a management tool to them to find out whether things are going well or not. This is periodically checked via the specific milestones. At the same time, the plan has given them motivation and engagement to move ahead and to reach their objective. As Jesper mentions in the story, they follow the plan amazingly well. Altogether, this story of Back11Basics's use of a business plan can easily be seen as a classical example of the business plan as a management tool.

The curb of creativity-perspective

However, the story can also be perceived differently. It is likely that Jesper and Peter wrote the business plan in order to fulfil the expectations that are often posed to new organisations about production and business plans. Thus, it is more to align with these implicit expectations than it is the explicit intention of using the plan as a management tool. Their planning process and the business plan can therefore be considered as an attempt to act appropriately and legitimately in a given business context. It can, for instance, be an external pressure – for example from the bank – to have a business plan.

In addition, in the story the business plan can be perceived as a possible curb of creativity. It is likely that the fact that they define their goal in terms of money have restricted them. In any case, it is a little remarkable that they stick closely to their budget, especially when they did not know their products or customers before they made the budget. It seems to indicate that they felt satisfied when they reached the goals and therefore reduced their speed and paused on creativity. We can only guess whether they would have managed to get much further in terms of their turnover if they had not defined goals in terms of money.

It is also possible to perceive the business plan as a curb of creativity that spoiled their adventure in Eastern Europe. The fact that they think so much in structure and are so planning-oriented might have prevented them from adapting and thinking creatively enough to redefine their approach to the market in Eastern Europe and gain success there.

■ Practical tests of the theory

Based on the above thoughts and discussions, you should be ready to make your own experiments in order to understand the importance of the business plan to the entrepreneurial process. The following are suggestions for exercises.

Exercise 1: Interviewing an entrepreneur

Make an interview-guide with interview questions that contain two overall parts. The first part focuses on the overall advantages that the entrepreneur is likely to experience in connection with his or her use of business plans. The other part contains the disadvantages and problems that an entrepreneur can be confronted with in connection with the use of business plans. Then contact an entrepreneur and interview him or her with respect to testing theory presented in this chapter about business plans. Based on this, make your own opinion about the paradox: management tool or curb of creativity?

Exercise 2: Interviewing a financial adviser
Do you know a financial adviser or others who are engaged in investments in new business opportunities? Interview them about how they evaluate a business plan, what information they want and how they want it to be shaped.

Exercise 3: The perception in the media
Enter a database of written media (for example www.infomedia.dk) and search for the word "business plan". You can choose to make your searching broad or narrow either by choosing a short or a long time period or by choosing whether the word "business plan" should be part of the heading of the article or not. After that, read and analyse the articles and categorise them with respect to their different views of the business plan. After that, on the basis of your analysis, conclude how business plans are generally perceived in the media. Do they consider the business plan as a management tool or as a curb of creativity?

Exercise 4: Make a disposition for a business plan
Are you puzzling with a small idea? If that is not the case, then search your network to find out whether you know someone who is thinking about starting his or her own organisation. Then try to make an enlarged disposition dealing with what a business plan pertaining to this opportunity should contain and whom it should address. After that, when you have finished the disposition, you can continue working and write a complete business plan.

Literature

Delmar, F. & Shane, S. (2003). Does business planning facilitate the development of new ventures?, Strategic Management Journal, 24, 1165-1185.

Honig, B. & Karlsson, T. (2004). Institutional forces and the written business plan, Journal of Management, 30, 29-48.

Kuratko, D. F. & Hodgetts, R. M. (2004). Entrepreneurship – theory, process, practice. Mason: Thomson.

Madié, D. (2007). Farvel til forretningsplanen! Start af virksomhed kræver handling, Iværksætteren, 7, 34-36.

March, J. G. (1995). Fornuft og forandring – Ledelse i en verden beriget med uklarhed. Frederiksberg: Samfundslitteratur.

Ohmae, K. (1982). The mind of the strategist: The art of Japanese Business. New York: McGraw-Hill.

Schilit, W. K. (1987). How to write a winning business plan, Business Horison, September-October, 13-22.

Simon, H. A. (1947). Administrative behaviour. New York: The Free Press.

Wickham, P. A. (2004). Strategic entrepreneurship. London: Prentice Hall.

De Witt, B. & Meyer, R. (1998). Strategy – Process, content, context. London: Thomson.

198

Chapter 9

Intrapreneurship

As promised in chapter 1, we are now going to introduce you for intrapreneurship. In a few words, this phenomenon covers entrepreneurship within the context of an existing company. In this context, new opportunities, which should be evaluated and organised, are also discovered or created. The result can be new organising units, strategic reorganising or innovations inside the existing organisation. As is the case when an independent organisation is started, the driving seat is here taken by an individual or a group of persons which are often called "intrapreneurs".

However, intrapreneurship is very different from entrepreneurship. The context of existing companies sets up certain conditions for the entrepreneurial process. The individuals, who discover or create, evaluate and organise new opportunities inside an existing company, depend on whether it accepts or rejects the new opportunities. Thus, the intrapreneur is restricted by the company context. On the other hand, intrapreneurs can benefit from the many different resources present in the existing company. This chapter offers you knowledge of what intrapreneurship is and how the entrepreneurial process is created and run within the context of an existing company.

■ Meet practice

Now, you will be presented with a story that emphasises how an existing company has tried its hand at intrapreneurship. The attempt is stretched over a long period because the company continuously works at implementing successful intrapreneurship.

A golden egg of considerable size

In the year 2000, an astonishing success based on intrapreneurial activities is announced. A Danish owned company group sells one of their high-tech subsidiaries to an American group. The Danish group is NKT, Scandinavian Cable & Wire A/S, a 100-year-old industry conglomerate. The success is the billion sale of the high-tech subsidiary Giga A/S. The media reported the following about the sale: *"Hardly any business news has in recent years amazed Denmark as much as the story last year about the almost unknown NKT-subsidiary Giga."* It is a striking sale which makes the surrounding world realise that the NKT-group is in the middle of a transformation process. Before the sale of Giga A/S, the NKT-group was considered as an old industry group. For decades, NKT produced wires and cables to be used for the power supply and the telemarket via NKT Cables A/S. In addition, NKT produced cleaning materials via NKT Nilfisk-Advance A/S. However, Giga is not the first NKT experience in the development of high-tech projects or companies. However, it is the first experience with a golden egg.

Giga awakens intention of intrapreneurship
From the beginning of the 1980s, the expectations of Giga are limited. The opportunity on which Giga is based has potential, but the potential is far from certain. Therefore, NKT only provides a modest venture-capital investment. NKT actually believes so little in the opportunity that the design-group behind Giga gain remarkable shares in the project. The manager of the design group is ambitious and committed. In spite of NKT's reticent attitude, the manager influences the employees towards a further technological and commercial development. The manager *"realized from the very beginning that his employees were very efficient technicians and then he started to teach them what the engineer education is not famous of: to become market oriented in a future oriented little niche"* (Berlingske Tidende, 22 May 2001). Quickly, Giga experiences to be considered as one of the most technologically leading groups in a market that is rapidly growing. This development results in the sale of Giga, which makes the team behind Giga multi-millionaires.

Intrapreneurship is organised
In the wake of Giga, NKT gives a higher priority to their focus on new high-tech projects and companies, and the financial preconditions of these are dramatically improved. Organising of intrapreneurship in the NKT-group now takes place through an internal incubator – a kind of hatchery in the company which helps supporting new organisational units in their first years. In the incubator, the new units are developed through three levels: 1) A project is created based on a recently developed technology. The project can be internally situated or externally in a research environment. 2) When the technology is evaluated and it is estimated that a commercial market exists for it, a subsidiary with its own manager is created. 3) When the subsidiary has redeveloped its technology to a level where prototypes of products are available, it is recognised as a company with growth potential. Now, the technology is going to be tested in the market. If NKT estimates that the subsidiary is capable of surviving and growing, a decision is made whether the company should be kept within NKT or whether the company should be sold to an external buyer as was the case with Giga.

Attached to the incubator, an IT-based knowledge management system is created – a system that is to support the entrepreneurial projects and companies with the necessary knowledge. This system consists of persons from the established business areas of the group. With about 80 employees divided between 16 different fields of expertise, the system provides the high-tech projects and companies with a wide range of knowledge, which effectively means that their development can accelerate.

Apparently, the incubator is a success. In the beginning of 2002, the NKT-group's portfolio of new projects and companies already includes nine investments. Now, there is space for new ways of thinking in NKT. A manager in a company explains, *"On the whole, we were free to do what we wanted. Of course, we should describe that what we were doing was rational and that it was not totally naive."* The projects and the companies develop within three high-tech areas: (1) optical communication, (2) life science and (3) material technology. However, at the end of 2002, new times seem to come for the NKT-group.

On the decline
After some years with a lot of activity in the telecommunications market, a crisis emerges in the market. The gloomy prospects force NKT to reconsider their present intrapreneurship-policy. NKT puts the brake on its expectations of hatching out a new golden egg. A number of projects are closed, replaced or sold. Emphasis is now primarily on optical communication. From having a portfolio consisting of 11 projects and companies, NKT only has five investments left in 2003.

The estimation of the value of the projects and the companies are also intensified. So far, the value of the projects and the companies has been estimated on the basis of management and board meetings where the project managers and teams present the obtained results. In order to make the estimation depend less on individuals, a "Key Performance Indicator"-system is injected. The system measures, for instance, the technological, commercial and procedural development of the projects and the companies.

NKT also has to realise that the above-mentioned IT-based knowledge system, that is supposed to supply the incubator's projects and companies with knowledge, does not function optimally. The employees do not use the system to the degree it was intended. An intrapreneur from a company says, *"Whether that (the IT-based knowledge system) is the right construction or not I do not know. To us, it is perhaps not the right as regards economy. There are things in it that are very good (...) but I also believe that things in it could be improved further."* Of course, the team attached to the projects make use of certain administrative, technical and organisational competences from the system. But when it comes to specific problems associated with developing sufficiently fast, technologically and commercially, the system is not helpful. The reason is that the projects and the companies are based on new high technologies, in which only a minority of persons have insight. Consequently, the system is played down. The number of service areas and employees is reduced by half.

■ Your immediate interpretation

What does the story tell you about NKT's experience with intrapreneurship? How will you perceive the development in the first instance? The exercises mentioned below will support you in creating your perception of what is at work in the story, and thus how you can perceive intrapreneurship.

- ■ Think about what kind of challenges NKT are confronted with in the story. Then prioritise the challenges according to which of them you think are the most crucial in terms of understanding intrapreneurship.
- ■ Now, you are going to handle and solve the challenge that you prioritised most in connection with the above-mentioned exercise. Try to put yourself in the place of the Giga-manager. How would he solve the challenge concerned? Then put yourself in the role of the top manager in NKT. How would he solve the challenge?
- ■ Now reflect upon whether the two solutions are influenced by the two roles you play. Have the two different roles made you handle the challenge differently? Why/why not?

■ Theories of entrepreneurship

In spite of the fact that the heading of this section is "theories of entrepreneurship", the pivotal point is actually theory of intrapreneurship. The theory will support you in obtaining an understanding of what mechanisms are essential to discuss in the situation where new opportunities emerge, are evaluated and organised within the context of an existing company.

The theory of intrapreneurship can basically be divided into two perspectives. One of the perspectives emphasises that intrapreneurship is initiated and impelled by the top management. Consequently, intrapreneurship is created top-down. The argument for a top-down process is that support and initiatives from the top management is indispensable if intrapreneurship is supposed to be a reality. It is the constant attention and control attributing to the top management that creates enterprise and success. Another perspective emphasises that successful intrapreneurship is created by the fact that employees who are enthusiastic and have self-confidence carry through intrapreneurship. Thus, intrapreneurship is created bottom-up. The argument is that intrapreneurship can only be pushed forward by means of enthusiastic and enterprising employees who in their daily work discover or create the potential of renewal and innovation. Effectively, in this chapter, you are going to discuss intrapreneurship in the light of the paradox:

Top-down or bottom-up?

The background history

Before we discuss the paradox thoroughly, we will, however, delve into the background of intrapreneurship. Basically, intrapreneurship is a phenomenon which has been promoted through three waves of popularity which can be explained by reference to the macro-economic development from 1960 to 2002. The waves show that it is especially in periods when the economy is growing that intrapreneurship is put on the agenda of existing companies. The good economic situation makes it possible to pursue new opportunities. On the contrary, periods with economic recession do not require such a focus. Birkinshaw et al. talk about the three waves of popularity: *"The first ended in 1973 with the oil price shock and the ensuing recession. The second began in the early 1980s (...) and came to an end in the late 1980s (again because of recession). The third wave began during the great 1990s technology boom, and it peaked in 2000 before falling steeply. The third wave was driven by a combination of new technologies and also a bubble economy"* (Birkinshaw et al. 2002: 10). In connection with each of the three waves, more and more existing companies have shown an interest in intrapreneurship. The question is whether the experiences associated with the three waves of popularity will influence how a fourth generation of existing companies runs intrapreneurship. In other words, the question is *"... whether organizations will have learned the lessons in making the idea work"* (Birkinshaw et al. 2002: 10).

The factors which have restricted the work with intrapreneurship in the three periods of growth can be identified as:

- Most companies worked with multiple objectives instead of a specific objective of intrapreneurship.
- The support from the management was not sufficient. The result was that necessary competences for the development of entrepreneurial ideas and opportunities were not developed.
- The remuneration systems, such as shares to the employees, were not in place. There was simply no carrot held out to encourage the team behind the new opportunity.

Consequently, apparently there are many potential impediments which are to be overcome when intrapreneurship is approached. But what are the success criteria? The main criteria seem to be, "... *develop clear goals – and a structure to deliver on them (...) build specialised capabilities (...) separate venture units and parent firm (...) committed sponsorship from the highest level*" (Birkinshaw et al. 2002: 12-15).

Denmark and intrapreneurship
In spite of the many potentially restricting factors, Denmark is a country with a big representation of intrapreneurs (Hancock & Bager 2003). Intrapreneurs made up 46 percent of the Danish entrepreneurial activity in Denmark in 2003 and, in comparison with other countries, Denmark takes over a rare leading position as regards the use of existing companies as the starting point for discovery or creation of new opportunities and for evaluation and organising of them. The high share shows that the Danish population is positive towards challenges associated with intrapreneurship. One of the reasons is that the wage earners in Denmark have a relatively bigger job-autonomy at their workplaces than is the case in other countries (Dobbin & Boychuk 1999). Many Danish wage earners experience that they are able to make decisions themselves in their work. They do not depend so much on acceptance from higher levels in a company. There is also a positive attitude towards intrapreneurship in Danish companies – an attitude which reigns among the employees and the management. Many big companies prioritise intrapreneurship to a great extent. For instance, we can mention Danfoss, TDC and Dong. But the same tendency is actually also to be found among smaller companies (Evald 2005). To cut a long story short – in Denmark, there is a great interest in intrapreneurship and the conditions for it are good.

A diverse concept

The concept of intrapreneurship appeared later than the concept of entrepreneurship understood as starting a new and independent organisation. Therefore, intrapreneurship does not have a long tradition to lean on like entrepreneurship. Intrapreneurship is still a phenomenon that is under development. Even the term intrapreneurship is often discussed because competing terms are employed such as "corporate entrepreneurship", "dependent entrepreneurship" or "entrepreneurship in existing companies". We perceive these terms synonymously but in this chapter we only make use of the concept intrapreneurship.

Ramifications in intrapreneurship

Similarities exist between entrepreneurship as the start-up of an independent organisation and intrapreneurship. Both research fields take their starting point in entrepreneurial behaviour and in entrepreneurial actions, which refer to the activities involving discovery or creation of opportunities and evaluation and exploitation of these through organising.

However, differences also exist. A crucial difference between the two fields is the fact that intrapreneurship does not necessarily involve all of the activities that an existing company is involved in. Intrapreneurship can appear as an extract of the activities at which a company aims. This is for instance the case in the NKT-story in which the core businesses are run at the same time as the activities in the incubator. By contrast entrepreneurship involves all of the activities needed to create a new and independent organisation.

Nevertheless, the most crucial difference between entrepreneurship and intrapreneurship is that in entrepreneurship the process involves the establishment of one or several new and independent organisations by an individual or a group of persons who are independent of connections to an existing company (Sharma & Chrisman 1999). On the contrary, it is characteristic of intrapreneurship that the process is driven by an individual or a group of persons who develop new opportunities inside an existing company (Collins & Moore 1970). Collins & Moore (1970) are among the first to divide entrepreneurship research in two parts according to where the entrepreneurial activity takes place, either independently or dependent on an existing company. This is illustrated in figure 9.1 which also divides the intrapreneurship concept into three different ramifications.

Figure 9.1: Ramifications in the research field of intrapreneurship

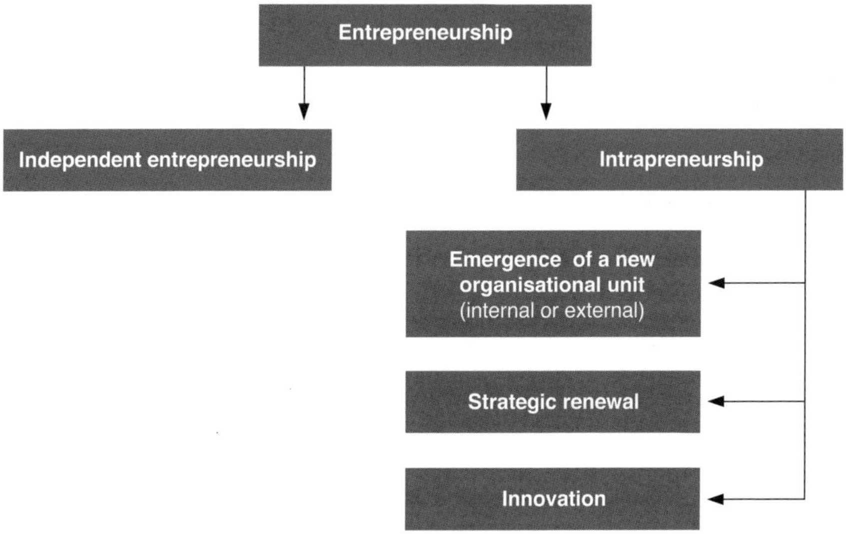

```
                        ┌─────────────────────────┐
                        │    Entrepreneurship     │
                        └─────────────────────────┘
                          │                    │
                          ▼                    ▼
┌──────────────────────────────┐   ┌──────────────────────────────┐
│ Independent entrepreneurship │   │       Intrapreneurship       │
└──────────────────────────────┘   └──────────────────────────────┘

                    ┌──────────────────────────────┐
                    │   Emergence  of a new        │◄───┐
                    │   organisational unit        │    │
                    │   (internal or external)     │    │
                    └──────────────────────────────┘    │
                                                         │
                    ┌──────────────────────────────┐    │
                    │      Strategic renewal       │◄───┤
                    └──────────────────────────────┘    │
                                                         │
                    ┌──────────────────────────────┐    │
                    │         Innovation           │◄───┘
                    └──────────────────────────────┘
```

As pinpointed, the figure illustrates that the intrapreneurship research field is influenced by three different ramifications or tendencies. To begin with, Guth & Ginsberg divide intrapreneurship into two big sub-groups which are: 1) the emergence of a new organisational unit and 2) strategic renewal (Guth & Ginsberg 1990). Strategic renewal means changes in an organisational strategy which can involve core competences, resource applications and competitive parameters at the level of project, company or group.

In 1999, the division is further refined by Sharma & Chrisman in the sense that they add a third sub-group: innovation. The addition happens because existing companies can create new organisational units or change their strategies without necessarily creating innovation. This is especially so if innovation is considered from a clear Schumpeterian perspective. In addition, a big organisation can create innovation without the two other elements as a part of that activity. For example, new combinations of knowledge can appear without the combinations necessarily resulting in new units or strategic renewal. In most cases, intrapreneurship will, however, involve all of the three aspects, which is also the case in the NKT story. The last refinement of intrapreneurship to be presented deals with the fact that the emergence of a new organisational unit can take place at an internal or external level in relation to the organisational settings of an existing company (Von Hippel

1977). This is marked with brackets in figure 9.1 under the category "emergence of a new organisational unit". Thus, the emergence of a new organisational unit can take place at an internal level when internal units are developed such as new working groups, projects or companies. The emergence of a new organisational unit can also take place at an external level when external units such as joint venture and spin-offs are established. In this chapter, we deal selectively with the perception of intrapreneurship as a matter of creating new units at an internal level. This approach is in accordance with Burgelman's (1983ab) definition of intrapreneurship. He perceives intrapreneurship as a process in which companies obtain differentiation through internal processes of development. This focus really puts the paradox: top-down and bottom-up on the agenda since intrapreneurship involves that the innovation should live side by side with the structures, routines and strategies pertaining to the existing organisation.

The extent of new thinking in intrapreneurship
The strengths and challenges which existing companies meet in their creation of intrapreneurship depend on the degree of innovation pertaining to the opportunities pursued. Are we dealing with an opportunity that is new to the existing organisation, new to the market or new to the world? The more innovative the opportunity the more the existing company is confronted with the challenge to create a new market for the opportunity. The result can be that the opportunity, which is to be exploited imposes a high degree of risk and complexity. On the other hand, the potential advantage of such an innovative opportunity is that the existing company obtains clear advantages in terms of differentiation and competition in comparison with its competitors.

In order to talk about the different degrees of innovation attached to intrapreneurship, the concepts incremental versus radical intrapreneurship are introduced. They should be perceived as a continuum. The first one refers to the fact that opportunities remain basically the same but are gradually being renewed. Company development is normally a gradual process in which products, processes etc. incrementally and slowly take new forms. On the contrary, radical intrapreneurship deals with how existing companies develop by leaps and bounds and come up with potential opportunities that are extremely different from the existing. This is illustrated in figure 9.2.

Figure 9.2: Incremental versus radical renewal

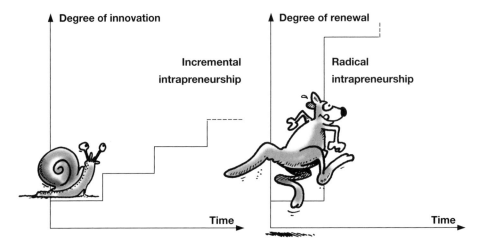

Degree of innovation

Incremental
intrapreneurship

Time

Degree of renewal

Radical
intrapreneurship

Time

The process behind intrapreneurship

What characterises the entrepreneurial process which is behind intrapreneurship? There are many different suggestions on how this process develops. Figure 9.3 is only one suggestion.

Figure 9.3: Intrapreneurship as a process

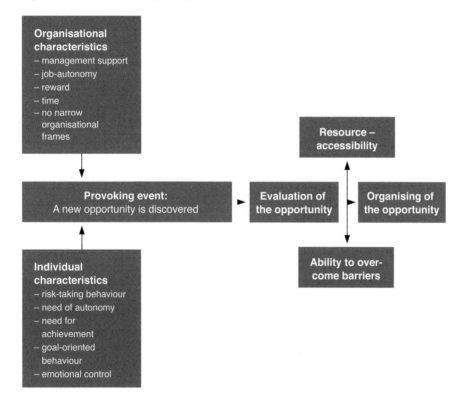

Source: Inspired by Hornsby et al. (1993), p. 31.

The figure illustrates what it takes to make individuals or groups of individuals take the initiative to intrapreneurship, discover or create opportunities and perhaps end up transforming these into concrete actions through evaluation and organising. Thus, the figure emphasises what happens through the intrapreneurship process.

The figure especially underpins how intrapreneurship is a product of two factors which still interact with each other, namely: The characteristics of the individuals and the organisational characteristics. In order to make these two factors interact with each other, a provoking event often appears: *"The decision to act intrapreneurially occurs as a result of an interaction between organizational characteristics, individual characteristics, and some kind of precipitating event. The precipitating event provides the impetus to behave intrapreneurially when other conditions are conducive to such"* (Hornsby et al. 1993: 33). To be more concrete, Zahra (1991) calls attention to how the provoking event, for example, can be development of new procedures or technologies, replacement of the management, a cooperation with or taking over of another company, a competitor's incipient taking over of market shares, rationalisations, changes in the customers' demand or economical changes. All this can result in individuals in an existing company discovering or creating a new opportunity. In the following, the contents of the figure will be explained in more detail.

Individual characteristics

In the course of time, a number of individual characteristics have been proven empirically to influence the process behind intrapreneurship. Many of the dimensions mentioned in figure 9.3 are obvious but two of them deserve elaboration. These are the need for achievement and emotional control. The need for achievement is, as mentioned in chapter 1, one of the first characteristics associated with entrepreneurs in the entrepreneurship research field. As a natural consequence, this character feature is also incorporated in the literature on intrapreneurship. Persons who prefer to be personally responsible for solving problems, to set up goals and reaching these goals are considered persons with a great need to achieve. The need for achievement is thus closely connected to other factors listed under individual characteristics such as goal-oriented behaviour and a need for autonomy. Emotional control is another type of character feature which is associated with intrapreneurs. This dimension deals with the way individuals or groups of individuals experience that they have control over every situation. They experience that they control what happens in the intrapreneurship process.

Organisational characteristics

As regards organisational characteristics, a couple of factors are considered important. They are, as a contrast to the individual characteristics, not so obvious and will therefore be dealt with more deeply. The support from the management includes for example fast adoption of the potential opportunities recognised by the employees, appreciation of persons who launch new potential opportunities, support of experimental projects and the accessibility of assuming venture capital. Job-autonomy refers to employees' opportunities to independently plan work-processes combined with absence of destructive criticism of mistakes made by the employees. Rewards refer to the recognition of personal challenge and responsibility, economic compensation depending on the effort, and the spread of the knowledge of potential opportunities that the employees have developed within the organisational hierarchy. The time-factor refers to the time the employees can spend on identifying new potential opportunities. This is for instance made possible through a moderate workload, avoidance of deadlines at every level of a person's work and support to time-consuming problem-solving projects. Hindering narrow organisational limitations is about avoiding standard procedures for all work-functions, reducing the dependence on narrow job-descriptions and rigid efficiency standards. All these aspects are considered as factors that promote the intrapreneurship process.

Activities in the intrapreneurship process
If no impediments appear in the interaction between organisational and individual characteristics, figure 9.3 suggests that individuals or groups of persons then initiate a number of activities. This can for instance be the making of business plans, market investigations and meetings with the top management about the size of the venture capital support. In other words, a lot of activities are started – activities which are about evaluation of the opportunity. Is it ready for the market and how? If the necessary resources are made accessible, and the number of organisational, cultural, business economic and individual barriers, which tend to appear through the process of emergence, are defeated, the process can result in an actual organising of the opportunity.

Top-down intrapreneurship
Now you know what the concept of intrapreneurship covers and you know the crucial events in the intrapreneurship process. However, the paradox of this chapter, which is top-down or bottom-up, pinpoints the existence of two different perspectives of what creates intrapreneurship.

From an overall perspective, the top-down processes are characterised by the fact that the management in existing companies takes the initiative through expressions of strategies, plans of actions and initiation of actual activities in the field. Thus, intrapreneurship is implemented from the top level of the organisation and down into the system which according to figure 9.3 above indicates that the organisational dimension dominates the intrapreneurship process. Top-down intrapreneurship means a controlled process since the management controls its development. Last but not least, a prevalent feature pertaining to top-down intrapreneurship is a close relation between the management of the existing company, the intrapreneurs and the development of the potential opportunity.

The close relation is, according to the top-down perspective, considered as appropriate. The relationship makes formal and informal sparring possible (Thornhill & Amit 2001). In addition, the intrapreneurs have easy access to the competences and resources, which the existing company has built up in the course of time.

Bottom-up intrapreneurship
As a contrast to the top-down perspective, the bottom-up perspective refers to the situation where intrapreneurship is created as a result of the initiative taken by the employees. Thus, intrapreneurship develops in existing companies from the bottom. According to figure 9.3, it implies that the individual dimension dominates in the explanation of the emergence of intrapreneurship in the organisation. In preference to control, the bottom-up perspective stresses autonomy more because the employees, through continuous renewal, break with the guidelines and plans performed by the management. In other words, the bottom-up perspective assumes a loose relation between the management of the existing company, the intrapreneurs and the potential opportunities which are discovered or created.

A too close relation between the mentioned players is, according to the bottom-up perspective, assumed to kill the entrepreneurial and innovative work environment which characterises the team behind the new potential opportunity (Birkinshaw et al. 2002). The reason is that it is explicitly or implicitly expected that the conventions, structures, rules and values applying to the existing company will be taken into account when new potential opportunities are developed (Day 1994). Consequently, this might result in a limitation of the creative development which the development of the opportunities requires. Thus, a high level of autonomy in connection with intrapreneurship is preferable.

Top-down and bottom-up
In order to go more thoroughly into the difference between top-down and bottom-up processes, we introduce Burgelman (1983ab). He is engaged in how strategies concerning intrapreneurship emerge and get shaped in large companies. Figure 9.4 shows in one figure both the top-down and bottom-up perspective.

Entrepreneurship in theory and practice

Figure 9.4: Top-down and bottom-up processes

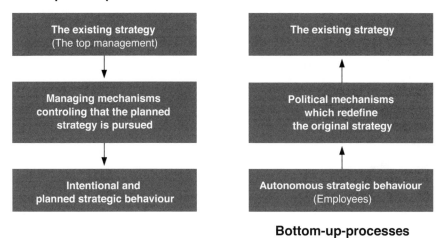

Top-down-processes

Source: Inspired by Burgelman (1983a), p. 225.

According to the left side of the figure, the point of departure for existing companies is a well-formulated and official strategy which tells the employees in which
direction the company wants to develop. To make sure that the employees in
the existing company act in accordance with the strategy, the top management
can carry out a number of administrative mechanisms. As such, the mechanisms
are behaviour controlling. They make the employee follow the direction which
is pointed out in the strategy. The administrative mechanisms either motivate or
punish the employees to display strategic behaviour, which the top management
wishes. That is what Burgelman considers as top-down controlled entrepreneurial
activities and processes.

Now to the right side of the figure. Since most employees are at the operational
level where day-to-day decisions are to be made, new potential opportunities
emerge all of the time – opportunities for how challenges can be solved, improved
or contested quite differently than hitherto. In some cases, the new potential opportunities can differ dramatically from the planned and intended strategy. If the
new opportunities turn out to be successful, a number of political mechanisms
unfold. The political mechanisms could be discussions of the existing strategy so
the top management becomes acquainted with the fact that there are alternative

ways of solving challenges. *"Political mechanisms through which middle managers question the current concept of strategy, and provide top management with the opportunity to rationalize, retroactively, successful autonomous strategic behaviour"* (Burgelman 1983b: 1352). In that way, the official strategy of the existing company is being re-evaluated and the new opportunities are integrated. In such cases, we are, according to Burgelman, dealing with a bottom-up process which creates and shapes the official strategy.

However, it is Burgelman's (1983b) main argument that strategies concerning intrapreneurship emerge from and are shaped by three connected activities that persons at different hierarchical levels in the existing company take care of. The behaviour and the actions, which top managers, middle managers and employees show, influence strategies about intrapreneurship. Strategies about intrapreneurship are not only either planned intentions that are created and formed top-down or strategies that emerge and are shaped bottom-up. They are a result of both top-down and bottom-up processes. Actually, it is a widespread assumption within the entrepreneurship literature that the balance between top-down and bottom-up processes is crucial for successful intrapreneurship. *"Many ventures fail because parent corporations provide the venture with inadequate support or autonomy. Paradoxically, to surmount this problem, some corporations grant ventures so free rein that the ventures incur large losses (...) how can corporations manage these extremes by providing autonomy while maintaining damage control"* (Simon et al. 1999: 145).

About creating a balance
In order to create successful intrapreneurship it is important to find a balance between top-down management and bottom-up initiatives. Thus, both control and autonomy are necessary to create intrapreneurship. Traditionally, the literature has primarily focused on how large companies can maximise the probability that new opportunities achieve success through a high autonomy level with ample room for bottom-up processes. However, there are several examples of how existing companies which give autonomy to their new projects and companies are not guaranteed the success of the new opportunities. Too much autonomy can be just as fatal to the realisation of new opportunities as too much control through top-down processes (Block & MacMillan 1993).

However, Thornhill & Amit (2001) emphasise that the need for social acceptance, support and control from the top management should be viewed over time. For the majority of the new ventures, the more they mature, the less the need for financial control. The social acceptance and support from the top management remains, however, important regardless of the age of the new ventures. However, there are also a few empirical results which oppose that idea. Over time, a few new companies experience an increased focus on financial targets simultaneous with diminished involvement from the top management. These results also make sense since financial independence often give rise to bigger financial responsibility. Finally, a company that achieves both independence and responsibility will have a reduced need for backing by the management.

But how is the balance between top-down and bottom-up processes to be created? There are many approaches. Simon et al. (1999) recommend that existing companies choose three persons to take care of the interests of new ventures and the existing company when intrapreneurship is being implemented. The combination of three persons should make sure that new ventures, on the one hand, get sufficient autonomy to develop. On the other hand, the combination should also secure continuous control of the new ventures.

One of the three persons should be the manager of the new venture. His or her task is to run the new venture and make sure that it provides the resources that are needed in order to secure its development. Thus, the purpose of the manager is primarily to take care of the interests of the new company. Another one is chosen as a "Godfather". Typically, it will be a centrally placed person whom the existing company points out to help the new company in its development. The Godfather's task is primarily to protect the new company from the bureaucracy of the existing company and make sure that the resources which are crucial for the development of the company are provided.

Finally, an "Ombudsman" should be selected by the existing company. Typically, it will be a centrally placed person in the existing company – for example a person from the management. The task of this person is primarily to take care of the interests of the existing company. This means that the investment which the new venture is an expression of is being evaluated all the time in relation to the interests of the existing company. The roles of the three persons are clarified in table 9.1.

Table 9.1: The balance between top-down and bottom-up

The Manager	The "Godfather"	The "Ombudsman"
Runs the new venture and makes sure that the need for autonomy will be met	Protects the new venture against organisational resistance from the existing company – helps providing autonomy	Keeps an eye on the progress made by each of the new ventures and balances the need for autonomy and control
Creates and develops new things	Argues for a high level of support and against removal of support during crisis periods	Decides which markets each of the new ventures should aim at. This is based on an estimation of what suits the interests of the existing company
Pursues aggressive strategies	Blocks the intervention of the existing company in everyday activities in the new venture	Decides number and size of the company-portfolio attributing to the existing company
Shapes the culture in the new ventures based on creativity and actions	Opposes insufficient rewarding systems and unfair punishment	Makes use of milestones in order to decide the support and reward of the new ventures

Source: Inspired by Simon et al. (1999), p. 157.

Intrapreneurship: top-down or bottom-up?

So far, you learned how the process behind intrapreneurship can be handled and what kinds of mechanisms create it. Especially two perspectives can be spotted – two perspectives which emphasise that a top-down or a bottom-up approach respectively is appropriate in order to obtain successful intrapreneurship. The two perspectives are summed up in table 9.2.

Table 9.2: The paradox: top-down or bottom-up?

	Top-down	Bottom-up
Hierarchical level	Top level	Operational level
Source of initiative	Top management	Employees
The process	Controlled behaviour	Autonomous behaviour
Tool	Administrative mechanisms	Political mechanisms
Mechanisms for implementation	Control and minimal autonomy	Autonomy and minimum control

The top-down perspective takes its starting point at the top level in the organisation. It is the top management that is supposed to take the initiative to the intrapreneurship process. The process is also a controlled process in which it is secured that the official objectives in the plans and strategies of the management are fulfilled. The management takes place through different administrative mechanisms such as different "whip/carrot"-mechanisms through which it is guaranteed that the operational level listens to the top level and understands the purpose of the official strategy. The success attached to the intrapreneurship process is secured through a high level of control and a very low level of autonomy.

The bottom-up perspective advocates a perception of the operational level as crucial to understanding how the process behind intrapreneurship emerges. It is the employees who take the intrapreneurial initiative. The actual process is controlled by autonomous behaviour. Thus, this approach leaves room for sudden brainwaves and renewing opportunities. Instead of administrative mechanisms, the process is controlled through political mechanisms through which the employees seek to create room, resources and support for the bottom-up process in the organisation. However, the precondition of a bottom-up process is that the management is reticent and leaves room for innovation by means of a high level of autonomy and a low level of control.

■ A theoretical interpretation

In the following, we will present you with our interpretation of the NKT case from the perspective of the theory and the paradox presented in this chapter.

The top-down perspective

According to a top-down interpretation, we will emphasise the following in the NKT story. Already before the official presentation of NKT's new strategy on intrapreneurship in 1999, the top management employs administrative mechanisms to motivate the employees to behave in accordance with the rules and systems that the top management thinks are necessary in order to create something new. The administrative mechanisms seem to regulate the behaviour of the employees. For instance, the team behind the subsidiary Giga is watched over so that the management can follow its technological and market development. In addition, the financial risk involved in the project is reduced at the same time as a remuneration system is introduced – a system which is to make the employees work more intensively on the development of the project. These administrative mechanisms follow, however, all the high technological projects which NKT starts up before introducing an official intrapreneurship policy. In the light of several years' experience with managing high technological projects, which by NKT is evaluated to be relatively radical and thus associated with a high degree of risk, the official intrapreneurship policy is finally introduced after a number of years. The provoking event is not necessarily the sale of Giga but perhaps rather a clarification of the fact that intrapreneurship can involve technological and commercial development which NKT is capable of controlling top-down to ensure a profit.

When the official strategy is finally introduced, the administrative mechanisms which are to control and support the carrying out of the intended and planned actions in accordance with the official strategy, are definitely helping to guarantee a precise course. The incubator functions as a supporting arrangement at the same time as the top management makes sure that the projects and the companies receive the necessary knowledge from the IT-based knowledge management system so that the technological market development can be optimised. And as soon as crises appear at the high technological markets that the projects and companies of NKT address, NKT is ready with interventions to ensure that their intrapreneurial initiatives are profitable all of the time. Thus, the projects and companies are under control so that the top management makes sure that they only keep their focus on the most profitable projects and companies.

On the basis of figure 9.4, we can conclude that the administrative mechanisms function all of the time and help keeping the employees on the right track. Thus, the NKT story can be perceived as an example of intrapreneurship which all of the time is created top-down, both before and after the introduction of the new official intrapreneurship strategy.

The bottom-up perspective

What does an approach to the NKT story from the perspective of a bottom-up perspective offer us? Such a perspective emphasises that it is only after a number of years with dedicated and ambitious employees who create new things, that intrapreneurship is officially put on the agenda in the top-management in NKT.

The way of gradually getting used to intrapreneurship, which NKT has been through, can be explained by the fact that NKT, when it starts, has no experience with intrapreneurship. Therefore, the company does not know how an official strategy should be shaped in the field. Thus, after some years the formulation of an official policy to aim at intrapreneurship can be seen as stimulated by the fact that the employees at the operational level have proved intrapreneurship possible. A bottom-up perspective will give reasons for the fact that existing companies and their top managers are reluctant to plunge into creating something new with no guarantee of success. Thus, new things are in most cases associated with lack of knowledge and uncertainty about the potential and therefore also a high risk. Due to the fact that NKT has gradually gained touch with what the intrapreneurship process involves, including how costly the process is, the company has become ready to implement an official strategy. Through the daily operations, the inspiration for the various elements associated with an official strategy is created. Once experiences in the field are collected, including convincing experience such as the Giga case, it is difficult for NKT to ignore the potential of creating something new and groundbreaking. Therefore, in this case, the provoking event is also the sale of the golden Giga-egg.

Even after the official strategy is adopted, with NKT aiming at intrapreneurship, the feedback from the operational level works. The IT-based knowledge system, which cannot satisfy the needs of the projects and the ventures, is changed and adjusted so that the system in a more purposeful way can support the projects and the ventures in their technological and commercial development. Thus, figure 9.4 seems to suggest that individuals or groups of persons with their autonomous behaviour influence the company strategy of NKT positively and create continuous change. The NKT story can therefore also be seen as an example of how intrapreneurship all the time is created bottom-up, both before and after a big revision of the official NKT strategy.

■ Practical tests of the theory

Now, time has come for you to develop your own understanding of intrapreneurship. The following exercises are for inspiration.

Exercise 1: Offer a bottom-up and top-down interpretation at the same time

What happens to the NKT story if you at the same time try to identify bottom-up and top-down processes? Which processes harmonise with each other and which are in conflict?

Exercise 2: Other companies which try their hand at intrapreneurship

Use the internet to find material about other existing companies which try their hand at intrapreneurship. Search at words such as "intrapreneur" and "intrapreneurship". Then discuss how different existing companies handle intrapreneurship and in what areas they share similarities with or are different from the NKT case.

Exercise 3: Strengths and challenges associated with intrapreneurship

On the basis of the collected material, you are now supposed to list the strengths and challenges which seem to influence existing companies when they try their hand at intrapreneurship. What strengths and challenges recur regardless of the size of the company, age and its attachment to a line of business? What strengths and challenges tend to be prevalent to a minor group of companies? Why is that apparently the case?

Exercise 4: Present your new knowledge to a company

Invite or visit an existing company which either wants to try intrapreneurship or already has experience with intrapreneurship. Present the knowledge that you have achieved on intrapreneurship. Together with the company, discuss how it handles intrapreneurship most effectively.

Literature

Birkinshaw, J., Batenburg, R. B. & Murray, G. (2002). Venturing to Succeed. Business Strategy Review 13(4), 10-17.

Block, Z. & MacMillan, I. C. (1993). Corporate Venturing: Creating New Businesses within the Firm, Harvard Business School Press, Boston, MA.

Burgelman, R. A. (1983a). A Process Model of Internal Corporate Venturing in the Diversified Major Firm, Administrative Science Quarterly 28(2), 223-244.

Burgelman, R. A. (1983b). Corporate entrepreneurship and strategic management: Insights from a process study, Management science 29(12), 1349-1364.

Collins, O. F. & Moore, D. G. (1970). The organization makers. New York: Appleton-Century-Crofts.

Day, D. L. (1994). Raising Radicals: Different Processes for Championing Innovative Corporate Ventures, Organization Science, 5(2), 148-172.

Dobbin, F. & Boychuk, T. (1999). National Employment Systems and Job Autonomy: Why Job Autonomy is High in the Nordic Countries and Low in the United States, Canada, and Australia, Organization Studies, 20(2), 257-291.

Evald, M. R. (2005). Corporate venturing blandt etablerede mindre danske virksomheder – en undersøgelse af tre casevirksomheder fra Kolding-området, udgivet i rapport-serien fra Center for Småvirksomhedsforskning: CESFO.

Evald, M. R. (2006). Corporate ventures kamp om politisk opbakning og legitimitet i nedgangsperioder, Ledelse og Erhvervsøkonomi, 3, 117-128.

Guth, W. D. & Ginsberg, A. (1990). Guest editors' introduction: Corporate entrepreneurship, Strategic Management Journal, 11.

Hancock, M. & Bager, T. (2003). Global Entrepreneurship Monitor: Denmark 2003, Børsens Forlag.

Hornsby, J. S., Naffziger, D. W., Kuratko, D. F. & Montagno, R. V. (1993). An interactive model of corporate entrepreneurship process, Entrepreneurship Theory and Practice, 17(2), 29-37.

Sharma, P. & Chrisman, J. J. (1999). Toward a reconciliation of the definitional issues in the field of corporate entrepreneurship, Entrepreneurship Theory and Practice, 23(3), 11-27.

Simon, M., Houghton, S. M. & Gurney, J. (1999). Succeeding at internal corporate venturing: roles needed to balance autonomy and control, Journal of Applied Management Studies, 8(2), 145-159.

Thornhill, S. & Amit, R. (2001). A dynamic perspective of internal fit in corporate venturing, Journal of Business Venturing, 16(1), 25-50.

Von Hippel, E. (1977). Successful and Failing Internal Corporate Ventures: An Empirical Analysis, Industrial Marketing Management, 6(3), 163-174.

Zahra, S. A. (1991). Predictors and financial outcomes of corporate entrepreneurship: An exploratory study, Journal of Business Venturing, 6(4), 259-285.

222

Chapter 10

Social entrepreneurship

In this chapter, we will deal with social entrepreneurship which is another context of entrepreneurship. As is the case with the building of an independent organisation and intrapreneurship in existing companies, social entrepreneurship is about discovery or creation of new opportunities, evaluation of these and finally it is about exploiting opportunities through the process of organising. From this perspective, there is nothing new under the sun. However, there are also differences between the types of entrepreneurship we have discussed so far and social entrepreneurship. The objective of entrepreneurship in the private commercial sector is normally to create economic value for the owners – to create profit. In social entrepreneurship, the objective is to create better conditions for people at a local as well as the global level while profit is a tool to obtain social objectives. In other words, the dictating vision of social entrepreneurship is social not economical.

When we are discussing social entrepreneurship in this case, it is in a broader sense of the concept "social" than the way it is normally used. It is not only about social sector services to socially weak persons. Our use of the concept "social" also takes into account activities in the culture and leisure life sectors as well as aid and projects aimed at people in the third world. All these aspects will be discussed more thoroughly in this chapter.

■ Meet practice

In the following, you will be acquainted with two stories about social entrepreneurship. At first sight, the two stories look very different because social entrepreneurship emerges so differently. The common denominator of the two stories is, however, that they can be interpreted as illustrations of social entrepreneurship.

Emphasising social and economic rights of elderly people

A new organisation, Ældre Sagen (In English: The Cause of Elderly People) is established in 1986 in continuation of an association called Ensomme Gamles Værn – EGV (In English: Lonely Elderly People), a voluntary association organising social work among old people. The overall purpose is: *"Elderly people should be acknowledged as equal citizens, elderly people should be able to make decisions about their own life, elderly people should have the opportunity to get by on their own conditions and weak elderly people should have proper and worthy care"* (www.aeldresagen.dk).

The protection of lonely old people already begins in 1910 with social and voluntary relief-work, primarily in the Copenhagen area. It involved students and women from the middle classes in Copenhagen who collected money at Christmas time for the poor old people in the city. Way into the 1960s, the association remained entirely based on private means and voluntary work but due to the rise of the Welfare State, it changed into a nationwide and more professional society in order to survive.

Bjarne Hastrup from Ældre Sagen.

Since the beginning of 1986, Ældre Sagen has obtained a strong position in Danish society and great political influence. All in all, approximately 2 out of 3 Danes know the association and a Gallup survey from 2007 shows that all in all 722,000 Danes read the members' magazine of Ældre Sagen. This means that the members' magazine of Ældre Sagen is among the five most read magazines in Denmark. Thus, Ældre Sagen is a society that is capable of attracting attention from the public to their cause. The number of members of Ældre Sagen has developed explosively. Already in 1987, 90,000 members had joined, far beyond the expected number of 10,000 members, and in 2007 there were 500,000 members. In 2008, Ældre Sagen had 520.000 members (every fourth Dane over 50 years was a member) and 10,000 active voluntary persons across 221 local groups all over the country. In addition, Ældre Sagen also has administrative head quarters in Copenhagen, counting approximately 100 employees, to service the groups and arrange excursions, communication and political initiatives.

Ældre Sagen offers a number of services to elderly people in the community. These are services such as free and impartial advisory service about social, legal, economic or housing matters, voluntary visitors, a "keep-fit" friend or a pc-supporter. In addition, the association arranges different activities all over the country and publishes, as mentioned before, a members' magazine and a newspaper which offers an overview over and analyses the discussion of politics concerning the elderly people. Finally, Ældre Sagen functions as a political pressure group on behalf of elderly people. Ældre Sagen asked, for instance, during the general election in 2007 *"all party leaders 6 crucial questions about health, welfare and the labour market. Now, it is a long time since the election came to an end. But the questions are the same. We will keep an eye on whether the politicians keep their words"* (www.aeldresagen.dk).

More than 89 percent of the income of the association comes from collected means, as for instance donations from partners, voluntary contributions, lottery, inheritance and membership fees. Thus, it is a considerable amount of money which Ældre Sagen administers. A personal membership, for instance, costs 220 Danish kroner (about 30 euro) a year. If we multiply by the 520,000 members, we find that the income from subscriptions counts no less than 114 million Danish kroner. According to the home page of Ældre Sagen, their financial means are used for the following activities: 16 percent for administration, 5 percent for projects, 8 percent for the member magazine, 29 percent for local and regional work and 43 percent for member advising, information, development and analysis.

The volunteers, who are attached to Ældre Sagen, do voluntary work, coordinate courses, talks and journeys or organise the political effort on the local authority level. An example of voluntary social work is the arrangement with voluntary visitors. A 27-year-old voluntary visitor to a 75-year-old woman says that it *"... is about human education and about feeling that you offer something and get something in return which can be used in your life (...) We have always had a close-knit family and I have enjoyed spending time with my grandparents. It is important to build on others' experiences and adventures. If we do not do that, we only understand a little of life even though we have all sorts of higher educations"* (www.aeldresagen.dk).

The architect behind the emergence of Ældre Sagen in 1986 through reorganisation of EGV is the former manager of Håndværksrådet (an association of SMEs in Denmark), Bjarne Hastrup. Håndværksrådet is a non-governmental organisation linked to the private commercial sector. The plan which he presents to reorganise

EGV is so convincing that he is requested to take the job as the first manager of the new organisation, Ældre Sagen – an offer which he accepts.

Bjarne Hastrup sees no gap between the overall social purpose of Ældre Sagen and running an effective and profitable organisation. The organisation has, however, in the 20 years of his leadership been able, year by year, to increase its total revenues. Since at the same time the costs have been under control, each and every year has shown a considerable profit which can be used to promote the overall social purpose. In 2007, he says, in connection with his 20th anniversary as manager of Ældre Sagen: *"I have learned how to earn money but also in which ways to spend the money"* (The news portal epn.dk, 5 July 2007).

IT-aids for cognitively disabled people

A student in pedagogy starts a website for persons with cognitive disabilities such as mentally retarded people, late developed people, people suffering from dyslexia and cognitively disabled people.

The idea of the homepage emerges when the pedagogue works in a social welfare institution where a user is not able to express himself linguistically: *"I (the pedagogue) had a job with an institution called Skovvænget. A user from Esbjerg (a provincial Danish town) lived there. He tried to explain that but his ability to express himself did not suffice. Then he showed me a picture of the four big white men [a sculpture which is the landmark of Esbjerg] and I asked if he meant Esbjerg. He said 'YES'!' That was the big redemption"* (JydskeVestkysten, 22 June 2005). By means of pictures, the user can communicate with the pedagogue. So, the pedagogue buys a digital camera and together they start using pictures as a helping tool in the communication. However, the problems are still not solved because the pictures are located on the computer in the institution. The visual support lacks when the user comes home. Therefore, the pedagogue develops the idea further and includes a home page which makes it possible for the user to use pictures in his communication regardless of where he is. At this point, Herbor.dk emerges, the simple home page with the big buttons.

The purpose of the home page is to make it possible for the users to maintain their own development, interests and experiences. Even in cases of turnover of staff members or moving, it will be possible to maintain the life story of the individual user: *"My job as self-employed in Herbor.dk is to develop IT-services for mentally disabled people, and in my professional life, I often meet the question: Why do mentally disabled people need to get on the internet? They have their comfortable*

A user and a pedagogue communicate via the homepage.

daily life in their welfare institutions, they do not need computers and internet! And every time I am asked the question, the audience must expect a committed talk from me. Because I think that all people in our society, disabled as well as not-disabled have the right to be a part of the general development and to profit by the new opportunities and technologies that emerge. And as a pedagogue, it is one of the fields of responsibility I have, namely to help influencing the technological development in a direction that is not only reserved for an elite or an A-team" (JydskeVestkysten, 6 October 2004).

There are almost 500 users of Herbor.dk. About 200 of them have bought subscription to the final product whereas approximately 250 are involved in projects. The projects are still an extraordinary activity associated with Herbor.dk. The users are helping to develop the program in cooperation with Herbor.dk. Users in the project still pay their subscription and in addition to this, they contribute to the further development of the site. A standard-private subscription costs 495 Danish kroner for six months or 949 for twelve months. It means that Herbor.dk, from an economic point of view, has made it possible for the pedagogue to deal with the company on a 100% basis. If we assume that approximately 500 users all take out a 12-month-subscription, it will result in an annual turnover of 474,500 Danish kroner. The payment from the development projects comes on top of this.

The program made by Herbor.dk resembles the email program Outlook. It is possible to keep a private calendar in Herbor.dk at the same time as email can be received and sent. However, the system is adjusted to the individual users so the only icons that are shown are those chosen by the user him- or herself. Since the system was presented for the first time in 2002, it has gone through several stages of development on the basis of input and good ideas from the users. It is, for instance, possible to have emails and picture-descriptions read aloud through synthetic speaking built in in all the functions. Furthermore, Herbor.dk has introduced a "pen-friend"-database in which the users can find friends through search criteria such as interests and geographic setting.

■ Your immediate interpretation

What do the two stories tell you about social entrepreneurship? The exercises mentioned below can support you in your process of understanding what characterises the phenomenon and of evaluating where the limit between social entrepreneurship and other types of entrepreneurship can be drawn.

- ■ Imagine that you wish to start a commercial organisation primarily with a view to profit. Mention the factors that you could imagine would motivate your engagement. Then imagine that you wish to start an organisation primarily for a social purpose. Then mention the factors that you could imagine would be motivating for your effort. Are there clear differences between the two lists? Try to explain similarities and differences.
- ■ Look at the two stories. Discuss to what extent and how they illustrate social entrepreneurship as an activity that creates better conditions for people at a local and a global level.
- ■ Social entrepreneurship is about creating better conditions for people through creation or discovery of new opportunities which are realised through the process of organising. Take a stand with respect to how innovative and new thinking the two stories are. Are the organisations to a high degree based on innovative opportunities? Is it, in your opinion, a demand that social opportunities be innovative by nature to qualify for social entrepreneurship?
- ■ Can you think of other examples of social entrepreneurship than the two represented in the two stories in which individuals or groups through creation or discovery of new opportunities have improved social conditions at a local or global level?

■ Theories of entrepreneurship

As mentioned, in its fundamental features social entrepreneurship resembles entrepreneurship which takes place in a commercial context. The main difference is that the motive behind social entrepreneurship is a wish of furthering social justice whereas entrepreneurship in a commercial context is aimed at profit (Johnson 2000).

A number of different perspectives on what social entrepreneurship covers exist. In this chapter, emphasis will especially be on two perspectives which consider the social and the financial element in social entrepreneurship differently in terms of being a means or a goal.

The first perspective on social entrepreneurship focuses on financial objectives as the final objectives and social objectives as a means to obtain the financial objectives. Emphasis of social entrepreneurship is, in other words, to create a business, and social elements are, in this perspective, reduced to a product in line with other commercial products. Since the final objective is to create a financially sustainable and profitable organisation, that type of entrepreneurship primarily takes place in a commercial context regardless of the fact that these organisations normally produce social services.

The second perspective primarily focuses on social elements. From this perspective, social objectives are the final objective and possible commercial exchanges only take place as a means to obtain the social objectives. Thus, social entrepreneurship is considered as an activity that is basically about creating a better world. This effort takes place within the context called the voluntary sector. It is called voluntary sector because a crucial part of the workload in these organisations originates from non-paid labour which, for instance, is the case of Ældre Sagen. The voluntary sector is also often called the non-profit sector.

Thus, in this chapter you will be presented with social entrepreneurship in the light of the paradox:

Business or a better world?

Introduction to social entrepreneurship

There are not many surveys showing how widespread social entrepreneurship is. This, however, is not the case in Great Britain. Here, the spreading of social entrepreneurship has been investigated several times (Harding & Cowling 2004; Harding 2006; Harding et al. 2007). The latest survey from 2007 shows that in 2005 almost 1.2 million people in Great Britain were engaged in social entrepreneurship. The entrepreneurs were about to start a social activity (less than 3 months old) or managed a new social activity (between 3 and 42 months old). If we compare the start-up rate within social entrepreneurship with commercial entrepreneurship understood as starting a new independent business organisation, it is approximately half as big (3.3 percent of the adult population are active within social entrepreneurship compared to 6.1 percent for entrepreneurship as the start-up of an independent business organisation). In addition, a further 1.5 percent of the workforce of Great Britain run well established social activities which are more than 42 months old. Thus, social entrepreneurship is a widely spread activity in Great Britain. Moreover, the way the activity influences society is pinpointed by the fact that the British Government has worked out that organisations with a social or environmental purpose account for a turnover of 27 billion pounds (Harding 2006).

The results from Great Britain indicate that social entrepreneurship in Denmark can also be a significant activity. That this is presumably the case is emphasised by a Danish investigation which has estimated the proportion of the voluntary sector in Denmark (Boje et al. 2006). The sector is defined in the investigation as social activities and types of organisations that are neither public nor commercial and which do not belong to the family. In a Danish context, the voluntary sector also contains a number of cultural activities and sports activities.

In the survey the proportion of the voluntary sector is estimated to *"... 65,000 associations, 6,800 independent institutions and 6,600 non-profit funds with a general purpose. In addition come almost 3,000 nationwide associations" (Boje et al. 2006: 74). It is further estimated that the sector creates value equivalent of "(...) 9.6 percent of the total Danish gross national product in 2004" or a "... total value of 134.5 billion kroner."* (Boje et al. 2006: 12). Thus, it is a considerable amount of the Danes who contribute to social activities within the voluntary sector, and the significance to the Danish economy is big.

However, these results about the dissemination of social entrepreneurship in Great Britain and in the voluntary sector in Denmark can be disputed because the proportion depends a lot on the definition of social entrepreneurship. Since social entrepreneurship is still an activity which is not particularly explored, there are disagreements as to how the phenomenon should be understood and defined. *"Social entrepreneurship (…) is not a tidy concept. Its untidiness has been argued to be a reflection of the way that the world is (…) It behooves anyone using the concept of social entrepreneurship to make it clear the sense he/she attaches to it"* (Peredo & McLean 2006: 64).

In spite of the disagreements about the definition of social entrepreneurship, it is widely believed that social entrepreneurship is about obtaining social objectives so that human conditions are improved at a local and global level. But this is where the agreement ends. The disagreement is about which priority social objectives have compared to financial objectives.

Social entrepreneurship as a continuum

For the purpose of clarifying which perceptions of social entrepreneurship exist, the continuum in table 10.1 can be used. The continuum contains two extreme perspectives of social entrepreneurship. The one perspective defines social entrepreneurship as activities that are basically dictated by social objectives – a better world. The other perspective perceives entrepreneurship as an activity where social objectives are only present to a certain extent but where business and thus financial objectives are actually the primary focus. In between the two perspectives exists a third perception of social entrepreneurship – a perception which combines social and financial objectives in a more balanced way even though the social purpose is basically the primary one.

Table 10.1: A continuum perception of social entrepreneurship

	Priority of aims	The importance of commercial exchange and profit	Examples
A better world	The formulated, overall objective is entirely social (but subordinate financial objectives can be found)	Commercial exchange and profit are only created with the purpose of supporting the social objectives	Doctors without Borders (Médecins Sans Frontières) (www.msf.dk)
	The formulated, overall objective is primarily social	Commercial exchange and profit are created for supporting social objectives and making the business financially sustainable	The Danish Merkur Bank (www.merkurbank.dk)
Business	The overall objective is entirely financial (but subordinate social objectives can be found)	Commercial exchange and profit are created for making the business financially sustainable	Vestergaard Frandsen (www.vestergaard-frandsen.com)

Source: Inspired by Peredo & McLean (2006), p. 63.

To create a better world

The one perspective which is illustrated in figure 10.1 emphasises, as mentioned, strongly that it is only social objectives which carry social entrepreneurship: *"At one extreme are those who hold that some goal(s) must be the 'exclusive' aim of the social entrepreneur"* (Peredo & McLean 2006: 59). The perspective is also expressed by Dees in the following way: *"For a social entrepreneur, the social mission is fundamental. This is a mission of social improvement that cannot be reduced to creating private benefits (financial returns or consumption benefits) for individuals. Making a profit, creating wealth, or serving the desires of customers may be part of the model, but these are means to a social end, not the end in itself. Profit is not the gauge of value creation; nor is customer satisfaction; social impact is the gauge"* (Dees 1998: 5).

The organisation "Doctors without Borders" is an example of a voluntary, non-profit organisation which is in accordance with Dees' definition of social entrepreneurship. The organisation is a *"... private, international, humanitarian organisation that provides medical relief to victims of conflicts and disasters all over the world"* (www.msf.dk). The organisation was established in Paris in 1971. The founders were a group of French doctors who in the previous years had assisted during the civil war in Biafra in Nigeria and journalists who supported the idea of independent and barrier-breaking relief in areas where nobody else could operate. As a result of annoyance towards strict rules and bureaucracy during the civil war in Nigeria and a consequence of the fact that the doctors felt that they were prevented from making decisions, they wanted an independent organisation that could provide the entire world with relief and put the humanitarian discussion of international solidarity on the agenda. In 2008, the organisation had offices in 19 countries and their projects were running in more than 60 countries.

In the intersection between social and financial objectives
As it appears from table 10.1, there is a modified version of the above-mentioned perspective. It emphasises that in social entrepreneurship, social as well as financial objectives can be combined with each other even though the social objective is still the primary one. Thus, it is wrong to restrict the phenomenon social entrepreneurship to the voluntary sector because social entrepreneurship can also be created in the commercial sector. In practice, social entrepreneurship can therefore involve social and commercial considerations at the same time which makes the border between the two sectors "not only vague but porous" (Peredo & McLean 2006: 61). Social entrepreneurship *"blur the traditional boundaries between the public, private and non-profit sector, and emphasize hybrid models of for-profit and non-profit activities"* (Johnson 2000: 1).

The argument for considering activities which combine social objectives with financial objectives are that *"... a lack of financial resources or capital can constrain social entrepreneurship and restrict the ability of social entrepreneurs to create social capital"* (Thompson et al. 2000: 330). Therefore, the definition of social entrepreneurship is not about restricting social entrepreneurship to a certain context. Instead, this perception of social entrepreneurship focuses on whether the activities which people get started actually create better social conditions or not.

A Danish example showing that it is possible to balance between social and financial objectives is the Danish "Merkur Bank". The bank can be seen as a hybrid type of organisation because it can be perceived as belonging to the private sector as well as to the voluntary sector: *"In Merkur, we do not only talk about common responsibility because it is topical. Since we established Merkur 25 years ago, we have maintained our wish to run a socially responsible company that shows consideration for people and the environment. And we will continue doing that (...) If you choose Merkur as your financial institution, you encourage a sustainable social development. In Merkur, it is possible for you as a deposit customer to influence what your money should be lent for. At the same time, we make an economic, social, ecological and cultural evaluation before we lend money to a project"* (www.merkurbank.dk). Actually, more than 75 percent of Merkur's total loans are lent to three main areas which cover ecology, social and cultural activities. The rest of Merkur's loans are spent on housing and loans taken over from other financial institutions. Thus, Merkur Bank attempts to balance between the objective of creating a better world and at the same time to create a profitable economic business. The balance between social and economic objectives is often referred to as the double bottom line (Dees et al. 2002: 173).

Social entrepreneurship as business

So far, we have looked at two versions that agree about the fact that social objectives are more important than financial objectives in social entrepreneurship. The disagreement among them finds expression in to what extent they acknowledge the use of financial objectives to fulfil social objectives.

However, there are also organisations where social objectives are not only mixed with financial objectives but are actually prioritised lower than the financial objectives. The argument for also understanding this type of activity as social entrepreneurship is that all activities, which in one way or another improve the social conditions of people, are worth acknowledging since, at the end of the day, it is this type of activity that is contributing to the creation of a better world (Austin et al. 2006) An example of a Danish organisation which, on the one hand, is helping to create better conditions for people in the Third World but which, on the other hand, makes no secret of the fact that the organisation is not a relief-project, is the company Vestergaard Frandsen. The products which Vestergaard Frandsen produces are, among other things, a mosquito net impregnated with chemicals that stop the ability of the mosquito to fly and thus to transmit malaria. It is, for instance, used at refugee camps. In addition, Vestergaard Frandsen is about to launch a water cleaning tool called Life Straw. The straw is approximately 25 cm long and contains an advanced filter that cleanses water. The filter makes it possible to drink water from polluted rivers or waterholes. This remarkably improves the access to water for poor people, especially in developing countries where the lack of access to clear water is a huge health problem. The managing director expresses the balance between financial and social objectives in this way: *"Our business is about 'doing business and doing good'. But business always comes first (...) It is possible to say that we show that the one thing does not exclude the other. But if the economy was of secondary importance, we might as well hand over the keys to the Red Cross. There are lots of problems in this world that call out for entrepreneurship. It is just a question of rolling up one's sleeves and get started"* (Børsen, 23 February 2007).

The emergence tradition and the opportunity tradition
So far, in the discussion of social entrepreneurship, we have primarily focused on how the social element and the balance between the social element and the business are likely to be perceived. However, there are other discussions that are essential. What has been discussed several times throughout the book is what it takes to be enterprising. In chapter 1, we discussed two different traditions with different views of what can be characterised as entrepreneurship: the emergence tradition and the opportunity tradition. According to the emergence tradition, behaviour can be characterised as enterprising if it involves the creation of a new organisation regardless of the extent of innovation. As opposed to this, the opportunity tradition characterises behaviour as enterprising if we are dealing with creation or discovery and exploitation of innovative and ground-breaking opportunities regardless of whether it will result in a new organisation or not. This discussion is also prevalent within the theory of social entrepreneurship.

Like the emergence tradition, Peredo and McLean define an activity as enterprising if it is realised with social goals in view and results in the creation of a new organisation. *"Social entrepreneurship is sometimes understood merely as the initiation and/or management of a social enterprise"* (Peredo & McLean 2006: 58).

Nevertheless, at the same time, some think that behaviour can only be characterised as social entrepreneurship if it involves activities with an innovative and social value. That understanding corresponds to the previously mentioned opportunity tradition. Dees pinpoints, for instance, that social entrepreneurs are innovative: *"They break new ground, develop new models, and pioneer new approaches (...) Those who are more innovative in their work and who create more significant social improvements will naturally be seen as more entrepreneurial. The truly Schumpeterian social entrepreneurs will significantly reform or revolutionize their industries"* (Dees 1998: 4). In order to characterise a new activity as social entrepreneurship, the activity should be innovative and represent new thoughts whereas it does not matter whether the activity involves the creation of a new organisation.

Social entrepreneurship: Business or a better world?

So far, we have discussed different perspectives of social entrepreneurship. These are summed up in table 10.2.

Table 10.2: The paradox: business or a better world?

	Business	A better world
Primary objective	Financial	Social
Sector	The for-profit sector	The voluntary sector/non-profit sector
Motive	To create a financially sustainable business	To create a better world and better conditions for people
The relevance of commercial exchange	Crucial for the success and development of the organisation	Supporting the primary social objectives
The relevance of social output	A product similar to other commercial products	The deeper purpose of creating social entrepreneurship

It appears from the table that the business perspective stresses that social entrepreneurship is considered as an activity which results in social services but where the overall objective is financial in the attempt to create a financially sustainable business. Thus, it is the commercial exchange that is considered as decisive to success and the social product becomes a product in line with other commercial products. On the contrary, the other perspective promotes that the overall objective associated with social entrepreneurship is to create a better world. Financial objectives are considered as tools to obtain the overall social objective. This type of social entrepreneurship belongs primarily to the voluntary sector where the entire purpose is to create better conditions for people.

Apart from the two perspectives, there are a vast number of variants that to different extents emphasise the relation between social and financial objectives. This actually means that social entrepreneurship can take place everywhere in society. The activities do not take place either within the voluntary sector or within the pro-profit sector. There are a vast number of hybrid forms of social entrepreneurship.

■ A theoretical interpretation

In the following, you will be presented with our interpretation of the two stories in the beginning of this chapter. At first, the stories will be interpreted in the light of the business perspective and after that, the perspective that focuses on social entrepreneurship as creation of a better world will be emphasised.

The business perspective

Both of the stories you were presented with in the beginning of this chapter can be interpreted from the business perspective. In both stories, it is obvious that the financial foundation plays a crucial role for the ability of people to get engaged in the social activities. With no sustainable business, improved social conditions cannot be achieved since people cannot live on good intentions alone.

Ældre Sagen originated in 1990. At that time, as is the case today, the financial foundation was crucial in the sense that it made it possible for the association to improve the quality of life of elderly people. In the beginning, especially private donations made it possible for the association to help elderly people. Today, it is the membership fees make it possible for it to operate nationally and to be capable of holding various arrangements and supply elderly people with services. The membership fees alone supply the association with an income of approximately 114 million Danish kroner a year, which indicates that the organisation has obtained its own independent life. Without a financially sustainable business, the work of the association would soon be starving and become remarkably complicated. Although the association sells itself as having a primarily social purpose, the financial purpose of it should not be underestimated since it is what keeps the wheels turning and motivates people to help.

The same goes for the home page Herbor.dk for cognitively disabled people. Also in this case, the foundation of the home page can be interpreted as profit. Without a financially sustainable business, the home page Herbor.dk would not exist and could not continue developing functions in the system which make sure that different groups of cognitively disabled people can use the tool. The idea behind Herbor.dk emerged some time ago by pure chance but the pedagogue soon sees an opportunity to shape his own organisation and profit from the good idea. The pedagogue sees opportunities to improve his quality of life by means of an economic improvement. The approximately 500 customers provide a turnover of 470,000 Danish kroner a year, and to this should be added the revenue from development projects that flow from the 250 projects.

The better-world perspective

At the same time, both stories can also be interpreted from the other side of the paradox which emphasises that entrepreneurship is about creating better conditions for people at a local and global level. In both stories, social engagement and a vision of creating better conditions can be seen as the driving motivation behind the activities that are started. At the same time, the economic objectives can be seen as secondary.

To Ældre Sagen, quality of life of elderly people has been the pivotal point as long as the association has existed. Ældre Sagen has mainly accomplished its social objectives by operating with a big and national voluntary corps of people who on their own initiatives and out of a desire try to create a better life at a local level for elderly people who need help. The membership fees are a financial help which makes sure that the nationwide work of the association through a central secretariat is supported and helped towards fulfilling the social objectives of Ældre Sagen.

Herbor.dk can also be seen as an example of the fact that social objectives are the driving force. The idea for the website for cognitively disabled people emerged when the needs of a user could not be satisfied. The pedagogue behind Herbor.dk experienced that the quality of life for many cognitively disabled people was not optimal since their daily life was characterised by misunderstandings and lack of communication and understanding between the users and the pedagogues. On his own initiative and with a desire to create better conditions for the cognitively disabled people, the pedagogue designed the home page Herbor.dk. Soon, the pedagogue experienced that the demand for the home page was enormous and that many different institutions experienced a need to develop the home page so that it could be adjusted to the exact needs of their users. Therefore, the pedagogue took the consequence and dedicated himself 100 percent to the development of the IT-tool so that the quality of life of cognitively disabled people could be improved. Thus, an independent organisation was established, but the salary which the pedagogue received was only a tool to reach the objective of improving the social conditions of cognitively disabled people.

■ Practical tests of the theory

Now once again time has come for you to enter into the research room and this time to test another crucial topic within the context of entrepreneurship, namely social entrepreneurship.

Exercise 1: The coverage of social entrepreneurship in the media

Find a number of articles about social entrepreneurship in different national newspapers. Then discuss the different attitudes that influence the discussion of social entrepreneurship. Which attitudes do you share and which do you not agree with? Argue why that is the case.

Exercise 2: "Uncle and aunt"

Watch the following video case at www.idea-textbook.dk: "Uncle and aunt". The case is about the start-up of a privately owned kindergarten. Does the case story deal with social entrepreneurship? To what extent does the story meet the requirement of creating value for other people by creating or discovering a new opportunity and realising it through the process of organising?

Exercise 3: Visit China

According to the weekly newsletter "MandagMorgen" published June 16 2008, the Chinese Government will invest billions of dollars in infrastructure improvement, education, health and new welfare systems. It is expected that the investments rise by 20-30 percent each year the following four years. The outstanding growth in China can create massive opportunities for organisations in Denmark and other countries that can supply solutions within this area. Your task is the following: Figure out, on the basis of the development in China, a social idea which you might profit from. Then investigate how you will turn the idea into an opportunity so that it can provide the background for a sustainable organisation.

Exercise 4: Skjødt's Publishing House

Watch the video case from Skjødt's Publishing House at www.idea-textbook.dk. The case deals with a 31-year-old student who starts her own consulting and publishing business with an ambition of translating and publishing the works of a certain author. Is this likely to be interpreted as social entrepreneurship? And how is the balance between social and financial objectives?

Literature

Austin, J., Stevenson, H. & Wei-Skillern, J. (2006). Social and commercial entrepreneurship: Same, different, or both?, Entrepreneurship, Theory and Practice, 30(1), 1-22.

Boje, T. P., Fridberg, T. & Ibsen, B. (2006). Den frivillige sektor i Danmark: Omfang og betydning, Copenhagen: Socialforskningsinstituttet.

Dees, J. G. (1998). The meaning of "Social Entrepreneurship." Standford University: Draft report for the Kauffman Center for Entrepreneurial Leadership.

Dees, J. G., Emerson, J. & Economy, P. (2002). Strategic tools for social entrepreneurs: Enhancing the performance of your enterprising nonprofit. New York: John Wiley & Sons. Inc.

Harding, R. & Cowling, M. (2004). Social Entrepreneurship Monitor: United Kingdom 2004, Barclays.

Harding, R. (2006). Social Entrepreneurship Monitor: United Kingdom 2006, Barclays.

Harding, R., Hart, M., Jones-Evans, D. & Levie, J. (2007). Global Entrepreneurship Monitor: United Kingdom 2007 Monitoring Report, London Business School.

Johnson, S. (2000). Literature Review on Social Entrepreneurship, Canadian Centre for social Entrepreneurship.

Peredo, A. M. & McLean, M. (2006). Social Entrepreneurship: A critical review of the concept, Journal of World Business, 41(1), 56-65.

Thompson, J., Alvy, G. & Lees, A. (2000). Social entrepreneurship – a new look at the people and the potential, Management Decision, 38(5), 328-338.

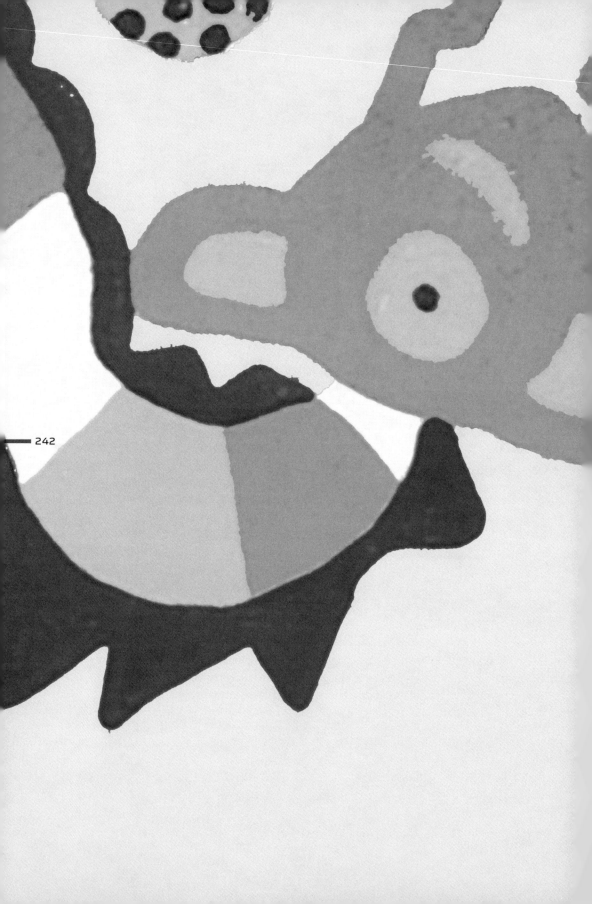

Chapter 11

Synthesis and conclusion

In your profession as an entrepreneur, you should prepare yourself for running the gauntlet between paradoxes. For instance, it is necessary to balance between planning and improvising. One moment, you are in the middle of a planning process, which means that you are dealing with paperwork and calculation. The next moment, you set free your inventive nature and your improvising behaviour. Sometimes, these processes take place synchronously and other times asynchronously. But regardless of the progress, as an entrepreneur you are a tightrope walker in the universe of paradoxes simply because these competences are needed if the entrepreneurial process is to be successful. In this closing part of the book, we want to cast a glance at the paradoxes which have been discussed throughout the book and pose the question: Is there a connection between them? Certainly, the entrepreneur experiences a connection in the practical world. But perhaps there is also a deeper theoretical connection in the sense that paradoxes might be connected in groups and perhaps it is possible to find a meta-paradox hidden in the pattern of the many paradoxes which have been presented in the preceding chapters.

■ The paradoxes in the book

To be an entrepreneur is about balancing in the universe of paradoxes. In other words, paradoxes are not a matter of choosing one thing in preference to another thing but a matter of finding the right balance in the specific situation. This choice varies depending on who you are and what process you aim to unfold. As an entrepreneur, you can well assume that it is not enough with one extremity regardless of how much you are attracted to it. It might be the case that a given entrepreneur loves the start-up process – the process in which the ideas start living, and there is room left for improvisation and nothing is finally decided. Another case might be an entrepreneur who is satisfied when the basic idea of the project is found and the process is about carrying out the idea through action, planning and organising. But regardless of the preferences, there are no entrepreneurial processes in which only one side of the paradox is present. Ideas are hardly conceived before the first immediate evaluation is made and in the organising process there is constantly a need for new ideas and solutions to how the products are likely to be presented, how the customers are cultivated, how the employees are recruited etc. Thus, entrepreneurs are, regardless of personal preferences and the stages of the process, in a universe of paradoxes where pragmatic "both-and" solutions rather than "either-or" solutions are needed. Therefore, it is possible to conclude that the entrepreneurs – or entrepreneurial teams – that control the paradoxes in the entrepreneurial process are the likely winners in the race between the many projects that are constantly started within every possible field.

That is the reason why in this textbook we have chosen to build up the chapters around some crucial paradoxes. We think that the paradoxes are important just as they are within organisation and management theory in general (Høbner et al. 2007). In addition, through the paradoxes we have pinpointed that certain paradoxes are crucial in the emergence phase whereas others are important in a later phase or related to certain contexts. Finally, we have aimed at focusing on the foundations of entrepreneurship, namely the discovery or creation of opportunities which are to be evaluated and exploited through organising in preference to more functional aspects such as financing and marketing. Let us begin with summing up the paradoxes as they have been presented in the introductory chapter of the book. The summing up is illustrated in table 11.1.

Table 11.1: The paradoxes in the book

Born	or	Made
Discovered	or	Created
Instrumental	or	Legitimate
Planning	or	Improvising
Exploit	or	Explore
Rational	or	Embedded
Management tool	or	Creativity curb
Top-down	or	Bottom-up
Business	or	A better world

Our point about presenting the paradoxes as two opposing perspectives on how entrepreneurship takes place is indicated by an "or" between the two perspectives of the various paradoxes. However, as is emphasised throughout the book, in most cases it is a matter of balancing between the apparently opposing perspectives on the same topic. Thus, it is not a choice to be made between extremities. The challenge to the entrepreneur or the team of entrepreneurs is to walk a tightrope between extremities. Therefore, both perspectives in a paradox can sometimes be extremely useful in the process of understanding what happens in the entrepreneurial process.

■ A synthesis of the paradoxes

Is there a connection between the paradoxes on the left side and the right side of the table, that is between, on the one hand: born, discovered, instrumental, planning, exploit, rational, management tool, top-down and business; and, on the other hand: made, created, legitimate, improvising, explore, embedded, curb of creativity, bottom-up and a better world? Is there a kind of meta-paradox hidden in this picture puzzle? Actually, it is possible to argue the existence of a meta-paradox. Where the left side of the above-mentioned table can be summarised by reference to an objectivistic approach, the right side is more likely to be summarised by reference to a subjectivistic approach (Burrell & Morgan 1979). Generally, the objectivistic and the subjectivistic approach refer to two different scientific traditions. The first-mentioned approach advocates the existence of an objective world that exists independently of human beings and their actions. On the contrary, a subjectivistic approach deals with how the world is created through the actions performed by human beings, their experiences and perceptions. In the following, we will explain more thoroughly how the meta-paradox mentioned finds expression in entrepreneurship.

An objectivistic approach

As mentioned, the left side of table 11.1 expresses the objectivistic approach to entrepreneurship. From this perspective, individuals and groups of persons act as economically and rationally as possible. The connection to the left side is characterised by the fact that entrepreneurs discover an opportunity, evaluate it through the use of instrumental tools and start organising it. An almost linear process can be written down beforehand. The activities happen for instance by the fact that the entrepreneurs adjust their network to the purpose and make a business plan. Thus, the entrepreneurs can more easily go rationally and safely through the entrepreneurial process. Therefore, the process is conscious, systematic and it is controlled through planning towards achieving a specific and predictable goal – a profitable organisation. Consequently, the entrepreneurial process is considered controllable. It is just a matter of providing the right knowledge, which also explains why top-down management and control from the top management become crucial to achieve entrepreneurial behaviour. According to this perspective there are actually optimal recipes for how entrepreneurs, whether single or in teams, approach the entrepreneurial process. All these features could be called an objectivistic approach to entrepreneurship because the entrepreneurial process is given beforehand and thus is independent of individuals. It is out there in the "real world".

As players, entrepreneurs are just a kind of "gear wheel" in the machinery that is to take care of reaching the goal as quickly and effectively as possible. The project is the crucial thing, not the person. The purpose of the entrepreneur is to develop and operate the entrepreneurial machine so that it is possible for him or her to reach the goals which are set beforehand. Through planning, control over the machinery, coordination, analysis etc., the entrepreneur is capable of controlling the machine in the desired direction. The "made"-perspective emphasises how the entrepreneur is considered as being born for that purpose.

Last but not least: The objectivistic approach also promotes that a "best practice" exists for developing a new organisation. The business plan considered as a management tool is an example of such a "best practice" for organisation creation. The objective character of the plan is reflected by the fact that from the beginning of the entrepreneurial process, it is possible to predict what destinations the entrepreneur must visit in the process in order to realise the objective. The different dimensions of the business plan (financing, marketing, strategy etc.) illustrate that the entrepreneurial process is made up by a number of activities which demand planning and coordination. In accordance with this, it is crucial to the objectivistic approach to present some universally applying structural tools and regularities that can support the entrepreneur in the process of operating the entrepreneurial machine.

Sarasvathy (2008) has characterised the objectivistic approach as "causal" since it takes its starting point in goals by which the entrepreneur is constantly controlled as for instance the selection of the means which he or she makes use of in the approach to the goals. It is assumed that the entrepreneur, more or less, has access to exploit the necessary means such as resources and network or to rationally single them out in the beginning of the entrepreneurial process. They are taken for granted.

A corresponding causal approach is to be found in classic organisation theory. Actually, back to Taylor, in the beginning of the twentieth century, a mechanical and rational approach to organisation creation and development emerges (Scott & Davis 2007). Correspondingly, the approach is reflected in decision-making theory where the rational theory tradition is crucial in early as well as recent decision-making theory (Bager et al. 2001). To organisations, however, the rationality is bounded rather than absolute as in macro-economic theory (Simon 1946). Bounded rationality involves that we do not know all alternatives and consequences of the choices we make, just as in practice we accept satisfying solutions in preference to optimal solutions. Such an understanding also makes sense in entrepreneurship.

A subjectivistic approach
The right side of table 11.1 expresses a subjectivistic approach to entrepreneurship. Here the entrepreneur is motivated and acts on behalf of many different logics which do not always fit into a traditional economic rationality logic. Emphasis is on the human player both at an individual and group level. The individual becomes an entrepreneur through a personal development and he or she has a decisive influence on emergence and shaping of the entrepreneurial process. The human being who creates opportunities and decides to pursue opportunities is a holistic human being who also has other priorities in life. Thus, the entrepreneurial process is far from fixed, given by something "out there". It is rather something that is created from the entrepreneur's thoughts, feelings, wishes and experiences.

The subjectivistic approach pinpoints, however, that the entrepreneur does not create the entrepreneurial process by himself. The process is created and recreated through constant interaction with other people which indicates how the entrepreneurial process is socially constructed. Thus, from this perspective, other people and networks are fundamental conditions in which the entrepreneurial process is embedded. They constantly influence how the entrepreneurial process unfolds. Therefore, from a subjectivistic approach, the entrepreneurial process is far from considered as a linear one which follows phases and goals given beforehand. It is rather considered as a process that is formed by jumps forwards and backwards and parallel sequences.

Another pillar in the subjectivistic approach is scepticism towards the value of planning and strictly defined goals. The future cannot be predicted, and actions and decisions should be made depending on which situations emerge. This lack of predictability does not only apply to entrepreneurs who are in an early stage of the entrepreneurial process where ideas and projects come into being and new organisations are created. In more mature organisations, which are characterised by fixed routines and systems, the planning and determination of goals can be just as complicated an activity to carry through, especially if the goals involve the creation of something new. Nothing can be predicted and therefore it is important to leave room for the entrepreneurs who carry out the everyday actions. Thus, according to the subjectivistic approach, it is crucial to let the innovation happen bottom-up because the creation of something new at times can be a chaotic process in which fixed objectives and planning do not always make sense and value. Actually, it could be argued that a strongly rational and planning approach can destroy the opportunities for the entrepreneur and the development of the idea. Consequently, the business plan is also often considered as a curb of creativity.

Instead of making plans at one's desk, it is, from this perspective, about getting into touch with the outside world. You should let the idea guide you and at the same time you should be prepared for possibly changing or adjusting it. For example, it might be redirected towards a completely different customer group. Instead of a predictable, universally valid and goal-oriented entrepreneurial process, the process becomes, within the subjectivistic approach, considered as a unique process which you do not know the result of beforehand. As Steyaert writes: *"... every entrepreneurial endeavour follows and writes its own story"* (Steyaert 1997: 15).

Only through interaction with other people and by acting, the entrepreneur can find out to what extent and how the opportunity can be organised – whether it is legitimate or not and how it more precisely should be adjusted. Weick has encapsulated this perception in the sentence: *"How do I know what I think, until I see, what I say"* (Weick 1969: 207). Thus, at first, you say and do something and then you grasp it and understand it. It emphasises how the starting points of the subjectivistic approach, which Sarasvathy (2008) has also pinpointed, are not pre-defined goals. On the contrary, the starting point of the subjectivistic approach is the actions which the entrepreneur performs and the means which he or she has access to. Sarasvathy calls this approach "effectual" as opposed to "causal" because the starting point is the means which the entrepreneur mobilises in order to achieve an overall effect.

Entrepreneurship in theory and practice

■ Advantages and limitations associated with the two approaches

Once again, it should be emphasised that both of the two outlined overall approaches to entrepreneurship are important, and they should not necessarily be seen as rivals. Theoretical evidence supports both of them and for the individual entrepreneur the crucial thing is the balance in the specific situation. Sometimes emphasis should be on the objectivistic dimension and at other times on the subjectivistic dimension. Something similar applies to the choice of study area and projects at the university. In this connection, there is also an objectivistic and a subjectivistic dimension which the student has to handle at the same time.

Thus, both dimensions are relevant. However, you can get a lot of benefit out of working with them separately – choosing the one side of a paradox and see the project or the process through this perspective. But it can certainly also be valuable to perceive the project or the process from both perspectives of the paradox. Applying this method, you get thoroughly into the material and you avoid more effectively the normative "blindness" we all carry with us in the sense that we find interest in certain perspectives. Some would for instance in the starting point be turned on by a rational perspective whereas others get frightened by this calculative perspective. Both need, so to speak, to put on "reverse glasses". By approaching entrepreneurship from several perspectives, a better understanding of why processes develop the way they do is obtained and, in particular, a better understanding of why success or failure is sometimes the result of an entrepreneurial process is generated.

■ Your journey begins now

We are approaching the end of our journey through this textbook and the learning universe which is attached to www.idea-textbook.dk. We hope that you have enjoyed the journey, that you have become inspired and feel that you are prepared to start your own entrepreneurial journeys. Whether you become an independent entrepreneur or end up unfolding entrepreneurial projects in existing organisations or in your leisure life we are sure that you, at some point, come to deal with new ideas, opportunities and their realisation, simply because it is so universal and important in human life.

In order to make headway, we recommend that you test your abilities through one or several entrepreneurial projects in practice. Not until then will you seriously understand what we have tried to communicate and only in that way will you discover your – perhaps hidden – talents and strengths. In practical projects, you will experience how difficult and frustrating it can be not to be able to find your way through the jungle of ideas and on the other hand, you will experience the feeling of victory when the entrepreneurial process is successful. It is somewhat like looking at the big dipper from below in the fun fair: Not until you have experienced it for real will you know how it feels.

You can find a practical project in many ways. Like approximately 5 percent of your fellow students you could start a student company while you are studying instead of having a study job; or together with others you could start a project within the field of social entrepreneurship for example headed towards world problems associated with the climate or poverty; or you could look for a student job – or an internship arrangement – in a company or organisation where you can work with the development of new opportunities in interdisciplinary project teams.

You can also redevelop your knowledge of the topics of the book by pursuing these within the educational system. If the book and the entrepreneurship field have caught your interest, in most cases you will be able to choose several related courses later on in your studies – courses in for instance innovation or creativity with focus on the topics which we have dealt with. An investigation from the United States has demonstrated that students who are trained in producing new ideas and discovering or creating opportunities get better at it than similar students who have not been exposed to such courses (DeTienne & Chandler 2004). Also in this case, the old platitude makes sense: "practice makes perfect." It can also be more advanced courses within specific topics such as the financing conditions that apply to start-up companies, management of growth or the special procedures and rules that deal with protection of immaterial rights.

You can also decide to participate in the many extraordinary offers at the institutions of higher education. It could be exciting innovation camps, which are typically arranged for 2-3 days with participation of business managers and other representatives of organisations (Bager 2008); it could be Venture Cup and other business plan competitions; and it could be offers of training courses and mentoring in your local student pre-incubator environment. A survey has illustrated that the majority of the students who participate in a student pre-incubator activity have strengthened their academic learning by participating (Laursen & Jørgensen 2008). So you do not need to lose concentration on your study by participating in these activities.

Perhaps you are not yet convinced that entrepreneurship is important to you. Therefore, let us finally sum up three main arguments:

■ Whether you wish to get a job when you have finished your studies or you want to start a new organisation, your chances of success are improved if you already in your student years have learned about the core elements of entrepreneurship which is the emergence, evaluation and organising of opportunities. Remember that in modern society, the vast majority of jobs designed for highly educated people involve interdisciplinary project-based work with new ideas, opportunities and their realisation. Much seems to suggest that this aspect will only become more important in the future since the speed of innovation keeps going up in our modern society.

- Should you feel like starting your own organisation, perhaps together with others, it is, of course, also important to prepare yourself for that during your student years. Here you have the chance to "play" the role before it becomes serious and can cost you a lot of money. The best argument for it is probably the message that the entrepreneurs, who have already started, send out. An example is the network for growth entrepreneurs attached to the business organisation Danish Industry – a network which in 2008 counted approximately 300 members and which calls for more education and training in entrepreneurship in the educational system (Sørensen 2007).
- A final argument is that it is funny to participate in entrepreneurial projects. Most of your time as a student, you are fed with knowledge. Entrepreneurship is fundamentally different even though an academic field also exists here. Basically, it is about developing an ability to catch yet-to-be phenomena and work in a future-oriented way. Most people seem to find this engaging and funny. The funny part is associated with the fact that you are working on developing something new and you typically do this in cooperation with others whose experiences and educational backgrounds are completely different from yours. Often it is in such connections that you really come to understand the field you have studied and how to use it.

Let us end up with Harvard professor Scharmer's argument for the fact that entrepreneurship and orientation towards the future are important: *"We also pour considerable amounts of money into our educational systems, but haven't been able to create schools and institutions of higher education that develop people's innate capacity to sense and shape their future, which I view as the single most important core capability for this century's knowledge and co-creation economy"* (Scharmer 2007: 3).

Literature

Bager, T. (2008). The camp model for entrepreneurship teaching, Paper til IntEnt Conference 2008 (can be found at www.idea-textbook.dk)

Bager, T, Obel, B., Søgaard, V. (2001). Strategi og organisation – en introduktion. Odense, Syddansk Universitetsforlag.

Burrell, G. & Morgan, G. (1979). Sociological paradigms and organisational analysis. Heinemann Educational.

DeTienne, D., G.N. Chandler (2004). Opportunity identification and its role in the classroom: A pedagogical approach and empirical test, Academy of Management Learning and Education, 3, 242-257.

Høbner, F., Jørgensen, T. B., Andersen, T. & Sørensen, H. (2007). Modstillinger i organisations- og ledelsesteori. Aarhus: Academica.

Laursen, S., Jørgensen, C. (2008). Evaluering af 10 studentervæksthuse. IDEA og Erhvervs- og Byggestyrelsen (can be found at www.idea-denmark.dk).

Sarasvathy, S. (2008). Effectuation: Elements of Entrepreneurial Expertise. Chelterham: Edward Elgar.

Scharmer, C.O. (2007). Theory U – leading from the future as it emerges. Cambridge, MA: SoL Press

Scott, W. R. & Davis, G. F. (2007). Organizations and Organizing: Rational, Natural and Open System perspectives. Prentice Hall. Simon, H. (1997 (1946)). Administrative Behavior. Free Press

Steyaert, C. (1997). "A Qualitative Methodology for Process Studies of Entrepreneurship – creating local Knowledge Trough Stories." International Studies of Management and Organisation: 3-33

Sørensen, T. M. (2007). DIs IværksætterNetværk – et tilbud til vækst-iværksættere. In Bager, T. & Klyver, K. (Ed.), Iværksætterne og deres netværk (pp. 23-32), Copenhagen: Børsens Forlag.

Weick, K. (1969). The Social Psychology of Organizing. Reading: Addison-Wesley.

Entrepreneurship in theory and practice

254

Index

Entrepreneurship in theory and practice